Early praise for *Rediscovering JavaScript*

JavaScript used to only have a few "good parts." Now most of the parts are good. Although legacy features still remain, new features provided in the ES6/7/8 standards can help you write safer, simpler, and more concise code...but only if you know about them. In this book, Venkat shows everyone, from beginners to experts, how to use the modern language that JavaScript has become.

➤ **Ben Rady**
Author of *Serverless Single Page Apps* and *Continuous Testing with Ruby, Rails, and JavaScript*

This concise and brilliant introduction to modern JavaScript keeps the reader engaged by employing simple and direct language, coupled with focused examples and exercises that facilitate rapid learning. Recommended for anyone who wants to discover the joys of ES6/7/8.

➤ **Suresh Iyer**
Polyglot Programmer and Senior Staff Applications Engineer, ServiceNow

Once again, Venkat manages to distill into a concise work the most important changes in the evolution of JavaScript. If you want to update your knowledge of the most ubiquitous language in record time, this book is for you.

➤ **Brian Sam-Bodden**
Integrallis Software

If you tried and abandoned JavaScript long ago, it's time to give it a fresh look. This book teaches you all the improvements that bring the language into the 21st century.

➤ **Kenneth A. Kousen**
Java Champion and author of multiple books, including *Modern Java Recipes*

Rediscovering JavaScript

Master ES6, ES7, and ES8

Venkat Subramaniam

The Pragmatic Bookshelf

Raleigh, North Carolina

Our Pragmatic books, screencasts, and audio books can help you and your team create
better software and have more fun. Visit us at *https://pragprog.com.*

The team that produced this book includes:

Publisher: Andy Hunt
VP of Operations: Janet Furlow
Managing Editor: Brian MacDonald
Supervising Editor: Jacquelyn Carter
Copy Editor: Liz Welch
Indexing: Potomac Indexing, LLC
Layout: Gilson Graphics

For sales, volume licensing, and support, please contact *support@pragprog.com.*

For international rights, please contact *rights@pragprog.com.*

ISBN-13: 978-1-68050-546-7

Book version: P1.0—June 2018

Contents

Part II — Nice Additions

Part III — OO and Modular Code

Part IV — Going Meta

Acknowledgments

This book project was possible largely because of the support, help, time, and generosity of many. My sincere thanks to everyone who gave his or her knowledge, time, and effort to help me improve this book, and along the way helped me to learn and improve as well.

Special thanks to Scott Davis, Suresh Iyer, Ben Rady, Brian Sam-Bodden, Nathaniel Schutta, Stefan Turalski, and Jim R. Wilson for their reviews. These kind developers and experts reviewed the book for technical correctness, identified gaps in my writing, and suggested ways to improve. Any errors that remain in the book are my own.

The alpha geeks who bought the beta of this book placed their trust in me and I am very thankful for that. Thanks to the readers who provided feedback through the book's website, and to early readers Richard L. Brownrigg, George S. Cowan, Brett DiFrischia, Carsten Hess, Richard Hoggart, and Felipe Sultani for taking the time to make this book better.

I had the luxury of teasing out many of the topics presented in this book at conference presentations, in front of live audiences. The No Fluff Just Stuff (NFJS)[1] conference series, in particular, generously gave me the platform to present different topics related to this book for a couple of years before I started writing. Many thanks to Jay Zimmerman, the director of NFJS, for his continued support.

Writing a book has ups and downs, and the editor can make or break the project. In spite of various challenges along the way, Jackie Carter tirelessly worked on this book to get it in its current shape. I thank her for the positive feedback when she found the writing was good and her guidance in places where improvements were needed.

---

1. https://www.nofluffjuststuff.com

Thanks to Andy Hunt and the entire Pragmatic Bookshelf team, many who work behind the scenes, for taking on this book project and their continued effort to get it to fruition.

Knowing very well that asking, "Did the code you were trying last night work?" will start a long rant and a demo, a tireless soul kept asking that question and continued to motivate me. Without her help, none of this would have been possible or even matter—thank you, Kavitha. Also thanks to my sons Karthik and Krupa for their understanding when Dad had to hide to work on the book.

Introduction

A few days before a corporate event, the company informed me that the developers attending would be a mixture of Java, C#, and PHP programmers. I was concerned that presenting examples in Java may frustrate C# and PHP programmers. Picking any of the other two languages might have similar consequences. I made an executive decision and used JavaScript for all my examples—that way, I frustrated them all equally. Just kidding. It turned out to be a good choice—JavaScript is truly one language used by programmers who otherwise use different languages for most of their work.

JavaScript is the English of the programming world—it's native to some people, it's arguably the most widely used language, and the language itself has heavily borrowed from other languages, for greater good.

JavaScript is one of the most powerful, ubiquitous, and flexible languages. A large number of programmers fear the language for many reasons. In the past it had become infamous for being error prone and idiosyncratic. Thankfully, through the newer versions, JavaScript has evolved into a respectable language; it has come a long way since Douglas Crockford wrote *JavaScript: The Good Parts [Cro08]*.

Unlike other languages, JavaScript does not have the luxury to deprecate features. Such a measure would be considered draconian—currently working legacy code will suddenly fail on newer browsers. The language had to evolve without breaking backward compatibility.

The changes in JavaScript comes in three flavors: alternatives, additions, and advances.

Features that are error prone and outright confusing have alternative features in the newer versions. For example, const and let are the new alternatives to the messy var declarations. The rest operator, which makes it easier to create self-documenting code, is a much better alternative to arguments, which lacks clarity and needs explicit documentation. Also, the enhanced for loop removes the burden of looping that is inherent in the traditional for loops. While the old way of doing things still exists, we should make a conscious effort to learn and use the newer alternatives.

When coming from other languages, programmers often say, "I wish JavaScript had…" A lot of those wishes have come true. JavaScript has adapted features found in languages like Java, C#, and Ruby, to mention a few. These additions to the language not only make the language more pleasant to use but also help solve a set of problems in a more elegant way than before.

In the vein of comparing with other languages, generators and infinite iterators in JavaScript make it possible to create lazy sequences as in languages like Haskell or Clojure. Arrow functions bring the power of lambda expressions with consistent lexical scoping while making the code concise and expressive. Template literals bring the feature of *heredocs* from languages like Ruby and Groovy to JavaScript. And the enhanced class syntax makes programming in JavaScript feel almost like any other object-oriented language…well, almost.

And what good is a language that does not allow you to create programs that can in turn create programs? JavaScript makes it easy to turn those meta-thoughts into useful programs using the advances in the area of metaprogramming. The Proxy class, along with many capabilities of the language to create dynamic, flexible, and asynchronous code, makes JavaScript a very exciting language to program in. If you have enjoyed metaprogramming in languages like Ruby, Python, and Groovy, JavaScript now has similar capabilities to create highly flexible and extensible code.

The changes in recent years bring an entirely different feeling and vibe to the language. It is a great time to be excited about programming in JavaScript. Whether you are programming the front end or writing code for the server-side back end, you can use the newer language features to make your code elegant, concise, expressive, and above all less error prone.

There is no better way to learn the language than practicing. This book has several examples for you to try out, as you learn about the new and exciting features.

Fire up your favorite IDE or text editor—let's get coding.

How to Run Modern JavaScript

JavaScript has evolved considerably but the runtime engines are still catching up. Different browsers have varied support for different features from the newer versions of JavaScript.

Sites like kangax.github.io[1] and caniuse.com[2] can help you find whether a particular browser supports a JavaScript feature you're interested in using. MDN[3] web docs is a good source for documentation of JavaScript features and support in a few different browsers. The good news is all browsers will be 100 percent features compatible within the next 20 years—or so it feels—but we can't wait that long.

If you are developing for the back end using JavaScript, you may have better control of the version of the runtime engine you use. If you are developing for the front end, you may not have much say about the browser and the version of browser your users have. The version they use may not support a particular feature, or it may be an old browser and may not support any of the features of modern JavaScript. What gives?

Here are a few options to run JavaScript in general and, in particular, to practice the examples and exercises in this book.

Run in Node.js

The easiest way to practice the code examples in this book is running them in Node.js.[4] Version 8.5 or later supports most of the latest features. I will guide you along where necessary if you need to use a command-line experimental option or an additional tool.

First, verify that Node.js is installed on your system. Point your browser to https://nodejs.org and download the latest version if you don't have it or have a fairly old version. To avoid colliding with versions of Node.js already installed on your system, use Node Version Manager[5] (NVM) if it's supported on your operating system.

Once you install the latest version of Node.js, open a command prompt and type

```
node --version
```

The version of Node.js used to run the examples in this book is

```
v9.5.0
```

The version installed on your machine may be different. If it's very old compared to the version mentioned here, consider installing a more recent version.

---

1. https://kangax.github.io/compat-table/es6/
2. https://caniuse.com
3. https://developer.mozilla.org
4. https://nodejs.org
5. https://github.com/creationix/nvm

If what you have is later than the version shown here, then continue using the version you have.

To run the program in Node.js, issue the `node` command followed by the file-name. For example, suppose we have a file named hello.js with the following content:

introduction/hello.js
```
console.log('Hello Modern JavaScript');
```

Use the following command at the command prompt to run the code:

```
node hello.js
```

The command will produce the desired output:

```
Hello Modern JavaScript
```

Most IDEs that support JavaScript offer ways to more easily run the code from within the IDE. Make sure that your IDE is configured to use an appropriate version of Node.js.

Run Using the REPL

Even though I use text editors and IDEs to develop applications, I am a huge fan of *REPL*, which stands for "read-eval-print-loop." I call it the micro-proto-typing environment. While in the middle of working on a function or imple-menting enough code to make a unit test to pass, I often reach for the REPL to quickly try out ideas. This is like how painters prime their brushes on the side of the canvas while painting.

Let's fire up the REPL and try out a snippet of code. The Node.js command `node`, when executed without any filename, runs in the REPL mode.

At the command prompt type the command `node` and press Enter. In the node prompt, which appears as >, type various JavaScript code snippets and press Enter to run immediately. The output from the execution of the snippet is shown instantly. To exit from the REPL, press Ctrl+C twice, press Ctrl+D, or type .exit.

Let's take the REPL for a ride. Here's an interactive session for you to try:

```
node
> languages = ['Java', 'Python', 'Ruby', 'JavaScript']
[ 'Java', 'Python', 'Ruby', 'JavaScript' ]
> word = 'Hello'
'Hello'
> word.st(hit tab)
word.startsWith   word.strike
```

```
> word.startsWith('H')
true
> languages.filter(language => language.startsWith('J'))
[ 'Java', 'JavaScript' ]
>
```

In the REPL, create a list of languages and the REPL immediately evaluates and prints the list. Now, suppose we want to pick only languages that start with J. Hmm, does string support a startsWith() function? Why guess? We can ask the REPL.

Create a variable named word and set it to the string 'Hello'. Then type word.st and press the Tab key. The REPL lists all methods of string that start with st. Then it repeats the command you had already typed. Type a after word.st and press the Tab key again. The REPL now will complete the code with word.startsWith. Proceed to complete that call and press Enter.

Finally, type the line with filter to pick words from the list that meet the expectation. The REPL immediately provides a feedback with the result of executing the call.

REPL is also a great tool to use when you are on a colleague's machine and trying to show something quickly and realize he or she is not using your favorite IDE. Instead of fiddling with his or her tool, you can open up the REPL and show some quick examples on it.

Run in the Browser Console

Much like Node.js's REPL, most browsers provide a developer console for interactive experimentation. Here's an example of using the console in Chrome, which can be invoked by choosing View > Developer > JavaScript Console or by pressing the appropriate keyboard shortcut key.

Much like an IDE, the console pops up a list of possible methods when you type a period and start typing the method. It provides an instant feedback like the REPL as well.

Run within a Browser Using Babel

In many cases, developers don't have control over the browser that their users use. Very old browsers obviously don't support any of the modern JavaScript features. The support of newer features in newer browsers also varies widely. Writing code using newer features, only to find that some browser a user is running chokes up, is no fun, especially once the application is in production. This is where transpilers come in—they translate the JavaScript you write to the good old JavaScript supported by browsers old and new.

If you are developing for the front end, you're most likely already using a transpiler like Babel.[6] Since most browsers support the older version of JavaScript, you get the best of both worlds; you can write the code using the features available in the newer versions of the language and let Babel compile it to code that will run on most browsers. With this approach, you can make use of the features without the worry of browser compatibilities, although you still need to test and verify that things actually work.

Since most examples in this book run in Node.js, we don't need to dive into Babel at this time. We'll revisit this topic toward the end of the book in *Using Decorators*, on page 219, when we need Babel.

What's in This Book?

The rest of this book is organized as follows.

Before we dig into the newer features of JavaScript, we'll quickly visit some old problem areas in Chapter 1, *JavaScript Gotchas*, on page 3. You'll learn about things to avoid and the safe alternatives to some nefarious features.

Chapter 2, *Variables and Constants*, on page 15 will encourage you to replace var with let or const and why you should prefer const where possible.

JavaScript has always had support for flexible parameters, but it was not intuitive and was also error prone. Chapter 3, *Working with Function Arguments*, on page 27 will show how the newer features of JavaScript make working with parameters safe, expressive, and pleasant.

---

6. https://babeljs.io

The enhanced for loop of modern JavaScript is the antidote for the boredom of the common loops. We discuss different ways to loop, along with the generators and how to create infinite sequences, in Chapter 4, *Iterators and Symbols*, on page 47.

The lexical scoping semantics of anonymous functions is inconsistent and confusing, to say the least. Arrow functions don't have majority of the problems that are inherent in anonymous functions. But arrow functions come with some limitations as well, as we'll see in Chapter 5, *Arrow Functions and Functional Style*, on page 69. In this chapter, we'll also see how arrow functions make it easy to create functional style code.

Hands down, one of the most exciting features of JavaScript is destructuring. In Chapter 6, *Literals and Destructuring*, on page 91 we'll unleash the power of destructuring along with features like template literals and enhanced object literals.

JavaScript has supported classes for a long time, but without the class keyword. Sadly, that created problems. The newer class-related syntax in JavaScript makes writing object-oriented code much simpler, as we'll see in Chapter 7, *Working with Classes*, on page 115.

Unlike many other languages that support class-based inheritance, JavaScript has prototypal inheritance. Even though this feature is highly powerful and flexible, using it has been hard in the past—with the syntax confusing and error prone. As we'll see in Chapter 8, *Using Inheritance*, on page 135, it's now much easier, and safer, to use inheritance.

In Chapter 9, *Using Modules*, on page 155, you'll learn to work with multiple JavaScript files and the rules of module import and export.

Asynchronous programming is a way of life in JavaScript, and you need a fairly good knowledge of how promises work to master that. Chapter 10, *Keeping Your Promises*, on page 169, has you covered, I promise.

There's something magical about *metaprogramming*—the ability to create programs that can create programs. In Chapter 11, *Exploring Metaprogramming*, on page 187, we'll explore one type of metaprogramming—injection.

Then, in Chapter 12, *Deep Dive into Metaprogramming*, on page 201, we dig into another type of metaprogramming—synthesis—and how to create highly dynamic code.

Appendix 1, *Answers to Exercises*, on page 229 has solutions for exercises at the end of each chapter, for you to compare notes with the solutions you create.

Finally, for your convenience, the URLs that are scattered throughout this book are gathered in one place in Appendix 2, *Web Resources*, on page 253.

Who Is This Book For?

This book is for programmers, full-stack developers, lead developers, software architects, technical managers, or just about anyone who dives into code and is interested in learning and applying modern JavaScript. If you feared JavaScript or if the language annoyed you in the past, this book will show how the language has beautifully evolved in ECMAScript 2015 (ES6), 2016 (ES7), and 2017 (ES8) and how it is now highly approachable. You can make use of these features to program the front or the back end using JavaScript.

This book assumes the reader is familiar with basics of programming—it does not teach the fundamentals of programming. Some prior knowledge of JavaScript will be helpful. Programmers who are familiar with languages like Java, C#, and Python but who are not familiar with JavaScript should be able to pick up the concepts presented fairly quickly.

If you're already familiar with the materials presented in this book, you may use this book to help train your developers.

Online Resources

You can download all the example source code for the book from the Pragmatic Bookshelf website for this book.[7] You can also provide feedback by submitting errata entries.

If you're reading the book in PDF form, you can click the link above a code listing to view or download the specific examples.

Thank you for reading this book.

---

7.   https://www.pragprog.com/titles/ves6

Part I

The Safe Alternatives

Defining variables and passing arguments is commonplace in programming. Yet, these fundamental operations were error prone in the past. In this part we explore the safe alternatives modern JavaScript offers for defining variables and passing arguments. Along the way, you'll also learn to avoid some common pitfalls in general programming with JavaScript.

CHAPTER 1

JavaScript Gotchas

JavaScript is full of surprises, not all of which are pleasant. When our under-standing of the semantics differs from the language's intentions, we lose. In this chapter you'll learn about some of the most fundamental unpleasant semantical idiosyncrasies in JavaScript. Knowing these first will help you stay clear of common pitfalls when coding in JavaScript.

We'll start by looking at the way the language treat semicolons. Then we'll look at the troublesome == operator, discuss the consequences of forgetting to explicitly define variables, and explore ways to cope with these issues.

Be Careful Where You Break Lines

A number of dynamically typed programming languages don't care about semicolons and treat them as optional syntax. JavaScript is not one of them—semicolons are not optional. In some places a semicolon is critical, while in other places it's more of a stylistic choice. However, if you leave out a semicolon where it's required, JavaScript will not complain. That's because JavaScript has this philosophy that it's more fun to take revenge than to complain.

Merely placing a ; is not sufficient. We have to truly understand JavaScript's *automatic semicolon insertion* (ASI) rules.

A valid program ends with a ;. If a given script does not end with a ;, then JavaScript inserts a ; automatically.

As the tokens are parsed from left to right, if an unexpected token is encoun-tered and a line break separates it from the previous token, then a ; is auto-matically inserted before the encountered token. For example, consider this code snippet:

```
gotchas/unexpected.js
//BROKEN CODE
const unexpected = function() {
  let first
  second = 1;

  console.log(first);
  console.log(second);
}

unexpected();

console.log(second);
```

We use let and const instead of var—that's the good part of this code. We'll see why in Chapter 2, *Variables and Constants*, on page 15. The bad part of the code, however, is that the token second is not expected after first, even though a line break separates the two. So, JavaScript quietly inserts a ; before the variable second. This results in first taking on a value of undefined and the variable second turning into a global variable—ouch. We can see this from the output:

```
undefined
1
1
```

If a candidate token is break, continue, return, throw, or yield, and a line break appears between the candidate token and the next token, then JavaScript automatically inserts a ; after the candidate token. For example, the second return in the following code is not written correctly:

```
gotchas/careful-with-semicolon.js
Line 1  //BROKEN CODE
   -    const compute = function(number) {
   -      if(number > 5) {
   -        return number
   5          + 2;
   -      }
   -
   -      if(number > 2) {
   -        return
   10         number * 2;
   -      }
   -    };
   -
   -    console.log(compute(6));
   15   console.log(compute(3));
```

Since the second return is followed by a line break, JavaScript automatically inserts a ; right after the return, thus returning nothing—that is, undefined, as we see from the output:

8
undefined

In the first return, even though there is no ; on that line, it is legal for + to follow number so no ; was inserted on that line. But try changing + 2 to 2 on line 5 and JavaScript will insert a ; before 2, resulting in an output of 6 instead of giving an error for seeing unreachable code.

If a line is relatively short, end it with a clearly visible semicolon. By convention we don't place ; after the } that ends a code branch. If a line is long, then break it into multiple lines, but do so in such a way that JavaScript does not deviate from your intentions by automatically placing semicolons.

As we see from the example, it's really not the question of whether ; is optional—it comes down to how we break a line of code. It's easy to fall into this trap, but you can prevent these kinds of errors by using the lint tools that we'll discuss soon in *Lint the Code*, on page 10.

Now that we know where to break a line, let's focus on a few things that go within a line.

Use === Instead of ==

Many JavaScript programmers, including your humble author, often repeat the mistake of comparing using ==, which is the type-coercion non-strict equality operator. Let's look at an example that shows why using == may be a bad idea.

gotchas/double-equals.js
```
//BROKEN CODE
const a = '1';
const b = 1;
const c = '1.0';

console.log(a == b);
console.log(b == c);
console.log(a == c);
```

In the short piece of code, the constants a, b, and c have values '1', 1, and '1.0', respectively. One value is of number type and the other two are of string type. The last three lines compare each combination of the constants. Suppose a is equal to b and b is equal to c; then logically JavaScript should tell us that a is equal to c. But the JavaScript == operator does not honor the transitive property of equality, due to type coercion, as we see in the output produced by running the code:

```
true
true
false
```

The == operator performs type coercion if the things being compared are not of the same type. If the objects or values being compared are both of type string, number, or boolean, then a direct equality check is performed.

When comparing a with b and b with c, type coercion was involved before the comparison. However, when a and c were compared, a lexical comparison was used. Hence we see a different result than what we may otherwise expect.

In the uncommon situation where you want type coercion before comparison for equality, then == is your operator. One situation where == may be a better choice than === is when you want to determine if a variable is either null or undefined—the check variable == null will yield true if variable is null or undefined and may be used instead of variable === null || variable === undefined.

In most of the situations, however, we generally would want a straight up strict equality check, with no type coercions. In that case, use === instead of ==. Let's rework the previous example using the identity strict equality operator—that is, ===.

gotchas/triple-equals.js
```
const a = '1';
const b = 1;
const c = '1.0';

console.log(a === b);
console.log(b === c);
console.log(a === c);
```

We replaced all uses of == with ===. We're asking JavaScript to perform comparison without any coercions, and it reports all three comparisons as false—consistently the same result for all three comparisons.

```
false
false
false
```

Just like the way we should most likely use === instead of == to check if two instances are equal, use !== instead of != to check inequality.

Declare Before Use

At first sight it may appear that JavaScript is highly flexible, but things can get tricky if we're not careful. Let's look at the following code as an example:

gotchas/no-declaration.js
```
Line 1  //BROKEN CODE
    2   const oops = function() {
    3     haha = 2;
    4
```

```
5    console.log(haha);
6  };
7
8  oops();
9  console.log(haha);
```

The function oops assigns a value to a variable haha and then prints it. As expected, the effect of calling oops() will be to print the value 2 to the console. But this function isn't as benign as it looks. JavaScript looks at line 3 and says, "Hey, look, the developer didn't explicitly declare the variable before use—what can I do to cause the most damage? Lemme make it global." Just kidding, no, it's not personal, but global variables make code hard to maintain and often lead to programming errors due to unpredictable or incomprehensible change.

To verify this, at line 9, after the call to oops(), we print the variable that was used inside the oops() function. The output from the code shows the consequences of not declaring the variable before using it—it is indeed global.

```
2
2
```

Now, let's change line 3 to declare the variable:

```
let haha = 2;
```

Then we'll get a failure at runtime that haha is not defined, thus confirming the variable haha is a local variable within the function oops and is no longer global.

We can't take this issue lightly. Mistyping a variable name creates an unintended global variable. Once a variable becomes global, its reach can have terrible consequences.

Consider the following code, and before you look at the output that follows, eyeball the code to see if you can figure out what the code will do:

gotchas/global-mess.js
```
//BROKEN CODE
const outer = function() {
  for(i = 1; i <= 3; i++) {
    inner();
  }
};

const inner = function() {
  for(i = 1; i <= 5; i++) {
    console.log(i);
  }
};

outer();
```

The code does not produce the intended or desired output but instead outputs:

```
1
2
3
4
5
```

Let's understand what caused this anomaly in the output. The function outer() uses a variable i but without declaring it first. As a result, that variable fell into global scope. After setting a value of 1 for i, the outer() function calls the inner() function. Sadly, inner() also uses i without declaring it first and so binds to the same global variable i. At the end of the call to the inner() function, i has a value of 5. When the control flows back to outer(), the variable is way over the bounding value of 3 and so the loop terminates after the first iteration.

Even more alarming, due to the same reason, this code can turn into a non-ending program if we change the value 3 to 8 in the outer function. Surprise.

Let's quickly fix the problem in the previous code—in the two loops, prefix the declaration of the variable i with let, like so:

```
const outer = function() {
  for(let i = 1; i <= 3; i++) {
    inner();
  }
};

const inner = function() {
  for(let i = 1; i <= 5; i++) {
    console.log(i);
  }
};
outer();
```

After this fix, the code will produce the intended result—printing values 1, 2,... 5 three times.

Falling into these traps is no fun; it can soon lead to loss of productivity and become a source of errors. Let's look at some options to proactively deal with these issues.

Stay One Step Ahead

The traps we saw have been part of JavaScript for a long time. Even though the language has evolved considerably, these gotchas are inherent and they're here to stay. Thankfully, we can make a preemptive strike to avert these issues using some tools and techniques.

Apply the use strict Directive

Placing 'use strict'; at the beginning of a JavaScript source file or within a function turns on the strict mode of execution. In this mode, the execution runtime does not tolerate, among other things, use of undeclared variables.

If the directive is placed at the top of a script, then all code in the script runs in the strict mode. If placed only within a function, then only the code within that function runs in the strict mode—the situation where we'll need this is quite rare.

One situation where you may try placing the directive within a function is when you're gradually refactoring large legacy code, one function at a time. Placing the directive at the top of the file may produce too many errors to deal with in one small refactoring session. In this case, you may start with the directive in a function you're refactoring and then gradually, as you clean up more code, broaden the reach of the directive. Eventually, you'll want the directive at the top of the file so all the code in the file runs in strict mode.

The syntax for the directive is an odd-looking 'use strict'; but was designed that way for a good reason. Since it appears as a string, the newer JavaScript engines can recognize it whereas the older engines can ignore it.

As a general rule, always place 'use strict'; at the top of your script, like this:

```
gotchas/preemptive-strike.js
//BROKEN CODE
'use strict';

const oops = function() {
  haha = 2;

  console.log(haha);
};

oops();
console.log(haha);
```

The example uses an undeclared variable, but it will not turn into a disastrous global variable. The 'use strict'; directive will cause an error, like so:

```
  haha = 2;
     ^

ReferenceError: haha is not defined
```

The directive does a lot more than look for undeclared variables. For example, it watches out for changes to read-only properties, the deletion of properties, and the use of some keywords that are reserved for the future...to mention a few.

All the remaining examples in this book use the 'use strict'; directive, except where the runtime automatically runs the code in strict mode—like module files, for example. To keep the code listings short, however, we do not show the 'use strict'; directive.

Lint the Code

The 'use strict'; directive certainly gives much needed relief, but it would be nice to know about some potential errors even before running the code. This is where the lint tools come in. Some of the notable lint tools are JSLint,[1] JSHint,[2] and ESLint.[3] These tools can be installed easily with an npm install command.

JSLint is an aggressive tool and, in fact, may be a bit overly so at times in veri-fying the code for compliance to the code quality standards it sets. As soon as you unleash it on a piece of code, it will probably hurt your feelings. JSHint is also an aggressive tool, but at least it will appear to give you a hug at the end of the ordeal. It's gentler and the more easily customizable of the two. ESLint is also easy to customize, and furthermore, it supports rules for ES6 modules.

We'll take a look at using ESLint on a piece of code. Let's first create a sample script with some badly written code in it:

gotchas/smelly.js

```
Line 1  const sample = function(number) {
          factor = 4;

          if(number == 2) {
    5         return
                number * factor;
          }

          return number * 10;
   10   };

        console.log(sample(2));
```

Here are the steps for you to try ESLint on this code. First, install ESLint on your system. Enter the following npm command at the command prompt:

```
npm install -g eslint
```

This will install the tool globally on your system. If you'd rather have it available in only one project or directory, remove the -g option from that command. Gen-erally it's better to install tools and libraries locally instead of globally.

---

1. http://www.jslint.com
2. http://jshint.com/
3. https://eslint.org

Once you've installed ESLint, create a configuration file using the following command:

```
eslint --init
```

If you installed ESLint locally instead of globally, then you'll have to prefix the command name with the path to the tool.

Run this command either in the current directory or one of the ancestor directories. Follow along the interactive setup to complete the configuration. Whenever you want to change the rules ESLint uses, edit the generated .eslintrc.js file. For example, let's edit the configuration file to add some rules, including the rule that'll require the use of === instead of ==. Here's the .eslintrc.js file after the change:

```
.eslintrc.js
module.exports = {
    "env": {
        "es6": true,
        "node": true
    },
    "extends": "eslint:recommended",
    "rules": {
        "eqeqeq": "error",
        "strict": "error",
        "no-var": "error",
        "prefer-const": "error",
        "no-console": "off",
        "indent": [
            "error",
            2
        ],
        "linebreak-style": [
            "error",
            "unix"
        ],
        "quotes": [
            "error",
            "single",
            "avoid-escape"
        ],
        "semi": [
            "error",
            "always"
        ]
    }
};
```

For a list of rules, see the Configuring ESLint[4] web page.

---

4.   https://eslint.org/docs/user-guide/configuring

To try ESLint on the script smelly.js, enter the following command at the command prompt, from within the directory where the file resides:

```
eslint smelly.js
```

If you want the tool to examine all JavaScript files in the current directory, replace the filename with a dot to represent the directory, like so:

```
eslint .
```

Here's the output of running ESLint on the previous example code:

```
1:1    error  Use the global form of 'use strict'           strict
2:3    error  'factor' is not defined                       no-undef
4:13   error  Expected '===' and instead saw '=='           eqeqeq
5:11   error  Missing semicolon                             semi
6:1    error  Expected indentation of 4 spaces but found 6  indent
6:7    error  Unreachable code                              no-unreachable
6:16   error  'factor' is not defined                       no-undef

✘ 7 problems (7 errors, 0 warnings)
  2 errors, 0 warnings potentially fixable with the `--fix` option.
```

ESLint points out several things; we didn't use the 'use strict'; directive, we're using == instead of ===, our code may cause trouble due to a missing semicolon, and a variable is used without being defined. We got all those error messages without running the JavaScript file—that's nifty.

Now that we know the issues in the code, let's fix these issues with the code in the smelly.js file.

```
'use strict';
const sample = function(number) {
  const factor = 4;

  if(number === 2) {
    return number * factor;
  }

  return number * 10;
};

console.log(sample(2));
```

Run the eslint command again, this time with the modified code:

```
eslint smelly.js
```

ESLint does not report any issues now. The output is empty—it follows the Unix philosophy of "Silence is golden."

By using ESLint from within the IDE and during the continuous integration build process, we can proactively detect and remove any error so that it never sneaks into production.

Wrapping Up

JavaScript is a very powerful language with some unpleasant surprises. You learned to be careful about automatic insertion of ;, to use === instead of ==, and to declare variables before use. We also discussed a few ways to proactively deal with the gotchas—by using the 'use strict'; directive and lint tools. In the next chapter we will discuss how a very fundamental task of declaring variables has changed, for the better, in JavaScript.

Exercises

Take a break and practice, using these code exercises, to identify some potential errors in code and ways to improve writing JavaScript. You can find answers to these exercises on page 229.

Exercise 1

What will be the result of each of the following return statements?

```
return
  2 * 3;

return 2
   * 3;

return 2 * 3
   ;
```

Exercise 2

Is it better to use == or === in the following comparison?

```
"2.0" / 2 * "2.0" == 2 / 2 * 2;
```

Exercise 3

Write a function named canVote() that takes age as a parameter and returns a string, as shown in the following example calls to the function:

```
console.log(canVote(12));       //no, can't vote
console.log(canVote("12"));     //no, can't vote
console.log(canVote(17));       //no, can't vote
console.log(canVote('@18'));    //no, can't vote
console.log(canVote(18));       //yay, start voting
console.log(canVote(28));       //please vote
```

Exercise 4

What is the output of the following code?

```
var isPrime = function(n) {
  for(i = 2; i < n; i++) {
    if(n % i == 0) return false;
  }

  return n > 1;
}

var sumOfPrimes = function(n) {
  var sum = 0;
  for(i = 1; i <= n; i++) {
    if(isPrime(i)) sum += i;
  }

  return sum;
}

console.log(sumOfPrimes(10));
```

Fix the errors in code to get the desired result.

Exercise 5

The code in this exercise is intended to determine if a given number is a perfect number.[5]

Eyeball the following code to detect the errors and jot them down. Then run ESLint on the code to display the errors. Compare with what you jotted down to see if you caught them all. Then fix the errors until ESLint is quiet.

```
gotchas/is-perfect.js
var isPerfect = function(number) {
  var sumOfFactors = 0;

  for(index = 1; index <= number; index++) {
    if(number % index == 0) {
      sumOfFactors += index;
    }
  }

  return sumOfFactors
    == number * 2;
};

for(i = 1; i <= 10; i++) {
  console.log('is ' + i + ' perfect?: ' + isPerfect(i));
}
```

---

5. https://en.wikipedia.org/wiki/Perfect_number

CHAPTER 2

Variables and Constants

Traditionally JavaScript has used var to define variables. Moving forward, we should not use that keyword. Instead, we should choose between using const and let.

In this chapter, you'll start by learning why var is a bad idea, why it's still there, and why we should avoid it. Then you'll learn about the strengths, capabilities, and some limitations of using let. Finally, we'll explore const and discuss when to use it instead of let.

Out with var

Prior to ES6, JavaScript required var to define variables. If we forget to define a variable explicitly before assigning to it, we'll accidentally define a global variable. The 'use strict'; directive saves us from that error. In short, all variables should be defined before their first use. However, var is not the right choice, as we'll see here.

var does two things poorly. First, it does not prevent a variable from being redefined in a scope. Second, it does not have block scope. Let's explore these two issues with examples.

Redefining

It's poor programming practice to redefine a variable in the same scope as that often leads to errors in code. Here's an example where a variable max is redefined.

```
variables/redefine.js
Line 1  'use strict';
     2  var max = 100;
     3  console.log(max);
     4
     5  var max = 200;
     6  console.log(max);
```

On line 5 the variable max, which already exists, is redefined. If the programmer intended to assign a new value to an existing variable, then there should be no var declaration on that line. It appears, though, that the programmer intended to define a new variable, which happens to have the same name as an existing variable, thus accidentally erasing the previously stored value in that variable.

If a function were several lines long, it's possible that by accident we may redefine a variable for a different purpose or intent. Unfortunately, JavaScript doesn't give us any hint of the variable being redefined when var is used—tough luck.

No Block Scope

Variables defined using var within functions have function scope. Sometimes we may want to limit the scope of a variable to a smaller scope than the entire function. This is especially true for variables that are defined within a branch or a loop. Let's look at an example with a loop to illustrate the point.

variables/no-block.js
```
'use strict';

console.log(message);

console.log('Entering loop');
for(var i = 0; i < 3; i++) {
  console.log(message); //visible here, but undefined
  var message = 'spill ' + i;
}
console.log('Exiting loop');

console.log(message);
```

The variable message was defined within the loop—what happens in a loop should stay in the loop, but vars are not good at keeping secrets (poor encapsulation). The variable spills over the loop and is visible outside the loop—var hoists the variable to the top of the function. As a result, both message and the loop index variable i are visible throughout the function.

Not only is the variable, defined using var, visible following the block, it's also visible before the block. In other words, regardless of where in the function a variable is defined, it has the scope of the entire function.

Here's the output of running the previous code:

```
undefined
Entering loop
undefined
spill 0
spill 1
Exiting loop
spill 2
```

In short, var is a mess; don't use it.

var is terrible, but programmers have used it extensively for a few decades in JavaScript. Changing its behavior to fix these issues or removing var entirely will create compatibility issues between old and new JavaScript engines. This will turn into a nightmare for developers who deploy code on different browsers. That's the reason why var is still lingering around in the language. Even though the language can't get rid of it, we can and should. Quit using var and choose from the new let or const.

In with let

let is the sensible replacement for var. Anywhere we used var correctly before we can interchange it with let. let removes the issues that plague var and is less error prone.

No Redefinition

let does not permit a variable in a scope to be redefined. Unlike var, let behaves a lot like variable definitions in other languages that strictly enforce variable declarations and scope. If a variable is already defined, then using let to redefine that variable will result in an error, as in the next example.

variables/no-redefine.js
```
'use strict';
//BROKEN_CODE
let max = 100;
console.log(max);

let max = 200;
console.log(max);
```

This example is identical to the one we saw earlier, except that var was replaced with let. The compiler gives an error that max can't be redefined, as we see in the output:

```
let max = 200;
    ^

SyntaxError: Identifier 'max' has already been declared
```

let brings variable declaration semantics in JavaScript on par with what's expected in general programming.

What if we define a variable using var and then try to redefine it using let or vice versa? First, we should avoid such immoral thoughts—no reason to use var anymore. Second, JavaScript will not permit redefining a variable when let is used in the original definition or in the redefinition.

The fact that let does not allow redefinition is mostly good. There is, however, one place where that may not be to our advantage—in the REPL. As we saw in *Run Using the REPL*, on page xiv, we can use node also as a quick experimentation tool. Likewise, as we saw in *Run in the Browser Console*, on page xv, we may also use the browser console to experiment and try out different code. When experimenting, we'd want to write and quickly change code to try out different ideas. In a few languages that have REPL and also prohibit variable redefinition, the rules of redefinition are favorably relaxed in REPLs for developer convenience. Sadly, node and the console in some of the popular browsers enforce the rule of prohibiting redefinition, thus making it a bit hard to retype chunks of code with variable definitions even within the console or REPL.

Block Scope

Variables declared using let have block scope. Their use and visibility is limited to the block of code enclosed by the {...} in which they're defined. Furthermore, unlike var, variables defined using let are available only after their point of definition. That is, the variables are not hoisted to the top of the function or the block in which they're defined.

Let's convert var to let in the code we saw earlier where we used a variable defined within a loop from outside the loop.

```
'use strict';

//console.log(message);  //ERROR if this line is uncommented

console.log('Entering loop');
for(let i = 0; i < 3; i++) {
  //console.log(message); //ERROR if this line is uncommented
  let message = 'spill ' + i;
}
console.log('Exiting loop');

//console.log(message);  //ERROR if this line is uncommented
```

This code illustrates the semantic difference between var and let. First, the variable defined within the block is not visible outside the block. Furthermore, even within the block, the variable is not visible before the point of definition. That's semantically sensible behavior—just the way it should be.

Perils of Mutability

let does not permit redefinition of variables, but it allows changing the value held in the variable. Without executing it, eyeball the following code to determine what the output will be.

```
variables/confusion.js
'use strict';
let factor = 2;

let product = function(number) {
  return number * factor;
};

factor = 0;

console.log(product(4));
```

Show the code to your colleagues nearby or far away—what good is technology if you can't bother someone with it—and ask them to determine the output. Did you or your colleagues gasp, shout out an answer, ending with "right?!" Were there inconsistency in the answers? Is the trouble worth it?

You might think that the result of the call to produce(4) should be 8. That would have been true if the value of factor were captured at the time of the definition of the inner function. However, the variable factor in the inner function is instead bound directly to the variable factor in the outer. As a result the call to product(4) will return 0. In any case, though, the code poses a cognitive load on any developer who has to read and/or maintain this code.

If a function will have access to variables defined outside its immediate scope, it's better to make those variables immutable. Not doing so may lead to confusion and error.

Mutability is common in imperative programming but is taboo in functional programming. When defining a variable, you have to decide whether it should be mutable. If you're in doubt, favor immutability since that's the safer of the two options.

const

The const keyword is used to define a variable whose value shouldn't change. If you intend to modify the value in a variable, then define it using let; otherwise, define it using const.

Here's an example that shows the difference between using let and const:

```
variables/letconst.js
//BROKEN CODE
'use strict';
let price = 120.25;
const tax = 0.825;

price = 110.12;

tax = 1.25;
```

There's no issue changing the value of the price variable. However, since tax is defined as a constant, we will get a runtime error when we try to modify the value:

```
tax = 1.25;
   ^
```

```
TypeError: Assignment to constant variable.
```

Reach of const

Before we declare const as one of the most awesome features in modern JavaScript, let's understand its limitations. Only primitive values, like number, and references to objects are protected from change. The actual object that the reference refers to does not receive any protection from the use of const.

Let's take a closer look at the limitations with an example:

```
variables/const-reach.js
const max = 200;
const ok = true;
const nothing = undefined;
const nope = null;
const sam = { first: 'Sam', age: 2 };

//max = 200; //Not allowed
//ok = true;  //Not allowed
//nothing = undefined; //Not allowed
//nope = null;  //Not allowed

//sam = { first: 'Sam', age: 2 }; //Not allowed

sam.age = 3;
```

The variable max, of type number, is defined as a constant variable and initialized to a value of 200. The value of max is now set permanently, like my opinions of politicians. We can't legally place max on the left-hand side of the equals sign, even under the pretense of resetting it to the value it already contains. The same is the case with ok, which is of type boolean, and nothing, which is of type undefined. nope and sam are references and can't be altered.

JavaScript const is like final in Java and readonly in C#—all of these protect only primitives and references. None of these protect the object being referenced. In the previous example, the reference sam is a handle to an object with two properties: first and age. While the const prevents us from changing the reference sam, it does not care about any change to the internals of the object. Thus, setting the age of sam to a different value had no issues.

To make a reference immutable, use const. However, to make an object itself immutable, we need some additional help from JavaScript.

Making Objects const

It's great that primitives and references can be made immutable using const. However, any arbitrary function may modify the properties of an object even if the object was intended to be unchanged. There's thankfully a way to prevent changes to an object. Let's examine an object that's already immutable before we see how to bring that feature to our own objects.

variables/change-string.js

```
//BROKEN CODE
const greet = 'dude';
console.log(greet);

greet[0] = 'r';
console.log(greet);
```

A constant variable named greet is given a value dude at the start of the function. Then we change the value of the first element in the string instance. Let's take a look at the output from the code:

```
dude
dude
```

The value held in the object referenced by the greet variable is the same before and after the change. Strangely, the change had no effect at all. That's because objects of string are immutable in JavaScript.

JavaScript silently ignored the change to the immutable object instead of yelling out—it treats us like we treat our guests. We can change this behavior by including the 'use strict'; directive, like so:

variables/change-string-strict.js

```
//BROKEN CODE
'use strict';

const greet = 'dude';
console.log(greet);

greet[0] = 'r';
console.log(greet);
```

Now, when we modify the string instance, we get a stern error:

```
greet[0] = 'r';
        ^

TypeError: Cannot assign to read only property '0' of string 'dude'
```

A code that fails loudly is better than the one that misbehaves quietly—'use strict'; came to our rescue yet again.

The reference greet is immutable since we declared it const, but the actual instance is also immutable. That's intriguing; if they can do that for string, we should be able to do that for our own instances. The answer is the freeze() method in Object. Let's use that to make immutable the sam object we saw earlier.

```
variables/immutable-object.js
//BROKEN CODE
'use strict';

const sam = Object.freeze({ first: 'Sam', age: 2 });

//sam = {}; //ERROR, the reference sam is immutable

sam.age = 3;

console.log(sam.age);
```

Right after we created the object, we passed it through the freeze() method of Object. This returns a reference to an object that is immutable. We assign the reference to a constant variable named sam. Now, the reference is immutable thanks to const. Furthermore, the object itself is immutable due to freeze(), as we see from the output:

```
sam.age = 3;
         ^

TypeError: Cannot assign to read only property 'age' of object '#<Object>'
```

There's a caveat in using the freeze() method, however. It is a shallow freeze, not deep. The freeze() method makes only top-level properties of an object read-only. If a property in turn refers to another object, instead of a primitive type, then that nested object is not made read-only by the call to the freeze() method.

Safer Code with let and const

var does not have block scope and, in the past, that led developers to use a JavaScript design pattern known as *Immediately Invoked Function Expression* (IIFE) or the Self-Executing Anonymous Function. This pattern was also used to hide variables and functions from outside visibility. In this pattern, lines of code are wrapped inside an anonymous function that is immediately executed.

For example, in the following code, the variable sqrt defined within the block is hoisted to the top of the file and becomes unintentionally available outside of the intended scope.

```
//BROKEN CODE
'use strict';

var result = 0;
```

```
for(var i = 0; i < 5; i++) {
  var sqrt = Math.sqrt(i);
  result += sqrt;
}
```

```
console.log(result);
```

```
console.log(sqrt); //sqrt is visible here, though not intended
```

To avoid issues like this, the IIFE design pattern was often used. For example, let's use the pattern to implement the previous code:

```
//BROKEN CODE
'use strict';

var result = (function() {
  var result = 0;

  for(var i = 0; i < 5; i++) {
    var sqrt = Math.sqrt(i);
    result += sqrt;
  }

  return result;
})();
```

```
console.log(result);
```

```
console.log(sqrt); //ERROR because sqrt is not visible here,
//that's the desired behavior
```

There's a reduced need for this pattern in ES6 and beyond. That's because let and const have block scope. Furthermore, as we discuss in Chapter 9, *Using Modules*, on page 155, modules have restricted visibility. Where you may have used the IIFE design pattern in the past to limit variables from being hoisted, you can rely instead on the language features to limit the scope. This greatly reduces the need to wrap lines of code in anonymous functions that are immediately executed. We can instead enjoy less ceremony, and write fewer lines of code—code that is more intuitive and less error prone.

Prefer const over let

We saw that JavaScript has three options to define variables: var, let, and const. When writing new code or refactoring existing code, take some time to replace the old way of declaring with var with the modern replacements let or const.

Here are a few rules to follow when working with variables:

- Don't use var
- Use const wherever possible
- Use let only where mutability is needed

In the industry, many developers tend to lean toward let and often assume that const may not be an option. For instance, when writing a for loop, consider whether const is suitable instead of let.

const is the go to keyword to define variables and let should be more of an exception. There are many benefits to using const instead of let:

- Code is less prone to errors.
- Code is easier to reason about.
- The code prevents accidental or unintentional change to variables.
- The code is safe to use in functional style code or with arrow functions—see Chapter 5, *Arrow Functions and Functional Style*, on page 69

When there's a choice, prefer const over let.

Wrapping Up

const and let are far better replacements for the old var to define variables. Moving forward, we should quit using var and use const where possible and choose let otherwise. These two have block scope, prevent accidental redefinition of variables, and offer much better programming safety. You also learned how to honor immutability when programming. Next you will learn about improvements in passing arguments to functions.

Exercises

The following exercise problems will let you hone your skills about using use strict, avoiding var, and when to use let rather than const. Give these a try before heading over to the next chapter. You can find answers to these exercises on page 231.

Exercise 1

What's the output of this code?

```
function first() {
  for(i = 0; i < 5; i++) {
    second();
  }
}

function second() {
  for(i = 0; i < 3; i++) {
    console.log(i);
  }
}

first();
```

Exercise 2

First modify the code in the previous exercise so it gives a runtime error due to the major issue. Then modify the code to produce a reasonably desired result.

Exercise 3

What are the benefits of using 'use strict';?

Exercise 4

Will this code result in an error?

```
const fourth = '4th';

fourth = fourth;

console.log(fourth);
```

Exercise 5

Will this code result in an error?

```
'use strict';

const person = Object.freeze(
  {name: 'John Doe', address: { street: '101 Main St.', City: 'New York' }});

person.address.street = '102 Main St.';

console.log(person);
```

CHAPTER 3

Working with Function Arguments

Calling functions is arguably one of the most frequent tasks you'll do when programming. As an author of a function, you have to decide on the parameters to receive. As a caller of a function, you have to pass the right arguments. And, from the extensibility and flexibility point of view, you may want functions to receive variable numbers of arguments. From the beginning, JavaScript is one of those few languages that has supported a variable number of arguments. But that support was very spotty—the syntax was unclear and inconsistent.

Modern JavaScript brings a breath of fresh air both for defining functions and for calling functions.

Now, when defining functions you can clearly and unambiguously convey if you intend to receive a few discrete parameters, or receive a variable number of parameters, or a mixture of both. Unlike the old arguments, the new rest parameter is a full-fledged Array object, and you can process the parameters received with greater ease; you can even use functional style code for that. And, if you choose to extend your function by adding new parameters, the default parameters makes that transition much smoother than in the past.

When calling a function, the spread operator removes the need to manually break down the values in an array into discrete parameters. That leads to less code, less noise, and more fluency. In combination with Array, you may also use the spread operator to combine values in arrays and discrete variables to pass arguments to functions that receive rest parameters.

In this chapter we'll quickly review the old arguments and how such a powerful feature is mired with issues. Then we'll see how the rest parameter replaces arguments, bringing all the power forward minus the perils. We'll then switch to the function calling side and take a look at the benefits of the spread operator. Finally we'll examine default parameters and how they interplay with rest parameters.

The Power and Perils of arguments

The ability to pass a variable number of arguments to a function is a feature that's esoteric in many languages but is commonplace in JavaScript. JavaScript functions always take a variable number of arguments, even if we define named parameters in function definitions. Here's a max() function that takes two named parameters:

```
parameters/max.js
const max = function(a, b) {
  if (a > b) {
    return a;
  }

  return b;
};

console.log(max(1, 3));
console.log(max(4, 2));
console.log(max(2, 7, 1));
```

We can invoke the function with two arguments, but what if we call it with three arguments, for example? Most languages will scoff at this point, but not JavaScript. Here's the output:

```
3
4
7
```

It appears to even produce the right result when three parameters were passed—what's this sorcery?

First, we may pass as many arguments to a function as we like. If we pass fewer arguments than the number of named parameters, the extra parameters turn up as undefined. If we pass more arguments than the number of parameters, then those are merely ignored. Thus the last argument 1 was ignored in the last call to the max() method.

JavaScript has always allowed passing a variable number of arguments to functions, but receiving a variable number of parameters has been messy until recently. Traditionally, the special arguments keyword is used to process the parameters, like so:

```
parameters/arguments.js
const max = function() {
  console.log(arguments instanceof Array);

  let large = arguments[0];

  for(let i = 0; i < arguments.length; i++) {
    if(arguments[i] > large) {
      large = arguments[i];
    }
  }

  return large;
};

console.log(max(2, 1, 7, 4));
```

This version of the max() function does not have any explicitly named parameters declared. Within the function we query if arguments is an Array and then iterate over each element in that "thingy" to pick the largest value. The output from the code is shown here:

```
false
7
```

While in the past arguments has been used extensively in JavaScript, there are many issues with its use, as we see in this example:

- The method signature does not convey the intent—worse, it's misleading. While it appears that the function does not take any arguments, the actions of the implementation are quite contrary to that.

- arguments is an Array wannabe—it may be used like an Array, but only on the surface; it's largely deficient in its capabilities.

- The code is noisy and can't make use of more elegant solutions that may be used if arguments were an Array.

arguments is beyond repair since JavaScript has to preserve backward compatibility. The rest parameter solves the issues—moving forward, don't use arguments and use the rest parameter instead.

Using the Rest Parameter

A rest parameter is defined using the ellipsis (...) to signify that that parameter is a placeholder for any number of arguments. The rest parameter directly addresses the issues with arguments. First, it stands for the *rest of the parameters* and so is highly visible in the parameter list. Second, the rest parameter is of Array type. Let's convert the max() function from the previous example to use a rest parameter.

parameters/restmax.js
```
const max = function(...values) {
  console.log(values instanceof Array);

  let large = values[0];

  for(let i = 0; i < values.length; i++) {
    if(values[i] > large) {
      large = values[i];
    }
  }

  return large;
};

console.log(max(2, 1, 7, 4));
```

The two versions of max, the one that uses arguments and the one that uses a rest parameter named values, look almost identical. First, instead of an empty parameter list, we have ...values—the rest parameter name is prefixed with the ellipsis. Second, anywhere arguments appeared in the code, now there is values. At first sight, the rest parameter greatly improved the method signature and left the rest of the function mostly unaltered, except for the variable name change. Let's look at the output of this code before discussing further:

```
true
7
```

The output shows that the rest parameter is an Array. This means we can use better, more fluent, and expressive functions on the rest parameter than we could ever use on arguments. For example, we can easily change the code to the following functional style:

parameters/functionalrestmax.js
```
const max = function(...values) {
  return values.reduce((large, e) => large > e ? large : e, values[0]);
};
```

You will learn about the functional style later in this book. For now, we can appreciate how concise this code is, thanks to the fact that the rest parameter is of Array type; we can't call methods like reduce() directly on arguments.

JavaScript has some reasonable rules for the rest parameter:

- The rest parameter has to be the last formal parameter.
- There can be at most one rest parameter in a function's parameter list.
- The rest parameter contains only values that have not been given an explicit name.

Overall the rest parameter is one of the good changes to the language. It makes a very powerful feature of receiving a variable number of arguments civil and sensible from both the syntax and the semantics point of view.

The ellipsis symbol used for the rest parameter on the receiving end can also be used on the function call side; let's explore that next.

The Spread Operator

The spread operator looks the same as the symbol (...) used for the rest parameter, but it appears on the calling side of functions instead of on the parameter or receiving side. The intention of the spread operator is the opposite of that of the rest parameter—spread breaks a collection into discrete values whereas rest gathers discrete values into an array. Since they are used in two different contexts, there should be no confusion.

Suppose we have a greet() function that takes a rest parameter, like so:

parameters/greet.js
```
const greet = function(...names) {
  console.log('hello ' + names.join(', '));
};
```

If we have discrete variables, we can readily send them to the greet() function:

parameters/greet.js
```
const jack = 'Jack';
const jill = 'Jill';
greet(jack, jill);
```

If we had the names in an array, then we could pass them to the function after indexing into the array:

parameters/greet.js
```
const tj = ['Tom', 'Jerry'];
greet(tj[0], tj[1]);
```

But that's boring—there's gotta be a better way. Enter the *spread* operator.

parameters/greet.js
```
greet(...tj);
```

The spread operator may be used with any iterable object, and it expands, or spreads, the contained values into discrete values.

The spread operator retires the apply() function that is available in Java-Script—there's no more reason to use that function:

parameters/greet.js
```
greet.apply(null, tj); //no more stinky null
```

While spread may appear to be a direct replacement for the apply() function, we actually can get more mileage out of spread than when using apply().

The power and versatility of the spread operator is impressive. The spread operator isn't limited to the calling side of the rest parameter, like in the call to the greet() function. It may be used to spread an array to discrete parameters too, even when no rest parameter is involved. For example, in the next piece of code the function doesn't use a rest parameter but the caller uses a spread operator.

```
parameters/norest.js
const names1 = ['Laurel', 'Hardy', 'Todd'];
const names2 = ['Rock'];

const sayHello = function(name1, name2) {
  console.log('hello ' + name1 + ' and ' + name2);
};

sayHello(...names1);
sayHello(...names2);
```

The function sayHello() takes two separate named parameters. We can use a spread operator to invoke this function. If we pass an array with more values than necessary, the extras are ignored. If we are shy, then the parameter becomes undefined. We can see this from the output:

```
hello Laurel and Hardy
hello Rock and undefined
```

We can also mix the spread operator with other discrete arguments and also when the receiver has a mixture of named parameters and the rest parameter. Here's an example to illustrate:

```
parameters/mixed.js
const mixed = function(name1, name2, ...names) {
  console.log('name1: ' + name1);
  console.log('name2: ' + name2);
  console.log('names: ' + names);
};

mixed('Tom', ...['Jerry', 'Tyke', 'Spike']);
```

The function has two named parameters and one rest parameter. The caller is passing a separate stand-alone value 'Tom' followed by a spread argument. The stand-alone argument binds to the first parameter, name1; the first value within the spread argument binds to the second named argument, name2; and the rest of the values in the spread argument go to the rest parameter.

```
name1: Tom
name2: Jerry
names: Tyke,Spike
```

The now out-of-favor apply() function was only useful to expand values in a iterable when used in a function call. It could not be used with constructors. The spread operator works with constructors too:

```
parameters/constructor.js
const patternAndFlags = ['r', 'i'];

const regExp = new RegExp(...patternAndFlags);
```

The spread operator can also be used to copy, concatenate, and manipulate arrays:

```
parameters/arrayspread.js
const names1 = ['Tom', 'Jerry'];
const names2 = ['Butch', 'Spike', 'Tyke'];

console.log([...names1, 'Brooke']);
console.log([...names1, ...names2]);
console.log([...names2, 'Meathead', ...names1]);
```

The argument passed to the first log() call creates a new array with all of the values from the array names1 and an additional value as the last element. The argument passed to the second log creates a new array by concatenating arrays names1 and names2. The last one creates a new array with all of the elements from names2 followed by one arbitrary new element, then again followed by all of the elements from the names1 array. The output reflects the action of the code:

```
[ 'Tom', 'Jerry', 'Brooke' ]
[ 'Tom', 'Jerry', 'Butch', 'Spike', 'Tyke' ]
[ 'Butch', 'Spike', 'Tyke', 'Meathead', 'Tom', 'Jerry' ]
```

The spread operator has yet another charming capability. It may be used to copy contents of an object while optionally providing new values for some field and/or adding new fields. This is a feature used quite extensively in the popular JavaScript state container library Redux,[1] for example, to conveniently make copies of immutable state. To see this excellent use of the spread operator, let's make copies of an object in the next example.

```
parameters/objectspread.js
const sam = { name: 'Sam', age: 2 };

console.log(sam);
console.log({...sam, age: 3});
console.log({...sam, age: 4, height: 100 });
console.log(sam);
```

---

1. https://redux.js.org/

We first print the original object created on the first line. Then we make a copy of the object while replacing the age field with a new value of 3. Then, we make another copy, this time replacing age with the value 4 while inserting a new height field. The last line outputs the original object to confirm it has not changed. Here's the output:

```
{ name: 'Sam', age: 2 }
{ name: 'Sam', age: 3 }
{ name: 'Sam', age: 4, height: 100 }
{ name: 'Sam', age: 2 }
```

Beyond looking elegant and concise, the spread operator when used in this context makes the code highly extensible. If later on we add more properties to the object, the copy automatically takes care of copying over the extra properties without us having to modify the code. That can eliminate quite a few errors and makes the code easier to maintain.

Next, we will visit another excellent addition to the language, the default parameters.

Defining Default Values for Parameters

Parameters can take *default* values that step in for any missing arguments. We can benefit from default parameters in one of three ways:

- As a user of a function, we don't have to pass in a value for a parameter if the value we intend to send is the same as the sensible default chosen by the creator of the function—resulting in less work and reduced noise/clutter in code.

- As the author of a function, we can evolve the function signature more freely, to add a new parameter, without breaking existing code.

- We can compensate for the lack of function overloading in JavaScript. Many modern languages provide function overloading, but JavaScript does not. With default parameters, the caller may pass a different number of parameters, giving the illusion of using overloaded functions.

Let's explore the default values for parameters feature with an example to evolve a function.

Suppose we want to implement a function to sort a given array of books based on their titles. We can readily write that function, like so:

parameters/sort-books.js
```
const sortByTitle = function(books) {
  const byTitle = function(book1, book2) {
    return book1.title.localeCompare(book2.title);
  };

  return books.slice().sort(byTitle);
};
```

Within the sortByTitle() function we sort the given books array, but instead of calling sort() directly on the array we first use slice() and then sort(). The reason for not using sort() directly is that it will modify the array on which it is called—changing the input given to a function is a poor programming practice. The slice() function makes a copy of the given array and the sort() function then sorts the copy, thus not affecting the original array given as input.

Let's call the sortByTitle() function with some sample data.

parameters/sort-books.js
```
const books = [
  { title: 'Who Moved My Cheese' },
  { title: 'Great Expectations' },
  { title: 'The Power of Positive Thinking' }
];

console.log(sortByTitle(books));
```

The output of this call is the books sorted by title:

```
[ { title: 'Great Expectations' },
  { title: 'The Power of Positive Thinking' },
  { title: 'Who Moved My Cheese' } ]
```

Now suppose after a few weeks we're asked to enhance the function. While the users of our function mostly sort the books in the ascending order of the title, sometimes they may want to sort them in the descending order. We could write a new function for that, but that will result in duplication of significant code. If we change the function to take in an additional parameter, that may break existing code.

Technically, if we suddenly throw in a new extra parameter, the existing code will actually not be affected—at least not immediately. When the call is made, the value for the newly added parameter will come in as undefined. The code will then have to do undefined checks on the value of that new parameter—friends don't let friends write code like that. Furthermore, when the user of the function revisits he or she will be quite confused and start providing the necessary parameter; that's no fun either. The solution: default parameters.

Let's rework the function to use a default parameter:

```
const sortByTitle = function(books, ascending = true) {
  const multiplier = ascending ? 1 : -1;

  const byTitle = function(book1, book2) {
    return book1.title.localeCompare(book2.title) * multiplier;
  };

  return books.slice().sort(byTitle);
};
```

We added a second parameter, ascending, but gave it a default value of true. If the caller does not provide a value for this parameter, then a value of true is assumed for it. If a value is given, however, then that value is used.

Within the function, we create a local variable named multiplier, which holds a value of 1 if the value of ascending is true and -1 otherwise. We used the ternary operator, to keep the code concise, for this evaluation of multiplier. The localeCompare returns a positive number, a zero, or a negative number depending on whether the first value is greater, equal to, or smaller, respectively, than the second value. The multiplier of 1 will preserve that ordering whereas a value of -1 reverses it.

Let's repeat the old call to the function, but also add a new call to pass the value of false to the newly added parameter.

```
console.log(sortByTitle(books));
console.log(sortByTitle(books, false));
```

Since the first call is not passing any value for the second argument, the default value kicks in for the second parameter and the sorting happens in the ascending order. However, since a value is passed to the second argument in the second call, that value will appear for the second parameter. Let's quickly take a look at the output of these two calls:

```
[ { title: 'Great Expectations' },
  { title: 'The Power of Positive Thinking' },
  { title: 'Who Moved My Cheese' } ]
[ { title: 'Who Moved My Cheese' },
  { title: 'The Power of Positive Thinking' },
  { title: 'Great Expectations' } ]
```

In this example we saw how the default parameter helped to evolve the function. However, it does not have to be an afterthought. We can also proactively design our functions with sensible default values. Such design decisions may help the users of the functions to pass only essential arguments and rely on the defaults for the obvious and intuitive values that they don't care to customize.

The previous example showed how we can pass a custom value for the default parameter or simply omit it. If we omit it, the parameter takes on the default value provided in the function declaration. That is pretty straightforward, but our experience tells us it can't be that simple—there has to be more things to it to make this at least a tad complex. Well, of course, as we'll see next.

Multiple Default Parameters

A function can have any number of default parameters. For example, let's define a function with one regular parameter and two default parameters.

```
parameters/multiple-default-parameters.js
const fetchData = function(
  id,
  location = { host: 'localhost', port: 443 },
  uri = 'employees') {

  console.log('Fetch data from https://' +
    location.host + ':' + location.port + '/' + uri);
};
```

The caller of this function may pass three arguments, pass two arguments and leave out the value of the last parameter, or pass one argument and leave out both of the default parameters.

```
parameters/multiple-default-parameters.js
fetchData(1, { host: 'agiledeveloper', port: 404 }, 'books');
fetchData(1, { host: 'agiledeveloper', port: 404 });
fetchData(2);
```

In the first call, the given values were used for all three parameters, as we see in the following output. In the second call, the default value was used for the uri parameter. In the third call, both uri and location received the default values.

```
Fetch data from https://agiledeveloper:404/books
Fetch data from https://agiledeveloper:404/employees
Fetch data from https://localhost:443/employees
```

That's simple and straightforward too, but we're not done with this topic yet.

Passing undefined

Pass what?! Yep, that nasty undefined.

What if the calling code of the fetchData() function wants to pass a value for the uri parameter but not for location—it wants to use the default value for that.

We can think of two possibilities, neither of which is true in JavaScript:

- Don't permit that. Some languages that provide default parameters follow this rule. They will require values for all parameters to the left if you specify the values for a default parameter. In other words, in these languages, if we choose to use the default value for a parameter, we are forced to use default values for all parameters that follow. JavaScript does not have that rule.

- Require an empty parameter, like for example, fetchData(3,, 'whatever'). Thankfully, JavaScript does not allow that—imagine a function call like foo(1,,, 7,,, 20), delivered straight from hell.

But JavaScript permits passing undefined, and that has a special horror effect.

Here are the JavaScript rules:

- If a good value is passed to the default parameter, then that given value is used.

- If null is passed, then the value for the parameter is null—fair deal. So, don't pass null; after all, null is a smell.

- If undefined is passed, however, then the default value is given to the parameter in place of undefined.

Due to this feature, we may call the fetchData() function to provide a value for uri and use the default value for the location parameter, like so:

parameters/multiple-default-parameters.js
```
fetchData(3, undefined, 'books');
```

That call will give this result:

```
Fetch data from https://localhost:443/books
```

The issue is that undefined does not quite reveal the intention. It may not be too bad if we used it sparingly, but certainly avoid something like foo(1, undefined, undefined, 7, undefined, undefined, 20) because it's not easy to read.

Passing undefined arguments in method calls is rather unpleasant, but the feature of mapping undefined to default values is quite powerful. When using the spread operator or when using destructuring—which we see in Chapter 6, *Literals and Destructuring*, on page 91—missing values in the arguments list will turn up as undefined and thus will readily map to the default values on the parameter side.

Position of Default Parameters

The fact that passing undefined is inferred as a signal to choose the default value for a parameter leads to another implication. Unlike languages that require default parameters to be in trailing positions, JavaScript does not care. Here's a function with default parameters in arbitrary positions.

```
parameters/mixed-default-parameters.js
const badFetchData = function(
  location = { host: 'localhost', port: 443 },
  id,
  uri = 'employees') {

  console.log('Fetch data from https://' +
    location.host + ':' + location.port + '/' + uri);
};
```

The badFetchData() function also has three parameters, like the fetchData() function; however, the first and last parameters have default values while the middle one is a regular parameter. Since a value for id is expected, the users of the function may either have to give a value for location or use the unpleasant undefined as an argument, like so:

```
parameters/mixed-default-parameters.js
badFetchData(undefined, 4, 'magazines');
```

Mixing default parameters and regular parameters is poor design. JavaScript will not stop us from doing that, but our wisdom should. As a good practice keep all the default parameters trailing.

Expressions as Default Values

The default values are not limited to literals. Expressions are welcome as well, and that's quite powerful—kudos to JavaScript for that.

In the following code, the fileTax() function needs a date of filing. If the caller does not provide it, the current date of execution is assumed as the default value.

```
parameters/expression-default.js
const fileTax = function(papers, dateOfFiling = new Date()) {
  console.log('dateOfFiling: ' + dateOfFiling.getFullYear());
};
```

Let's call this function to verify the behavior of the expression in the default value.

parameters/expression-default.js
```
fileTax('stuff', new Date('2016-12-31'));
fileTax('stuff');
```

In the first call, we pass the last day of the year 2016 as the second argument. However, in the second call we leave it out. As we see from the output, the expression was evaluated on call and the year 2018 is used:

```
dateOfFiling: 2016
dateOfFiling: 2018
```

The value of the expression used for the default value is evaluated at the time of the call.

The expression that evaluates a default value for a parameter may use other parameters to the left. This gives the ability to compute the default value for a parameter based on other parameters' values, default or not.

Let's put that idea into a concrete—again a tax-related—example:

parameters/compute-default.js
```
const computeTax = function(amount,
  stateTax = 15, localTax = stateTax * .10) {
    console.log('stateTax: ' + stateTax + ' localTax: ' + localTax);
};
```

The computeTax() function takes a required parameter followed by stateTax, which has a default value. The last parameter, localTax, uses an expression to compute the default value. The expression computes the value based on the current value of stateTax.

If the user gives a value for stateTax and localTax, then those given values are used and neither the default value nor the expression has any effect. If the user gives a value for the stateTax only, then the localTax is computed based on the given value for stateTax. If both stateTax and localTax are left out by the caller, then localTax is computed based on the default value for stateTax.

Let's see these in action with a few calls to the function:

parameters/compute-default.js
```
computeTax(100, 10, 2);
computeTax(100, 10);
computeTax(100);
```

Let's glance at the output:

```
stateTax: 10 localTax: 2
stateTax: 10 localTax: 1
stateTax: 15 localTax: 1.5
```

The first call to computeTax() provides arguments for all three parameters and so the defaults don't have any effect. In the second call, the value for localTax is one-tenth of the value given for stateTax. In the last call, it is one-tenth of the default value for stateTax.

Don't use a parameter that's to the right in the computation of the default value for a parameter. But if you grew up as one of those curious kids who won't take "no" for an answer, don't change now; go ahead and try.

Try changing

```
const computeTax = function(amount,
  stateTax = 15, localTax = stateTax * .10) {
```

to

```
const computeTax = function(amount,
  stateTax = localTax * 10, localTax = stateTax * .10) {
```

Then, with a wicked smile, run the code, with the three calls to computeTax(). Remember, JavaScript is both naughty and lazy. On the naughty side, it does not complain much; it simply likes to watch the code crash and burn. On the lazy side, it will wait until the last minute to tell you *oops*.

There will be no errors on the first two calls; after all, we provided the value for stateTax and are not using the default value—why complain about what is not used? However, in the last call where we are not passing stateTax, it will complain, as we see in the output:

```
stateTax: 10 localTax: 2
stateTax: 10 localTax: 1
...
  stateTax = localTax * 10, localTax = stateTax * .10) {
                ^

ReferenceError: localTax is not defined
```

Programmers used to statically typed languages and rich compile-time checking will find this kind of behavior frustrating. Good automated testing of JavaScript code is highly critical to avoid runtime blowups—see *Test-Driving JavaScript Applications [Sub16]*.

We've seen in isolation two features related to parameters. The question is, do they play well with each other? We'll answer that question next.

Interplay of the Default and Rest Parameters

We can have any number of default parameters, and they can appear on (almost) any parameter. Rest parameters have some rules to follow—there must be at most one of them in the parameter list and it has to be the last one if present. What happens if we mix them together? For some reason this brings back memories of mixing barium with another chemical back in the high school chemistry lab—that was the last day they let me in there.

parameters/default-and-rest.js

```
const product = function(first, second = 1, ...moreValues) {
  console.log(first + ', ' + second + ', length:' + moreValues.length);
};
```

The product() method names a required parameter, a default parameter, and a rest parameter. There are a few consequences of this design.

Recall that the default parameter may be omitted and the rest parameter may receive zero or more values. Since the rest parameter has to be the last, when present, there is no way to omit the default parameters if the function also uses a rest parameter. So, in short, the default value is pretty useless, unless the user wants to use undefined—but we know that results in pungent smelling code.

Having discussed default values and the rest parameter, it's hard to avoid the nefarious thought of giving a default value to the rest parameter. Let's give that a try:

parameters/rest-and-default.js

```
//BROKEN CODE
const notAllowed = function(first, second, ...moreValues = [1, 2, 3]) {}
```

If we do not provide any values for the rest parameter, then we want it to assume the values [1, 2, 3]. And JavaScript says:

```
const notAllowed = function(first, second, ...moreValues = [1, 2, 3]) {}
                                                          ^
```

```
SyntaxError: Rest parameter may not have a default initializer
```

The good news here is we get an error at the point of declaration of the function, so it's instant rejection and that's good. When values are omitted for the rest parameter, it is required to be an empty array—no default values permitted there.

Wrapping Up

The rest parameter is a good replacement for arguments—just as powerful minus the perils. The same symbol (...) when used on the calling side becomes the spread operator. In addition to these two additions related to function parameters/arguments, JavaScript now has the ability to assign default values to parameters. This last feature especially is very useful to extend existing functions for adding new parameters. In the next chapter, we will look at nice ways to iterate over collections of data.

Exercises

This chapter covered some significant ground and touched on many useful features in JavaScript. Before you move on to the next chapter, spend some time on these practice exercises as a way to review what you have learned in this chapter. You can find answers to these exercises on page 232.

Exercise 1

An amountAfterTaxes() function returns the total amount after all the taxes are applied. Let's implement that function so the output for each call in the next code shows up as expected.

```
//the function goes here.

const amount = 25.12;
const fedTax = 10;
const stateTax = 2;
const localTax = 0.5;

console.log(amountAfterTaxes(amount)); //25.12
console.log(amountAfterTaxes(amount, fedTax)); //27.63
console.log(amountAfterTaxes(amount, fedTax, stateTax)); //28.13
console.log(
   amountAfterTaxes(amount, fedTax, stateTax, localTax)); //28.26
```

Exercise 2

The purchaseItems() function merely prints the parameters it receives, after a little formatting. Two calls to the function are shown. Let's implement a third call to the function so that it produces the desired result.

```
const purchaseItems = function(essential1, essential2, ...optionals) {
   console.log(essential1 + ', ' + essential2 + ', ' + optionals.join(', '));
};

purchaseItems('bread', 'milk');
purchaseItems('bread', 'milk', 'jelly');

const mustHaves = ['bread', 'milk'];
const andAlso = ['eggs', 'donuts', 'tea'];

//call purchaseItems so it prints bread, milk, eggs, donuts, tea
```

Exercise 3

Let's reimplement the purchaseItems() function from the previous exercise so that milk and bread are assumed for the first two parameters, respectively, if a value is not provided for the argument in that position.

```
const purchaseItems = //function declaration goes here
  console.log(essential1 + ', ' + essential2 + ', ' + optionals.join(', '));
};

const items = ['cheese', 'milk'];
purchaseItems('cheese'); //cheese, bread,
purchaseItems(...items); //cheese, milk,
purchaseItems(); //milk, bread,
```

Exercise 4

The placeOrder() function assumes values for shipping and date if those values are not given. Let's fix the parameter list so the function behaves as expected.

```
const placeOrder = function(//...let's complete the parameter list...
  )
  console.log(' shipping charge for id: ' +
    id + ' is $' + shipping + ' Date:' + date.getDate());
};

//shipping, if not given, is $5 if amount less than 20 else $10
//date is today's date unless given
placeOrder(1, 12.10, 3, new Date('05/15/2018'));
placeOrder(1, 25.20, 10);
placeOrder(1, 12.05);
placeOrder(1, 25.30);
placeOrder(1, 25.20);
```

Exercise 5

In the previous example, how can we pass the value for the date parameter without passing a value for the shipping parameter?

Part II

Nice Additions

In this part we dive into some of the most elegant and aesthetic features of modern JavaScript. You'll learn about features like arrow functions that reduce noise in code, about iterators and powerful generators that provide excellent capabilities to work with collections of objects, and about the most charming destructuring facility.

CHAPTER 4

Iterators and Symbols

Iterating over a collection of values is commonplace, yet the code to loop through and process elements has been cumbersome in the past. In this chapter you'll learn to use the new enhanced loop. This improvement to the language reduces noise, making iteration more fluent and pleasant to maintain.

We will then look at Symbol, the new primitive type added to the language, and see how it fills the void of interfaces in JavaScript. Finally, we'll work with generators and see how they help to create infinite sequences.

The Convenience of Enhanced for

The for loop is arguably one of the most widely used constructs in C-like languages. Here's an example of using the for loop to iterate over a list of names and print each element.

iterators/traditional-for.js
```
const names = ['Sara', 'Jake', 'Pete', 'Mark', 'Jill'];

for(let i = 0; i < names.length; i++) {
  console.log(names[i]);
}
```

The output from this code is the expected listing of the names:

```
Sara
Jake
Pete
Mark
Jill
```

That loop is very familiar but far from being simple—it has way too many moving parts. We first had to initialize the variable i, then set its upper bound, pause to grimace, wonder if it should be < or <=, then decide between pre-increment and post-increment. The assault of the complexity continues within the loop—we have to access the element in the collection based on the value of the index variable i.

No doubt, the for loop is quite powerful and capable. We can use it to iterate in forward or reverse order, we can break out of the loop at any time, we can step in increments of 2, and so on. However, we use it for the common forward iteration most of the time, and that's tedious.

Simple Iteration Over Elements

For straightforward iterations, the enhanced for loop is a better choice. Let's convert the previous loop to use this newer facility.

iterators/enhanced-for.js
```
const names = ['Sara', 'Jake', 'Pete', 'Mark', 'Jill'];

for(const name of names) {
  console.log(name);
}
```

This code produces the same result as the previous one, but it needed far less typing and is easier to read as well. Unlike the index variable i in the traditional for loop, the variable name used in the enhanced loop is a constant. It also has block scope and directly represents the selected element in each iteration. This code is not only concise, it is less error prone as well—we will discuss this further later in this chapter—a simple solution for a simple problem.

We can use for...of on any object that is iterable—that is, any object that implements the [Symbol.iterator]() method—we'll learn more about this in *Implementing an Iterator*, on page 58.

Getting the Index

The traditional for loop forced us to use the index variable even if we did not care for it. The enhanced for loop directly gets us the desired element in each iteration, but it does not prevent us from getting the index. To access the index, first we have to use the entries() function; let's explore that function first.

The entries() function of Array returns an iterator, which has the key plus the value. Let's iterate over the iterator returned by entries to get a feel for it.

iterators/using-entries.js
```
const names = ['Sara', 'Jake', 'Pete', 'Mark', 'Jill'];

for(const entry of names.entries()) {
  console.log(entry);
}
```

The variable entry represents the elements returned by the entries() method in each step of the iteration. Printing its content reveals that entry has two pieces of information: an index and the value at that index in the original array. We can see this in the output:

```
[ 0, 'Sara' ]
[ 1, 'Jake' ]
[ 2, 'Pete' ]
[ 3, 'Mark' ]
[ 4, 'Jill' ]
```

To get the index more conveniently while iterating over the array, we can use the enhanced for loop along with the facility to destructure arrays—we will explore destructuring in Chapter 6, *Literals and Destructuring*, on page 91.

Let's rewrite the example with enhanced for loop to get the index and the value while iterating.

```
iterators/enhanced-for-with-index.js
const names = ['Sara', 'Jake', 'Pete', 'Mark', 'Jill'];

for(const [i, name] of names.entries()) {
  console.log(i + '--' + name);
}
```

Instead of specifying only the name, we include the index variable i as well, but in an array. Then instead of iterating over names we iterate over the iterator returned by entries. Through each iteration, when the entries iterator provides an entry, the index and the value in the entry are destructured and placed into the variables i and name, respectively.

Here's the output from the previous code:

```
0--Sara
1--Jake
2--Pete
3--Mark
4--Jill
```

The enhanced for loop is the surefire replacement for the traditional for loop for simple iterations. It does not force us to deal with the index. Furthermore, even if we need the index, we don't have to mess with the bounds or alter the index.

Again, unlike the variable i used in the traditional for loop, this variable i is immutable—that reduces the chances of errors in code.

The entries() method returns an iterator, but JavaScript relies on a special method of Symbol for iteration. Let's dive into that new primitive type next.

Symbol—A New Primitive Type

JavaScript previously had five primitive types: number, string, boolean, null, and, undefined; now it has one more. Symbol is a new primitive type in JavaScript intended for limited specialized use. Symbols can be used for three distinct purposes:

- To define properties for objects in such a way they don't appear during normal iteration—these properties are not private; they're just not easily discovered like other properties.

- To easily define a global registry or dictionary of objects.

- To define some special well-known methods in objects; this feature, which fills the void of interfaces, is arguably one of the most important purposes of Symbol.

Interfaces in languages like Java and C# are useful for design by contract and serve as a specification or a listing of abstract functions. When a function expects an interface it is guaranteed, in these languages, that the object passed will conform to the specifications of the interface. There's no such capability in JavaScript, however. We'll see how Symbol helps fill the gap.

Let's explore each of the benefits with examples.

Hidden Properties

Until Symbol was added to JavaScript, all properties of an object were visible when iterated using for...in. Symbol changes that behavior; a Symbol property is not visible during such iteration.

If a property is intended to be visible during normal iteration, then define it as usual. However, if you like for a property to store some special data, like metadata about an object, that should not be visible using normal iteration, then you may hide it as a Symbol property.

Let's take a look at the behavior of a Symbol property using an example.

iterators/symbol-property.js
```
const age = Symbol('ageValue');
const email = 'emailValue';

const sam = {
  first: 'Sam',
  [email]: 'sam@example.com',
  [age]: 2
};
```

age is defined as a Symbol using the Symbol() function. The argument passed to this function has no real use other than for debugging purposes. A Symbol created using this function is unique and distinct from any other Symbol created using the function. Symbols can't be created using the new operator.

email is defined as a string. Within the sam object, first is a property and it is assigned the string value 'Sam' representing the name. Had we defined the next property as email: ... then the property name will be email. But our intention is to define the property name as emailValue, which is held inside the variable named email. Thus, we wrap the variable named with []. In effect, [email] defines a property named emailValue. Likewise, we define a third property with [age], but unlike email, which refers to a string, age refers to a Symbol. Thus we defined the third property where the property itself is of Symbol type while the value held by that property is of type number.

Let's iterate over the properties of the instance sam next.

```
iterators/symbol-property.js
console.log('iterating over properties:');
for(const property in sam) {
  console.log(property + ' : ' + sam[property]);
}

console.log('list of property names:');
console.log(Object.getOwnPropertyNames(sam));
```

First we iterate over the properties of the instance sam using for...in and print both the property names and the corresponding values. Next we query for all the property names on the object using Object's getOwnPropertyNames() method. The result for these two actions is shown next:

```
iterating over properties:
first : Sam
emailValue : sam@example.com
list of property names:
[ 'first', 'emailValue' ]
```

Both the properties first and emailValue are displayed, but the property ageValue, which is of type Symbol, is not exposed.

A Symbol property is hidden from normal iteration. However, it is not private or encapsulated. Any code with access to the object can both access and change the value for a Symbol property. Also, Object's getOwnPropertySymbols() method will give a list of all the Symbol properties, like so:

iterators/symbol-property.js
```
console.log('list of symbol properties');
console.log(Object.getOwnPropertySymbols(sam));

console.log('accessing a symbol property:');
console.log(sam[age]);

console.log('changing value...');
sam[age] = 3;
console.log(sam[age]);
```

The getOwnPropertySymbols() method does not hold back any Symbol properties. If an object has no Symbol properties, the method will return an empty array. Otherwise, it returns an array of Symbols with one element for each Symbol property.

The syntax sam.age will try to access a property named age, which does not exist in the instance. Our intention is to access a property whose name is held within the age variable. To achieve this, we use the [] syntax, like so: sam[age]. Likewise, to set the value of the property whose name is held within the age variable, we place sam[age] on the left-hand side of the assignment expression. The output of the code shows the list of Symbol properties and the result of our efforts to access/change the value of the ageValue Symbol property:

```
list of symbol properties
[ Symbol(ageValue) ]
accessing a symbol property:
2
changing value...
3
```

We played with our own instance sam in the previous example. Next, let's examine a built-in object for Symbols.

iterators/examine-regex.js
```
const regex = /cool/;

process.stdout.write('regex is of type RegExp: ');
console.log(regex instanceof RegExp);

process.stdout.write('Properties of regex: ');
console.log(Object.getOwnPropertyNames(regex));

process.stdout.write('Symbol properties of regex: ');
console.log(Object.getOwnPropertySymbols(regex));

console.log("Symbol properties of regex's prototype: ");
console.log(Object.getOwnPropertySymbols(Object.getPrototypeOf(regex)));
```

As an aside, in the code, in addition to using console.log() we're using process.stdout.write(). The log() function produces a new line. In this example, to stay on the same line after printing output, we use the write() method that's available in node.js. The variable regex holds a reference to an instance of the RegExp regular expression class. We first confirm that the instance is of the type we expect it to be. Then we query for all its properties using the getOwnProperty-Names() method. Then we query for all its Symbol properties. Finally we perform the query on the instance's prototype, accessed through the Object.getPrototypeOf() method, which returns the same instance as RegExp.prototype.

The output from the code is shown next:

```
regex is of type RegExp: true
Properties of regex: [ 'lastIndex' ]
Symbol properties of regex: []
Symbol properties of regex's prototype:
[ Symbol(Symbol.match),
  Symbol(Symbol.replace),
  Symbol(Symbol.search),
  Symbol(Symbol.split) ]
```

The little experiment we ran reveals that RegExp has a handful of Symbol properties. These properties are actually special methods. We'll soon see how we can benefit from special methods for our own classes. Before that, let's explore the uniqueness property of Symbol.

Global Registry with Symbol

When we create a Symbol using the Symbol() function, the argument passed to it has no significance and each call to Symbol() creates a unique Symbol. Let's quickly verify this behavior with an example.

```
iterators/creating-symbols.js
const name = 'Tom';
const tom = Symbol(name);
const jerry = Symbol('Jerry');
const anotherTom = Symbol(name);

console.log(tom);
console.log(typeof(tom));
console.log(tom === jerry);
console.log(tom === anotherTom);
```

We created three Symbols. Two of those were created using the same argument name. However, since the arguments passed to the function have no significance and the Symbol created by each call is unique, we can see in the output that the Symbol instances are all unequal:

```
Symbol(Tom)
symbol
false
false
```

The aforementioned behavior changes a bit when the Symbol.for() method is used to create a Symbol instead of the Symbol() function. The for() method takes a *key* as argument, creates a Symbol if one already does not exist for that key in a global registry, and returns either the newly created instance or the preexisting one. At any time we may obtain the pre-created Symbol for a given key using the keyFor() method. Let's explore these two methods with an example.

iterators/symbol-registry.js

```
const masterWizard = Symbol.for('Dumbledore');
const topWizard = Symbol.for('Dumbledore');

console.log(typeof(masterWizard));
console.log(masterWizard);
console.log(masterWizard === topWizard);

console.log('Dumbledore' === Symbol.keyFor(topWizard));
```

We first create a Symbol using the for() method, passing an argument to it, and assign the result to the variable masterWizard. We repeat this step, using the same argument for the for() method, but assign the result this time to the variable named topWizard. In the last line of the code we invoke the keyFor() method, passing to it the second Symbol we created. Unlike the Symbol() function, the argument passed to for() has significance—it represents a unique key for Symbol that is being created or fetched from the global registry. In this example, the first call to for() creates a new Symbol instance whereas the second call to for() fetches the Symbol created by the first call, since the argument is the same as in the first call. The call to keyFor() returns the key associated with the Symbol in the registry. We can verify the code's behavior from the output:

```
symbol
Symbol(Dumbledore)
true
true
```

This feature of uniqueness of Symbol is used in JavaScript to define special well-known functions, as we'll see next.

Special Well-Known Symbols

In languages like Java and C# we expect classes to collaborate with each other through interfaces. For example, if a class expects another class to have a compare() method, it would expect that class to implement a Comparator interface. JavaScript does not follow such traditions or ceremony. The contracts are rather informal and relaxed. If a class expects another class to have a method, it simply expects to find that method—as simple as that.

While there is merit to that simplicity, from the documentation point of view a single source of truth is still useful. Furthermore, not having a clear way to specify that you expect a class to implement a particular method or a property can lead to errors.

Suppose you expect a programmer using your library to create a class with a special method named myWonderfulMethod. It's hard to track if a programmer makes a typo and creates a method with the name myWonderfulmethod. Also, since the name myWonderfulMethod is not a standard name, a class may have already implemented that method for some other purpose than what you expected. A lack of a clear way to uniquely specify a method or property name can lead to errors and confusion. This is another place where Symbol comes to rescue.

Since a Symbol is unique, instead of expecting a class to implement a method named myWonderfulMethod, if you expect it to implement a special method [Symbol.for('myappname.myWonderfulMethod')] then there's no ambiguity.

JavaScript has nearly a dozen well-known Symbols, like Symbol.iterator, Symbol.match, Symbol.replace, and Symbol.search, to mention a few. Some functions and methods expect classes to implement methods with one or more of these well-known Symbol names in order to pass instances of those classes as arguments.

One example of a function that depends on a special well-known Symbol is String's search() method. If the argument given to search is not an instance of RegExp, it then creates a RegExp using the given argument as the constructor argument. However, that's true only if the given argument to search() does not support the special method named Symbol.search. If that method is available on the instance, then that method is used to perform the search. Let's create a class with this special method to learn about this behavior.

```
iterators/search.js
class SuperHero {
  constructor(name, realName) {
    this.name = name;
    this.realName = realName;
  }

  toString() { return this.name; }

  [Symbol.search](value) {
    console.info('this: ' + this + ', value: ' + value);
    return value.search(this.realName);
  }
}
```

We created a class named SuperHero using the new class syntax. It's much like what you may be used to in languages like Java and C#. We will explore the class syntax in Chapter 7, *Working with Classes*, on page 115.

An instance of the class SuperHero holds two fields: name and realName. The Symbol.search() method takes in a value as parameter and searches it for the contents present in the realName field. In addition, the method prints an informational message about the current context object this and the passed-in value argument.

Let's now make use of this class to see the power of the special search() method:

```
iterators/search.js
const superHeroes = [
  new SuperHero('Superman', 'Clark Kent'),
  new SuperHero('Batman', 'Bruce Wayne'),
  new SuperHero('Ironman', 'Tony Stark'),
  new SuperHero('Spiderman', 'Peter Parker') ];

const names = 'Peter Parker, Clark Kent, Bruce Wayne';
for(const superHero of superHeroes) {
  console.log(`Result of search: ${names.search(superHero)}`);
}
```

The code creates an array of SuperHero instances. Finally, it loops through the instances and invokes the search on a names variable, passing in the instance at hand.

The output from the code shows that the specially defined method in the class SuperHero is called during the call to the search() method on names.

```
this: Superman, value: Peter Parker, Clark Kent, Bruce Wayne
Result of search: 14
this: Batman, value: Peter Parker, Clark Kent, Bruce Wayne
Result of search: 26
this: Ironman, value: Peter Parker, Clark Kent, Bruce Wayne
Result of search: -1
this: Spiderman, value: Peter Parker, Clark Kent, Bruce Wayne
Result of search: 0
```

Each of the special well-known Symbols serves as a special method in places where its presence is expected. For a complete list of the well-known Symbols and their purpose, refer to the appropriate section in the ECMAScript 2015 Language Specification.[1]

---

1. https://www.ecma-international.org/ecma-262/6.0/#sec-well-known-symbols

We discussed the three benefits that Symbol provides. One of the most common Symbols in JavaScript is the well-known Symbol.iterator. You will learn to use it for creating custom iterators next.

Using Custom Iterators and Generators

The built-in collections in JavaScript, like Array, Set, and Map, are all iterable. We can iterate over them, using the for loop, to process the elements. But what about user-defined classes? You may create, for example, a Car class and may want the user of your class to iterate over its wheels or doors. Thankfully, JavaScript makes it quite easy to define custom iterators for user-defined classes. Before we jump in to writing custom iterators, let's examine iterators for built-in classes.

We can easily iterate over a collection of objects. For example, the following code iterates over an array of strings:

```
iterators/iterate.js
const names = ['Tom', 'Jerry', 'Tyke'];

for(const name of names) {
  console.log(name);
}
```

We can readily use the for...of syntax on an Array because it implements a function named [Symbol.iterate]. The previous code produces the expected output:

```
Tom
Jerry
Tyke
```

We can't, however, iterate on arbitrary instances. For example, let's create a class named CardDeck and iterate over an instance of that class.

```
iterators/no-iterator.js
class CardDeck {
  constructor() {
    this.suitShapes = ['Clubs', 'Diamonds', 'Hearts', 'Spaces'];
  }
}

const deck = new CardDeck();

for(const suit of deck) {
  console.log(suit);
}
```

The class CardDeck has a field named suitShapes of type Array with four String values in it. deck is an instance of CardDeck that we iterate over using the for...of loop. Not so fast, says JavaScript, as we see in this output:

```
for(const suit of deck) {
                      ^

TypeError: deck is not iterable
```

The error is fairly descriptive and intuitive; it clearly tells us what's missing or expected.

Implementing an Iterator

To satisfy JavaScript and allow iteration over an instance of CardDeck, we need to create a method that will serve as an iterator. But that's easier said than done—buckle your seat belts before looking at the code.

```
class CardDeck {
  constructor() {
    this.suitShapes = ['Clubs', 'Diamonds', 'Hearts', 'Spaces'];
  }
  [Symbol.iterator]() {
    let index = -1;
    const self = this;
    return {
      next() {
        index++;
        return {
          done: index >= self.suitShapes.length,
          value: self.suitShapes[index]
        };
      }
    };
  }
}
```

The code implements a method with the special name [Symbol.iterator]. JavaScript looks for this method to be present in an instance to use that instance as an interator. That's the good news. Unfortunately, though, the code is very verbose and has many levels of nesting, enough to drown us—hang on to those }s and climb to safety; we'll revisit this method shortly after some preparation.

We will significantly improve this code shortly. Don't feel perturbed at the sight of the verbosity in that code—you almost never have to write such code thanks to *generators*, as you will see soon.

First, even though this code exposes the ugly bare metals, let's use it to understand how the iterator works. A flowchart of the steps JavaScript takes to perform the iteration is shown on page 59.

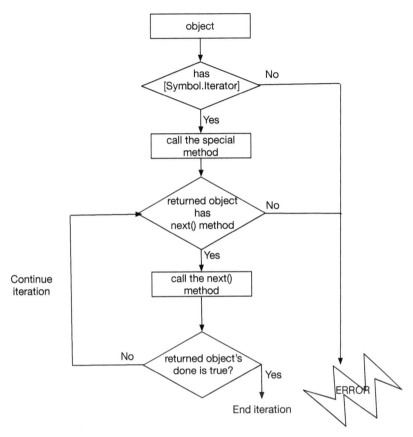

We defined a method with a special name [Symbol.iterator](). When we pass an instance of the modified class CardDeck to for...of, JavaScript will immediately look for, find, and invoke this special method.

In the [Symbol.iterator]() method, we return an object with one method named next(). On the calling side, internally for...of invokes the next() method and checks on the object returned by next() to see if that object's done property is false. By convention, a value of true means the end of the iteration; false tells it to continue with the iteration.

If next() returned an object with the done property set to false, then the value property is used as the current value through the iteration. After the current value is used in the loop, the iteration continues with another call to the next() method. This continues until the value of done in the result returned by next() turns out to be true.

Now it's time to put on your underwater breathing apparatus—we're going to dive into the [Symbol.iterator]() method.

Let's start with the first two lines of the method:

```
let index = -1;
const self = this;
```

As soon as for...of calls the iterator method, the method initializes a variable index to a value of -1. The function will return an object to the caller, but that object needs access to the instance of CardDeck—for this purpose we save the this reference for the instance to a variable self. The self variable will be available in the lexical scope for the object we'll soon create.

Let's now look at the next step in the iterator method.

```
return {
};
```

After defining index and self, the iterator quickly returns an object. At this point, the caller of the iterator method, for...of, will examine this returned object and look for a next() method in that object. If it finds the method, then for...of calls the next() method. Let's take a look at the next() method that is perched nicely inside the object we just returned.

```
next() {
  index++;
  return {
    done: index >= self.suitShapes.length,
    value: self.suitShapes[index]
  };
}
```

When for...of calls the next() method, the method increments the variable index that's in its lexical scope and, in turn, returns an object with two properties: done and value.

At this moment in the execution sequence, the value of index is 0. Thus, the value of the done property is false and the value of the value property is 'Club', which is the first value in the suitShapes field in the instance referenced by the self variable.

for...of will assign the property value to the iteration variable and examine the value of done. Since the value is false, for...of will call the next() method yet again. The value of index now increments to 1. This sequence of execution will continue until the next() function returns an object with the done property set to true.

Let's rerun the code with the newly added iterator method and see the output of the iteration:

```
Clubs
Diamonds
Hearts
Spaces
```

If we set aside the verbosity, we can appreciate the dynamic nature of this code, its power, and flexibility. We will soon see how this can help us create more dynamic, lazy iterators. But first, we have to clean up the code and make it more fluent and concise. In short, we have to remove the noise.

Using Yield

Let's put into words what the iterator method is doing. As the caller iterates over the object, the iterator *yields* the next value. To achieve that, we wrote quite a bit of code. We can get rid of most of it using the special yield keyword.

The caller of the iterator function should know if it should merely expect an object with the next() function or if it should do some extra work to process the result returned by yield. To help guide the caller, JavaScript relies on a special syntax—if the iterator will use yield, then the method should be decorated or marked with a *.

Let's convert the previous implementation of the iterator method from using the object with next() to a much more fluent and concise version using yield.

```
*[Symbol.iterator]() {
  for(const shape of this.suitShapes) {
    yield shape;
  }
}
```

That's a lot better—fewer moving parts and fewer levels of nesting. The code looks almost like functions we normally write. Using a simple for loop, we iterate over the values in the suitShapes array. Within the loop, we use the yield keyword to pass the value over to the caller, taking a pause in the iteration and giving an opportunity for the caller to process the value.

yield greatly simplifies the implementation of the iterator. We can use for, while, or other forms of iterations, or even simply place multiple yield calls within the function, like so:

```
*[Symbol.iterator]() {
  yield this.suitShapes[0];
  yield this.suitShapes[1];
  yield this.suitShapes[2];
  yield this.suitShapes[3];
}
```

When the execution runs into a yield, it switches the flow of execution to the caller side. When the caller is done with processing the yielded value, the execution resumes right after the yield call that was already processed.

The code is almost good except for the use of the somewhat verbose [Symbol.iterator]. The generators can cure that.

Using Generators

A generator, as the name indicates, generates values. For a function to serve as a generator, its name should lead with a * and its body should have one or more yield calls. Let's convert the iterator method to a simple generator.

iterators/generator.js
```
*suits() {
  for(const color of this.suitShapes) {
    yield color;
  }
}
```

We replaced the *[Symbol.iterator]() syntax with *suits() and the rest of the function stays intact—we may also use the multiple yield version if desired. This change will break the iterator. The class CardDeck no longer implements an iterator function. So, we can't quite perform for(const suit of deck) anymore. Instead we have to call the generator function directly to perform the iteration, like so:

iterators/generator.js
```
const deck = new CardDeck();

for(const suit of deck.suits()) {
  console.log(suit);
}
```

On the one hand, we can't iterate directly on the object, unless we write an iterator method in the class. On the other hand, we can have multiple generators —for example, one for suits, one for pips like Ace, King, Queen, and so forth.

Here's the implementation of a pips generator for the CardDeck class:

iterators/generator.js
```
*pips() {
  yield 'Ace';
  yield 'King';
  yield 'Queen';
  yield 'Jack';

  for(let i = 10; i > 1; i--) {
    yield i.toString();
  }
}
```

Using separate calls to yield, we return the non-number pips first and then loop through to return the number pips. We can use this generator much like how we used the suits generator.

```
iterators/generator.js
for(const pip of deck.pips()) {
  process.stdout.write(pip + ', ');
}
console.log();
```

Let's quickly take a look at the output from using the pips() generator.

```
Ace, King, Queen, Jack, 10, 9, 8, 7, 6, 5, 4, 3, 2,
```

Each of the generators we created so far created a series of values. That's nice, but what if we want to create suits and pips, all in one series? We'll explore an option for that next.

Combining Generators

In the CardDeck class, we have two generators: one to create the suits and the other for pips. It would be a shame if we have to duplicate the code to create one series that contains both suits and pips. Thankfully, we don't have to endure such guilt—JavaScript provides a way to combine generators.

Let's create a method, suitsAndPips(), in the CardDeck class.

```
iterators/generator.js
*suitsAndPips() {
  yield* this.suits();
  yield* this.pips();
}
```

In the suitsAndPips() method, we want to return the series of suits first and then the series of pips. That's exactly what we do, using the yield* syntax. While yield returns a single value, yield* explores the given collection and yields one value at a time from the collection.

Let's use the new suitsAndPips() method to iterate over the entire series.

```
iterators/generator.js
for(const value of deck.suitsAndPips()) {
  process.stdout.write(value + ' ');
}
```

The output from the call to the suitsAndPips() method shows the combined values:

```
Clubs Diamonds Hearts Spaces Ace King Queen Jack 10 9 8 7 6 5 4 3 2
```

In the suitsAndPips() method, we used yield* on the result of a generator. We may also use yield* on any iterable, like Array. Let's apply this knowledge to refactor the CardDeck class to use yield* in all three methods.

```
class CardDeck {
  constructor() {
    this.suitShapes = ['Clubs', 'Diamonds', 'Hearts', 'Spaces'];
  }

  *suits() {
    yield* this.suitShapes;
  }

  *pips() {
    yield* ['Ace', 'King', 'Queen', 'Jack'];

    yield* Array.from(new Array(9), (ignore, index) => 10 - index);

    //or using regular functions
    //yield* Array.from(
    // new Array(9), function(ignore, index) { return 10 - index; });

    //the above two use functional style. We may also use a more verbose
    //yield* Array.from(Array(11).keys()).reverse().splice(0, 9);
  }

  *suitsAndPips() {
    yield* this.suits();
    yield* this.pips();
  }
}
```

The refactored suits() method operates directly on the suitShapes array. Within the pips() method we first work on the array ['Ace', 'King',...]. Then we need numbers from 10 to 2 in descending order. There are multiple ways to achieve this. One approach is to use the functional style with arrow functions—you'll learn about this style in Chapter 5, *Arrow Functions and Functional Style*, on page 69. We may also use the functional style with a regular function for the values, as shown in the commented-out part. The last commented-out line shows a solution without using the functional style. You may discover more ways to generate the array of descending numbers. Pick the one you're most comfortable with.

The iterators we've seen so far worked off a collection of bounded size. However, iterators are flexible enough to allow iteration over unbounded or unknown size, as you'll see next.

Creating Infinite Iterators

Iterators in JavaScript are inherently lazy. They yield a value, wait for it to be consumed by the caller, and then, when requested for more, go on to produce the next value. While we can yield values from a known collection of data, we can also exploit this flexibility to create infinite sequences of data.

As an example, let's create an infinite sequence of prime numbers. As a first step, we'll define an isPrime() function that will tell us whether a given number is a prime number.

iterators/infinite-sequence.js
```
const isPrime = function(number) {
  for(let i = 2; i < number; i++) {
    if(number % i === 0) return false;
  }

  return number > 1;
};
```

The isPrime() function is a rather rudimentary implementation that determines if any number greater than 1 is a prime number—our purpose is not to optimize that function but to create an infinite series, so we'll keep our focus on that. Let's use this function to create a generator, like so:

iterators/infinite-sequence.js
```
const primesStartingFrom = function*(start) {
  let index = start;

  while(true) {
    if(isPrime(index)) yield index;
    index++;
  }
};
```

The variable primesStartingFrom refers to an anonymous generator function—we use * after the function keyword to define this function as a generator. Within the function we have an infinite loop that yields prime numbers, starting from the given start value, one at a time, forever. The generated sequence is infinite, but where would we store it? On the cloud of course!

The key idea here is laziness. Within the loop, when the flow of execution meets the call to yield, the control transfers to the caller side of the iteration immediately. If and only when the iteration returns to the iterator function, the index value is incremented and the while loop takes the next iterative step.

Let's now use the generator in an iteration. The sequence is infinite, but on the calling side, we have to control how many values the generator will yield—we can break out of the iteration whenever we like; for example:

iterators/infinite-sequence.js
```
for(const number of primesStartingFrom(10)) {
  process.stdout.write(number + ', ');
  if(number > 25) break;
}
```

The for loop iterates over the values returned by the generator, but it breaks out of the loop when number is greater than 25, thus terminating the iteration. Let's run the code and take a look at the output generated:

```
11, 13, 17, 19, 23, 29,
```

The generator produces 11 as the first prime number and proceeds to produce the sequence of prime numbers that follow, one at a time, until we break out of the loop when the value received is greater than the threshold we set.

The ability to easily create an infinite sequence is quite useful. We don't have to eagerly compute results a priori. Computation may be postponed for evaluation until the results are actually needed. That, in turn, can make the execution of code more efficient.

Wrapping Up

The newly introduced Symbol primitive type is useful to define properties and methods with unique names, like [Symbol.iterator], for example. The enhanced for loop provides an elegant, less noisy syntax, to iterate over collections of objects. To facilitate iteration over user-defined classes, JavaScript supports custom iterators and generators. The generators are lazy evaluators and may be used to create infinite streams of data.

So far we have used regular functions. In the next chapter you'll learn about the pros and cons of arrow functions.

Exercises

You learned about Symbols, iterators, and generators, and these are some of the most important and highly used features of JavaScript. These practice exercises will help you to review these concepts before you move on to the next chapter. You can find answers to these exercises on page 234.

Exercise 1

The code in this exercise prints every third letter, starting with the first, using the traditional for loop. Let's convert the loop into an enhanced for loop:

```
const letters = ['a', 'b', 'c', 'd', 'e', 'f', 'g', 'h'];

for(let i = 0; i < letters.length; i = i + 3) {
  console.log(letters[i]);
}
```

Exercise 2

Let's complete the following code to explore the Symbol properties in an Array:

```
const numbers = [1, 2, 3];

console.log("The Symbol properties in arrays are:");

console.log(//...code goes here...
  );
```

Exercise 3

Let's implement a method with the special name Symbol.replace to achieve the desired result in the following code:

```
class Message {
  constructor(text) { this.text = text; }

  //Your code goes here
}

const message = new Message('There are no stupid questions.');

console.log('stupid'.replace(message, 's*****'));
//There are no s***** questions.

console.log(''.replace(message, 'Yes, '));
//Yes, There are no stupid questions.
```

Exercise 4

Let's create a generator function to produce a Fibonacci series not exceeding the desired value:

```
//Your code goes here

for(const value of fibonocciSeries()) {
  if(value > 25) break;
  process.stdout.write(value + ", ");
}
```

Exercise 5

In the previous exercise, we terminated the iteration when the value in the series exceeded 25. Let's modify the fibonocciSeries() function so that we can terminate the series when a certain number of values has been obtained:

```
//Your code goes here
```

```
for(const [index, value] of fibonocciSeries()) {
  if(index > 8) break;
  process.stdout.write(value + ", ");
}
```

CHAPTER 5

Arrow Functions and Functional Style

Anonymous functions have been in JavaScript from day one. Arrow functions, which are new, reduce the clutter and make the code more expressive. At first sight, they may appear to be a direct replacement for anonymous functions, but significant semantic differences exist between them. Learning these differences is critical to avoiding surprises when you're refactoring code to use arrow functions.

The simplest of tasks can sometimes end up being incredibly difficult when the wrong set of tools are used. You will see how internal iterators and some convenience methods can save a lot of effort and remove accidental complexity from code. Along the way, you'll learn about the functional style of programming and its benefits.

From Anonymous to Arrow Functions

JavaScript has three different ways to define a function.

A named function uses the function keyword followed by the name of the function. For example, the following code defines a function named sqr:

```
function sqr(n) { return n * n; }
```

An anonymous function has the same structure, except it does not have a name—it's anonymous. An anonymous function can be passed to another function as an argument or stored into a variable. For example, here's an anonymous function that is stored into a variable named sqr:

```
const sqr = function(n) { return n * n; };
```

The third relatively new function form that JavaScript supports is an *arrow* function. An arrow (=>) separates the parameter list from the short body of the function. An arrow function, like an anonymous function, can also be passed as argument to another function or can be stored into a variable. For example, let's rewrite the previous anonymous function as an arrow function:

```
const sqr = (n) => n * n;
```

Arrow functions do not have a name and are a lot more concise than anonymous functions. Let's discuss using arrow functions compared to anonymous functions.

Passing functions as arguments to other functions is a common practice in JavaScript. Here's an example of passing a small anonymous function as an argument to the setTimeout() function:

```
arrow/anonymous-to-arrow.js
setTimeout(function() { console.log('greetings'); }, 2000);
```

When run, this code will produce the following output after a 2-second delay:

```
greetings
```

The call to setTimeout() is a bit cluttered. The feature of *arrow functions* was introduced to address situations like this—to make function passing short and code more expressive. Let's change our code to use an arrow function:

```
setTimeout(() => console.log('greetings'), 2000);
```

There is less clutter and less noise, and the code is crisp.

The structure of a short, single-line, anonymous function is

```
function(parameter1, parameter2, ...) { return ...body... }
```

The structure of the corresponding arrow function is

```
(parameter1, parameter2, ...) => ...body...;
```

Arrow functions have a parenthesized parameter list, an arrow, =>, and either a single-line body or a compound multiline body surrounded by {}. The return keyword is implicit and should be omitted if the body is not surrounded by {}.

JavaScript permits us to deviate from that syntax slightly on special occasions; let's explore a few of those.

Dropping the Parentheses

The parentheses around the parameter list are required if the arrow function has an empty parameter list or takes two or more parameters. However, the parentheses are optional if the function takes only one parameter.

For example, let's pass to setTimeout() a function that takes one parameter:

```
arrow/single-parameter-arrow.js
const greet = (subject) => console.log('Hello ' + subject);

setTimeout(greet.bind(null, 'Earthling'), 2000);
```

The code first shows that an arrow function, like an anonymous function, can be saved into a variable, such as greet. The arrow function has a parenthesized parameter list with one parameter named subject, followed by the arrow and the single-line body. In the call to setTimeout(), we bind the value Earthling to the parameter using the good old bind() function.

Since our arrow function takes only one parameter, we can drop the parentheses, like so:

```
const greet = subject => console.log('Hello ' + subject);
```

If your team prefers consistency, use the () around the single parameter. If they prefer less clutter, drop the parentheses where possible.

Multiline Arrow Functions

Arrow functions are not restricted to having a single-line body. JavaScript permits arrow functions to be multiline.

Multiline arrow functions are not as crisp, concise, and expressive as single-line arrow functions. The multiple lines in the body should be enclosed within {}, each statement or expression is expected to end with ;, and if the body intends to return a value, then the return keyword is required. Here's a piece of code that computes a factorial, defined as an anonymous function:

```
const factorial = function(number) {
  let product = 1;

  for(let i = 1; i <= number; i++) {
    product *= i;
  }

  return product;
};
```

We may write this function as a multiline arrow function if we desire, like so:

```
const factorial = (number) => {
  let product = 1;

  for(let i = 1; i <= number; i++) {
    product *= i;
  }

  return product;
};
```

Compared to writing as an anonymous function, we merely replaced

```
function(number)
```

with

```
(number) =>
```

There was hardly any benefit, other than less typing. Arrow functions have less noise and are concise and expressive when compared to regular and anonymous functions, but that's true only when the body is single line. Multiline arrow functions don't have those benefits. In appearance, the body of a multiline arrow function is no different from the body of the corresponding regular/anonymous function, but semantic differences do exist.

Since multiline arrow functions don't offer any syntactical benefit over regular/anonymous functions, should we ever choose them? Certainly we should not choose them to appear more fashionable. The decision to pick one or the other should be based on the semantic benefits that arrow functions offer compared to anonymous functions—we will discuss these in *Anonymous vs. Arrow Functions*, on page 74. At the same time, be mindful of the limitations of arrow functions when making that decision—see *Limitations of Arrow Functions*, on page 78.

Resist the urge to pass multiline arrow functions as function arguments—this makes the code hard to read. Consider the following example where the use of multiline arrow functions, I argue, is smelly.

```
navigator.geolocation.getCurrentPosition(
  (position) => {
    const latitude = position.coords.latitude;
    const longitude = position.coords.longitude;

    document.getElementById('location').innherHTML =
      `${latitude}, ${longitude}`;
  },
  (error) => {
    document.getElementById('location').innherHTML =
      `Error: ${error}`;
  });
```

Compare that to the following call:

```
navigator.geolocation.getCurrentPosition(onSuccess, onError);
```

It's a lot easier to see what we're passing to the getCurrentPosition() function: two arguments, one to deal with the success scenario and the other with the error scenario. The variables onSuccess and onError may refer to a regular function, an anonymous function, or a multiline arrow function, but must be defined before the call to getCurrentPosition(). This removes the clutter in code and makes the code expressive, easier to understand, and easier to maintain.

Using the Rest Parameter

In *Using the Rest Parameter*, on page 29, we saw how functions can take a rest parameter. Arrow functions' parameters can also have a rest parameter. Let's create another version of the greet() arrow function that takes multiple subjects.

```
arrow/rest-parameter-arrow.js
const greet =
  (message, ...subjects) => console.log(message + ' '+ subjects.join(', '));

greet('Hi', 'Developers', 'Geeks');
```

The function takes two parameters, message and subjects, where subjects is a rest parameter. The caller may pass a value for message and zero or more values for the second parameter. Here's the output of directly calling the arrow function:

```
Hi Developers, Geeks
```

In this example, since we had two arguments, we had to use the parentheses. Even if we had only one parameter, the relaxed rule for parentheses for a single parameter does not hold if it is a rest parameter. We have to use () if we use a rest parameter.

Using Default Arguments

In *Defining Default Values for Parameters*, on page 34, we saw how functions can take default arguments. Arrow functions can also take default arguments. Here's a short function that takes two parameters, the second with a default value.

```
const power = (number, exp = 2) => Math.pow(number, exp);

console.log(power(4, 3));
console.log(power(4));
```

We can call the power() function with two arguments, as in the first call, or leave out the second argument, as in the second call. The default value kicks in when the argument is omitted, using the same rules for default arguments here with arrow functions as with regular functions. The output of this code confirms that behavior:

```
64
16
```

Again in this case, the parentheses are required when default arguments are involved, even if there is only one parameter.

We saw how arrow functions are useful to reduce clutter for short functions. They reduce noise where anonymous functions are passed as arguments. Before looking at some benefits of using arrow functions, let's discuss some semantic differences between arrow functions and traditional functions.

Anonymous vs. Arrow Functions

At first sight, it may appear that arrow functions are direct replacements for anonymous functions. You may be tempted to readily replace anonymous functions with arrow functions. But that may result in code that behaves differently than you intend. There are many semantic differences between anonymous functions and arrow functions, and we have to carefully choose between them based on the context. Learning about the key differences between the two types of functions will help you pick the right one.

Lexical vs. Dynamic Scoping

Most variables used in any function either come from the parameters or are defined locally. However, some variables can be defined in an external context. Let's consider a short example.

```
[1, 2, 3].map(function(e) { return e * 2; })
```

The map() function takes an anonymous function as an argument. Within the anonymous function, we refer to a variable e in the expression e * 2. The e variable comes from the parameter passed to the anonymous function. No surprises here. Now, let's consider a small variation to this code.

```
[1, 2, 3].map(function(e) { return e * factor; })
```

The anonymous function passed to the map() function still receives only one parameter—map() will pass only one argument when it calls the function passed as an argument to it. However, within the anonymous function we use two variables, e and factor. The e variable is still the parameter passed to the function. However, the factor variable is neither a parameter nor a locally defined variable. Where does that come from?

There are two possibilities. The variable may come from the scope where the function using the variable is defined—that's called *lexical scoping*. Alternatively, the variable may be provided by the caller for the function—that's called *dynamic scoping*.

Most programming languages favor lexical scoping. A few languages use dynamic scoping. JavaScript is special—it does both, depending on the variable—and that has been a source of errors in anonymous functions.

JavaScript scopes all non-parameter, non-local variables to lexical scope for anonymous functions, except for this and arguments. Arrow functions have consistent lexical scoping for *all* non-parameter, non-local variables.

Lexically Scoped this and arguments

Anonymous functions use dynamic scoping for this and arguments and uses lexical scoping for all other variables. This behavior is often a source of error and unpleasant workarounds—recall that rest parameters are preferable to arguments in modern JavaScript, but the this keyword is still a nemesis. Let's look at an example that illustrates the odd behavior of this.

```
this.stuff = 'from lexical scope';
const someValue = 4;
const self = this;

setTimeout(function() {
  console.log('someValue is ' + someValue); //lexical scope for someValue
  console.log('this...' + this.stuff); //dynamic scope for this
  console.log('self...' + self.stuff); //lexical scope for self
}, 1000);
```

Outside of the anonymous function we have assigned a value from lexical scope to a stuff property of this—the context object. We also created a local variable named someValue and a variable named self, then we assigned the reference this to self. Within the anonymous function passed to setTimeout(), we have not defined someValue, this, or self, but we readily use those three. Let's look at the output of this code:

```
someValue is 4
this...undefined
self...from lexical scope
```

The variable someValue has lexical scope inside the anonymous function, so it gets the value assigned from outside the anonymous function. The variable this, however, is dynamically scoped—it's whatever setTimeout() passes. Since the this passed by setTimeout() does not have a stuff property, it gets printed as undefined. Finally, self also has lexical scope within the anonymous function, and we're able to get the stuff property of it—which is the value set into this in the outside scope.

Since this has a different scope compared to other variables, programmers often have to use workarounds like self to access this from the outside scope. It's easy to miss and use this directly without the intention of using dynamic scoping, and that leads to errors in programming.

Arrow functions keep scope consistent for this.

Let's change the previous anonymous function into an arrow function to see this behavior.

```
setTimeout(() => {
  console.log('someValue is ' + someValue); //lexical scope for someValue
  console.log('this...' + this.stuff); //lexical scope for this
  console.log('self...' + self.stuff); //lexical scope for self
}, 1000);
```

The only change to this code was replacing

```
function() {
```

with

```
() => {
```

It's a small change to the syntax but a big change to the semantics. Now, this within the arrow function is lexically scoped much like someValue, as we see from the output:

```
someValue is 4
this...from lexical scope
self...from lexical scope
```

The example illustrates a few key differences. It is very safe to use this within arrow functions and count on it being the value in the lexical scope. When using arrow functions, we do not need workarounds like the self or that variable that programmers often assign this to.

If your code relied on this from dynamic scoping, then arrow functions are not the right choice. You'll want to continue to use anonymous functions in such cases. Use your judgment.

In addition to this, anonymous functions use dynamic scoping for arguments. Here's an example to illustrate that difference in scoping of arguments between anonymous functions and arrow functions.

```
Line 1  const create = function(message) {
     2    console.log('First argument for create: ' + arguments[0]);
     3    return function() {
     4      console.log('First argument seen by greet: ' + arguments[0]);
     5    };
     6  };
     7
     8  const greet = create('some value');
     9  greet('hi');
```

The create() function creates and returns to the caller an anonymous function. It also prints the first argument passed to it before returning the anonymous function. Outside of the create() function, we store into the greet variable the function returned by a call to create(). Finally we invoke that function, passing the argument hi. Here's the output of this code:

```
First argument for create: some value
First argument seen by greet: hi
```

The output confirms that the anonymous function uses dynamic scoping for arguments—it reports the value hi passed by its caller and not the value some value from the context in which the function is created—that is, the create() method. In other words, the variables that are both named arguments on lines 2 and 4 are not the same.

Now, let's replace the anonymous function created within the create() method with an arrow function.

```
const create = function(message) {
  console.log('First argument for create: ' + arguments[0]);
  return () => console.log('First argument seen by greet: ' + arguments[0]);
};

const greet = create('some value');
greet('hi');
```

The code is concise compared to the previous version, but the difference is not just in syntax. Let's look at the output after this change:

```
First argument for create: some value
First argument seen by greet: some value
```

The variable arguments within the arrow function is lexically scoped. Thus the variable arguments within the arrow function now refers to the same variable that is visible within the create() function. The value hi passed to the call is not bound to the arguments in this case.

At first sight this might appear like a hindrance at the least and possibly an error. However, this is the intended behavior of arrow functions—they want to use lexical scoping consistently for this, arguments, and any other non-parameter, non-local variable.

If your function relies on using arguments, then stick with the anonymous function instead of converting it to an arrow function. If you do decide to convert to an arrow function, then change arguments to a rest parameter.

From here on, when writing JavaScript, don't use arguments—as we saw in *Using the Rest Parameter*, on page 29, rest parameters are far better than arguments.

Differences in bind, call, apply

The bind() function is useful to attach or curry arguments to functions so that the attached values are used in calls to the bound or curried function. Here's an example.

```
arrow/using-bind.js
const greet = function(message, name) {
  console.log(message + ' ' + name);
};

const sayHi = greet.bind(null, 'hi');

sayHi('Joe');
```

sayHi is a reference to a function that has curried or saved away a value for the message parameter of greet(). Later, when sayHi is called, it passes the curried value hi to message to the greet() function. The result of the previous code is

```
hi Joe
```

While bind() is a powerful function to curry arguments, there is one sore point about it: the first parameter. If we want to curry n parameters, we pass n + 1 arguments to bind(), and the first argument binds to this. Since arrow functions use the lexical this, we can't bind this if bind() is called on arrow functions. So the first parameter of bind() makes little sense when used in the context of arrow functions, and so the irrelevant first argument passed is largely ignored.

While the bind() function may be used to bind this and its parameters, when used on an arrow function, for example, anArrowFunc.bind(null, someinput), bind() can only bind parameters and not this—the first argument, irrespective of whether it is null or something else, is ignored.

If a function relies on this, the call and the apply functions help to pass values for this in addition to the parameters of the function. Since arrow functions already bind this to their lexical scope, it makes little sense to use call or apply with arrow functions. Furthermore, since we have the spread operator, apply has fallen out of favor. Don't use call or apply with arrow functions.

Limitations of Arrow Functions

Due to their concise and expressive nature, we'll be tempted to use arrow functions rather than anonymous functions. However, the choice should not be due to infatuation. Learning about the limitations of arrow functions will help us make an educated choice between anonymous functions and arrow functions.

Only Anonymous

Named anonymous function sounds like an oxymoron, but a function created in the argument list of a method call may be given a name. Here's an example of naming a function that's created just in time in the argument list.

```
arrow/named-anonymous.js
setTimeout(function repeat(count) {
  console.log('called...');
  if(count > 1)
    setTimeout(repeat.bind(null, count - 1), 1000);
}.bind(null, 5), 1000);
```

The function passed as an argument to the setTimeout() function has a name, repeat. This name is useful to make recursive calls to it.

A named function may be stored into a variable as well, like so:

```
arrow/named-anonymous.js
const repeat = function repeat(count) {
  console.log('called...');
  if(count > 1)
    setTimeout(repeat.bind(null, count - 1), 1000);
};

setTimeout(repeat.bind(null, 5), 1000);
```

Unlike traditional functions, arrow functions can't be named—they're truly anonymous. Arrow functions can be stored into a variable, but we can't give them a reliable name like we can non-arrow functions.

Not a Constructor

Functions may be intended to serve as constructors and the callers may use them with new to create instances. For example, the following function represents a class—the way we once defined classes in JavaScript.

```
arrow/car.js
//function Car(year) {
//or
const Car = function(year) {
  this.year = year;
};
```

Traditionally, function names were capitalized to convey they represent classes and regular functions otherwise. Regardless of how we name the functions, all are constructors. We can create an instance from this function, like so:

```
arrow/car.js
const car1 = new Car(2018);
```

Arrow functions can't serve as constructors and can't be used to instantiate objects. Let's examine what happens if we try to use new on an arrow function:

arrow/no-constructor.js
```
const Car = (year) => this.year = year;

const car1 = new Car(2018);
```

Any attempt to run this code will end up with an error:

```
const car1 = new Car(2018);
                 ^

TypeError: Car is not a constructor
```

If your intention is to create a class, anonymous functions will not serve that need. Thankfully, the alternative in modern JavaScript is not to use regular functions but to use the class keyword, as we'll see in Chapter 7, *Working with Classes*, on page 115.

new.target Is Lexically Scoped

Functions may use new.target to determine if they were called as a constructor or as a regular function. In the following code we use the new.target property to check how the function was called.

arrow/new-target.js
```
const f1 = function() {
  if(new.target) {
    console.log('called as a constructor');
  }
  else {
    console.log('called as a function');
  }
};

new f1();
f1();
```

If the function is called as a constructor, then new.target refers to the constructor function; otherwise it's undefined. The output from the previous code confirms this:

```
called as a constructor
called as a function
```

When it comes to arrow functions, the short answer is they don't have the new.target property. That makes sense because arrow functions can't be invoked as a constructor. However, if we reference this property within an arrow function we will not get a "new.target is not defined" error. That may surprise you, but the reason is that property takes on lexical scope.

Here are a few examples to illustrate this behavior. Let's first define an arrow function and call it.

arrow/arrow-new-target.js

```
const arrow = () => {
  console.log(new.target);
};

arrow();
```

The arrow function is directly defined in this file. In the lexical scope, the new.target property has a value of undefined. The reference to this property within the arrow function binds to the property in the file scope. Hence we get the following output:

```
undefined
```

If the arrow function is defined within the context of another function, it will take on the new.target property of that function. Let's verify this with the next example.

arrow/embedded-arrow-new-target.js

```
const outer = function() {
  return () => console.log(new.target);
};

const arrow1 = new outer();
const arrow2 = outer();

arrow1();
arrow2();
```

The outer() function returns an arrow function in response to a call. We first invoke outer() as a constructor and store the result into the variable arrow1. We then invoke outer() again, but this time as a function instead of a constructor, and store the result into the variable arrow2. Finally we call the two arrow functions, using the variables arrow1 and arrow2.

Since the first arrow function, referenced using arrow1, was created within a constructor call, its new.target property binds to the variable within the constructor. As a result, the print of this property to the console shows the reference to the constructor function. On the other hand, since the second arrow function, referenced using arrow2 was obtained from a function call, and not a constructor invocation, the new.target property is undefined. The output illustrates this scenario.

```
[Function: outer]
undefined
```

If you're converting functions to arrow functions and you see references to new.target, pay attention as the semantic behavior of this property goes from a locally defined variable to lexical scoping. If the function relies on new.target, it may really be intended to be used as a constructor, at least in some context, and that may no longer be valid after converting to an arrow function.

No prototype Property

Unlike many object-oriented languages, JavaScript provides prototypal inheritance instead of class-based inheritance. Each class has a prototype that can carry common methods and properties for the instances of the class. Since classes are traditionally represented as functions, each function has a prototype property that refers to the function's or class's prototype. However, arrow functions don't have the prototype property.

In the next example, we create a function and an arrow function and examine the prototype property.

```
arrow/arrow-prototype.js
const aFunc = function() {};
const anArrow = () => {};

console.log(aFunc.prototype);
console.log(anArrow.prototype);
```

While the regular function, referenced by aFunc, has a valid prototype, the arrow function referenced by anArrow does not, as we see in the output:

```
aFunc {}
undefined
```

If an existing code makes heavy use of the prototype property of a function and injects properties and methods using prototype, it may not be a good candidate to be replaced with an arrow function.

Can't Be Generators

In *Using Generators*, on page 62 we created a generator function that produced an infinite sequence of prime numbers. The code is repeated here for your convenience.

```
const primesStartingFrom = function*(start) {
  let index = start;

  while(true) {
    if(isPrime(index)) yield index;
    index++;
  }
};
```

The variable primesStartingFrom is referring to an anonymous function, which is marked with * to indicate it is a generator. Since the function is anonymous, you may be tempted to replace the anonymous function with an arrow function, like this:

```
const primesStartingFrom = *(start) => { //Will not work
  //...
```

Wishful thinking, but that does not work. The code will produce the following error:

```
const primesStartingFrom = *(start) => { //Will not work
                           ^

SyntaxError: Unexpected token *
```

There's no good reason for this except the support for arrow functions being generator functions has not been implemented. This may change in the future, and then it may be possible to use arrow functions as generators. Until then we have to continue to use regular or anonymous functions as generators.

throw Needs Wrapping

Single-line arrow functions are highly expressive, concise, and less noisy, and they don't need return. For example, here's a cute little arrow function:

```
const alwaysTrue = () => true;
```

The body of this arrow function returns true and there's hardly any ceremony in that code. Sometimes we may want to throw an exception from the body of an arrow function. This is especially useful when evolving code; an exception can serve as a placeholder to remind us that a real implementation is necessary at a later time.

Here's an arrow function that just throws an exception in its single-line body:

```
const mapFunction = () => throw new Error('fail'); //BROKEN CODE
```

That is also a concise piece of code, but it will not work; the code will produce the following when run:

```
SyntaxError: Unexpected token throw
```

For the body of an arrow function to be a single line, it should be either a statement that returns nothing or an expression that returns some value—throw can't be part of a single-line body. As a workaround, wrap the code snippet in {}, like so:

```
const madFunction = () => { throw new Error('fail'); };
```

Prefer a single-line no-noisy body over arrow functions wherever possible and switch to wrapping with {} as an exception, like when throwing exceptions.

Caution Returning Object Literals

When a language's syntax from different contexts collide, we have to bear the pain. Let's create a small arrow function that returns an object literal.

```
const createObject = (name) => { firstName: name };

console.log(createObject('George'));
```

That looks benign—what could possibly go wrong? The arrow function takes name as a parameter and returns an object literal, which has a firstName property with the given name as value. Let's run the code, in good faith, and look at the output:

```
undefined
```

Not what we would like to see. JavaScript notices the body of the arrow function starts with { and so decides it's a compound body instead of a single-line body. Once it steps into the body, it notices there's no return, so it returns undefined. But what about the firstName: name—what did JavaScript do with that? JavaScript decided to treat firstName: as a label to the expression name. "But I rarely use labels," you may protest. Well, we just did in this example, according to JavaScript.

One solution to this issue is to wrap the right side of => with a return {...}, but instead we can tell JavaScript that { is not the start of a compound body but part of an expression. To do this, use (), like so:

```
const createObject = (name) => ({ firstName: name });

console.log(createObject('George'));
```

Let's take a quick look at the output of running the code after this change.

```
{ firstName: 'George' }
```

When JavaScript sees (right after =>, as opposed to {, it decides the body is a single-line expression or statement. So by placing the { after (, we are able to convey the intent in a way JavaScript understands as we meant. That's much better—well, not really, but that's the workaround.

When to Use Arrow Functions

There are pros and cons of using arrow functions instead of regular or anonymous functions. We discussed the benefits and limitations of arrow functions throughout this chapter. Let's wrap up this discussion with the answer to the question: when should we consider using arrow functions?

Here are some recommendations that will help you make the right choice:

- Don't use arrow functions to define methods of a class, in an object literal, or through Object.prototype. The major hiccup here is the lexical scoping of this. If the method were defined using an arrow function, when the method is called, this will not refer to instance on which the method is called.

- Avoid multiline arrow functions as arguments to functions—see *Multiline Arrow Functions*, on page 71.

- Use arrow functions if the function is a short one-liner. The reduced noise of arrow functions shines here.

- When registering event handlers, don't use arrow functions if this needs dynamic scoping instead of lexical scoping. But if you want lexical scoping instead of dynamic scoping for this, then arrow functions are a great choice.

- Use single-line arrow functions as arguments to functions. The readability of code isn't lost, especially if we break the lines and indent on each argument.

Follow these recommendations only when doing so will result in semantically correct code.

Arrow Functions and Functional Style

The fluency of single-line arrow functions truly shines in the functional style of programming. In this style of programming, we use function composition—a series of transformations—to make the code expressive and easier to maintain. Functional style code removes accidental complexity that's present in the imperative style of programming.

Let's explore this with a few examples. Suppose we're given a list of names and asked to create a comma-separated result string with names of length five, all in uppercase. Try implementing that code using the traditional for loop. It's a simple problem but not a simple solution—that's accidental complexity. Here's an imperative implementation:

```
const pickNamesInUpperCaseOfLength = function(names, length) {
  let result = '';

  for(let i = 0; i < names.length; i++) {
    if(names[i].length === length) {
      result += names[i].toUpperCase() + ', ';
    }
  }
  return result.substring(0, result.length - 2);
};
```

The imperative style code has two major smells:

- It involves mutability; the variable result is being mutated throughout the iteration.

- We have to tell it what to do and also every step of how to do it.

We can remove this complexity by writing code in the functional style.

The functional style of programming is not new in JavaScript. It's been around since the beginning of JavaScript, but most programmers using JavaScript preferred the imperative way instead of the functional style. One reason for this is most programmers used some other mainstream language, like C++, Java, or C#, in addition to JavaScript. Since most mainstream languages, until recently, supported the imperative style—it was easier to use the same style across the board.

The functional style uses higher-order functions, where a function may receive a function as an argument or return a function as result. We're used to receiving and/or returning primitive types and instances of classes. With higher-order functions, we can extend that to receiving/returning functions. This leads to a nice way to perform function composition.

JavaScript provides higher-order functions like filter() and map() on arrays. Let's rewrite the previous code using higher-order functions, but by passing traditional functions as arguments instead of using arrow functions:

```
const pickNamesInUpperCaseOfLength = function(names, length) {
  return names.filter(function(name) { return name.length === length; })
    .map(function(name) { return name.toUpperCase(); })
    .join(', ');
};
```

Instead of using the traditional for loop to iterate, we use internal iterators like filter() and map(). The filter() function cherry picks the elements from the collection that satisfy the given predicate—the anonymous function argument to filter(). The map() function then transforms the selected names to uppercase, again using the anonymous function passed as an argument to map(). Finally, the join() function concatenates the strings in the collection into a single string separated by commas.

The arrow functions were largely introduced to remove the noise in code like this. The anonymous functions passed to filter() and map() are short, yet so much ceremony is there—function, return, and the ;. We can readily replace the anonymous functions in the previous example with arrow functions.

```
const pickNamesInUpperCaseOfLength = function(names, length) {
  return names.filter((name) => name.length === length)
    .map((name) => name.toUpperCase())
    .join(', ');
};
```

In most languages that support the functional style of programming, lambda expressions—JavaScript calls them arrow functions—have lexical scope for any variable not defined as a parameter or locally. JavaScript arrow functions are semantically aligned with that expectation and work well for short single-line functions in functional pipeline.

Like many programmers, including your humble author, if you're used to the imperative style of programming, it will take a bit of time and learning to start coding in functional style. With practice it gets better, and the thinking in functional style becomes more natural and eventually second nature.

Wrapping Up

When compared to traditional functions, arrow functions make code concise and expressive, and require less typing. However, they are not simple replacements for anonymous functions—significant semantic differences exist between anonymous functions and arrow functions. In this chapter you learned about the benefits and the limitations of arrow functions, how to create them, and when to use them. You also saw how arrow functions reduce noise when creating functional style code. In the next chapter, we'll explore one of the most charming features of modern JavaScript—destructuring.

Exercises

Use the following exercises to review the differences between anonymous functions and arrow functions. You can find answers to these exercises on page 235.

Exercise 1

Does JavaScript use lexical scoping or dynamic scoping for anonymous functions? How about for arrow functions?

Exercise 2

Refactor the following code to make it concise and to use arrow functions.

```
'use strict';

const success = function(value) {
  return { value: value };
};

const blowup = function(value) {
  throw new Error('blowing up with value ' + value);
};

const process = function(successFn, errorFn) {
  const value = Math.round(Math.random() * 100, 2);

  if(value > 50) {
    return successFn(value);
  } else {
    return errorFn(value);
  }
};

try {
  console.log(process(success, blowup));
} catch(ex) {
  console.log(ex.message);
}
```

Exercise 3

Make an effort to convert the following function to an arrow function:

```
'use strict';

const greet = function(...names) {
  console.log(this + ' ' + names.join(', '));
};

const helloJackJill = greet.bind('hello', 'Jack', 'Jill');

helloJackJill(); //hello Jack, Jill
```

Exercise 4

What's wrong with this code? Fix it so the code produces the correct/desired result.

```
'use strict';

const sam = {
  name: 'Sam',
  age: 2,
  play: (toy) => 'I am ' + this.name + ', age ' + this.age + ' with ' + toy
};

console.log(sam.play('ball'));
```

Exercise 5

Rewrite the following imperative code to functional style.

```javascript
'use strict';

const numbers = [1, 5, 2, 6, 8, 3, 4, 9, 7, 6];

let totalOfDoubleOfEven = 0;

for(const number of numbers) {
  if(number % 2 === 0) {
    totalOfDoubleOfEven += number * 2;
  }
}

console.log(totalOfDoubleOfEven);
```

CHAPTER 6

Literals and Destructuring

There's a new *noise ordinance* in JavaScript—it advises us to use elegant, concise, and pleasant code in place of noisy, verbose, repetitive boilerplate code. In this chapter you'll learn how template literals, multiline strings, object literals, and destructuring can help reduce code and clutter.

Using Template Literals

Single quotes and double quotes are used interchangeably in JavaScript, and both can only contain string literals. To embed the value of a variable or a result of an expression into a string, we traditionally used + to concatenate. But that can get verbose and noisy, as in the following example.

```
literals/template-literals.js
const name1 = 'Jack';
const name2 = 'Jill';

console.log('Hello ' + name1 + ' and ' + name2);
```

Code with multiple +s often gets unwieldy, unpleasant, hard to maintain, and boring to write. This is where template literals come in.

Template Literals

Template literals are strings with embedded expressions. The expressions may be a single variable, multiple variables with operators, a function call, or combinations of them—any valid JavaScript expression.

In languages like Ruby and Groovy, single quotes are used for string literals and double quotes for template literals. Since JavaScript has used both single and double quotes for string literals, it's too late to change the behavior or the semantics of either one. Thus, JavaScript has introduced a new syntax for template literals: the backtick.

Let's convert the last line of the previous code to use a template literal instead of the multiple + operator.

literals/template-literals.js
```
console.log(`Hello ${name1} and ${name2}`);
```

The output of this line of code is the same as the last line of code from the previous code snippet:

```
Hello Jack and Jill
```

Syntax of Template Literals

Within the pair of backticks, string literals appear as is. Expressions, on the other hand, appear within ${}. The curly braces {} surrounding the expressions in template literals are not optional. Without them, the expressions are treated as string literals. For example, let's remove {} in the second expression of the previous line of code:

literals/template-literals.js
```
console.log(`Hello ${name1} and $name2`);
```

Here's the result:

```
Hello Jack and $name2
```

Don't forget to embed the expressions with {} and also prefix with $.

You can use a backslash to embed a backtick within a template literal. For example, `\`` will result in `. Single and double quotes may also appear within template literals, like so:

literals/template-literals.js
```
const item = 'cake';
console.log(`The kid asked, "how's the ${item}?"`);
```

Template literals preserve the quotes, as we see from the following output:

```
The kid asked, "how's the cake?"
```

The combination of ${ causes template literals to treat what follows as an expression. The appearance of one or the other of those two symbols alone will be treated as literals, like so:

literals/template-literals.js
```
const price = 1;
console.log(`The price of a { symbol is $${price * 0.01 }.`);
```

The output shows that the first { and the first $ appear as is:

```
The price of a { symbol is $0.01.
```

Template literals may include function calls as well, like so:

literals/template-literals.js
```
console.log(`Shout out greetings: ${'hello'.toUpperCase()}`);
```

const, let, and Template Literals

In the examples so far, the variables used in template literals were declared as const. However, they may be declared using let as well, but use caution as this may lead to confusion. For example, try to determine the output of the following code without running it:

literals/template-confusion.js
```
let value = 4;

const msg1 = `The value is ${value}`;
const print = () => `The value is ${value}`;

value = 0;

console.log(msg1);
console.log(print());
```

The expressions within template literals are evaluated when the template literal is evaluated. As a result, msg1 will contain the value 4. However, since the template literal within the arrow function will be evaluated later, only when the function is invoked, the value there will be zero. This is because the value has changed by the time that template literal is evaluated. We can see this from the output:

```
The value is 4
The value is 0
```

This is another reminder why we should honor immutability wherever possible—see *Perils of Mutability*, on page 18 and *Prefer const over let*, on page 23.

Nested Template Literals

Template literals may be nested as well. Here's an example of nesting one template literal within another:

literals/nested.js
```
const hours = 14;
const event = 'meeting';

console.log(`The ${event} will happen ${hours < 12 ? 'in the morning' :
  `later in the day, in the ${hours < 20 ? 'evening' : 'night'}`}.`);
```

The top-level template literal relies on the nested template literal to create a string with an alternative embedded word "evening" or "night." The output of this code is

The meeting will happen later in the day, in the evening.

Use your judgment to decide if after nesting template literals the code is readable or hard to understand. If it is the latter, then break the nested template literal into a separate regular function or an arrow function, like so:

```
const when = (hrs) =>
  hrs < 12 ? 'in the morning' :
    `later in the day, in the ${hrs < 20 ? 'evening' : 'night'}`;

console.log(`The ${event} will happen ${when(hours)}.`);
```

If you decide to use nested literals, then inserting line breaks, as in the previous nested example, may help improve readability. That brings us to the next topic: multiline strings.

Multiline Strings

Creating a multiline string in the past involved effort and resulted in a lot of noise in code. Template literals may be single line or multiline—there is no special syntax to set the two apart, except for line breaks.

Here's a multiline string with expressions in it.

```
literals/multiline.js
const name = 'John Doe';

const message = `Dear ${name},
We're delighted to let you know that you have been included in
our routine spam starting with this one.

  You can thank us later.
`;

console.log(message);
```

Start the string with a backtick, continue each new line with a line break, and end the string with the ending backtick. Expressions in the string are optional.

The output of this code is

```
Dear John Doe,
We're delighted to let you know that you have been included in
our routine spam starting with this one.

  You can thank us later.
```

Multiline strings preserve indentations, and that can be inconvenient if we have the template literals in an indented region, like within a function or an if condition. We'll look at a possible workaround for that issue in the exercises at the end of this chapter.

Tagged Template

A template literal may be untagged or tagged. Tags are functions that receive the contents of the provided template literal in two parts: the template object and the evaluated expressions. The template literals we saw so far are untagged, but we may optionally place a tag in front of a template literal.

Before you learn how to write your own tagged template functions, let's make use of a built-in tagged template function called raw(). Suppose we want to create a string with some embedded special characters. In the next example we create a regular string, but by escaping each special character with a backslash.

literals/using-raw.js
```
console.log('some special characters: \\ \\n \\b \'');
```

The output from this code is

```
some special characters: \ \n \b '
```

The string captures all the special characters in the output, but creating those characters required repetitive use of \ before each special character. Let's try to remove those extra \s and see how that goes.

```
console.log("some special characters: \ \n \b '");
```

That's less noisy. By using a double quotes, we were able to include the single quote with no backslash. That's the only good part of this version. Getting rid of the backslash for other special characters, sadly, does not help, as we see from the output:

```
some special characters:

 '
```

To achieve the desired result while keeping the code less noisy, instead of using a regular string in the previous version we can use a template literal and tag it with the String class's raw() method. Let's change the previous code to use template literals and the raw tag:

```
console.log(String.raw`some special characters: \ \n \b ''`);
```

Even though a tag is written as a function, we do not invoke it like a function. Instead we *tag* a template literal by placing the tag literally in front of the template literal—no parentheses.

The string placed inside the template literal does not have extra backslashes. But the output created from this version is the same as the output from the first version where we used the extra backslashes:

```
some special characters: \ \n \b '
```

The raw tag is useful to get a raw form of string from a template literal. We can generalize the purpose of the tag from this example. A tag is useful to perform some special processing on a template literal. A tag does not have to return a string; it may return a string, a number, an object, or nothing at all.

Let's see how to create a tag by writing a function that prints what it receives when used as a tag on a template literal.

```
literals/print-template-literal.js
const printDetails = function(texts, ...expressions) {
  console.log(texts);
  console.log(expressions);
};

const name = 'John';
printDetails`Hello ${name}, how are you?`;
```

The printDetails() function takes two parameters. texts is an array of all the string literals in the template literal. The second argument, expressions, is an array of all the evaluated expressions. When the printDetails() function is used as a tag on the given template literal, the texts array will hold two strings: the string part before the expression and the string part after the expression. The expressions array will hold one value: the result of the expression in the template literal given, 'John' in this example. The tag function printDetails() does not return any result and that's fine. Here's the output for the code:

```
[ 'Hello ', ', how are you?' ]
[ 'John' ]
```

The length of the texts array will always be one more than the length of the expressions array. If a template literal is empty, then texts will hold one empty string. If a template literal has only one expression, then the value of the expression will be the single element in the expressions array, but the texts array will contain two empty strings—the empty string before the expression and the empty string after the expression.

A tag may be used to perform transformations on the given template literal. Here's a tag that masks the expressions:

```
literals/mask.js
const mask = function(texts, ...expressions) {

  const createMask = (text) => '*'.repeat(text.length);

  const maskedText = expressions
    .map((expression, index) =>
      `${texts[index]}${createMask(expression.toString())}`)
    .join('');
```

```
  const closingText = texts[texts.length - 1];

  return `${maskedText}${closingText}`;
};

const agent = 'Bond';
const organization = 'MI6';

console.log(mask`Hi, I'm ${agent}, with ${organization}.`);
```

We iterate over the expressions array using the map() function and, for each expression, create a string of the text before the expression and a series of *s of the length of the value, converted to a string, in the expression. Finally we append to the result the string after the last expression in the template literal. The previous code produces the following output:

```
Hi, I'm ****, with ***.
```

Try changing the template literal passed to the mask tag to different values—an empty template literal, one with no expressions, one with only expressions, expressions that are numbers, and so forth.

Since tags may transform template literals into various representations, the possibilities of its application is endless. Different JavaScript libraries may use tags for different purposes.

Enhanced Object Literals

Creating an object by assigning fields with values from existing variables is a common operation. In the past this involved a lot of noisy code. Let's consider the old way to create an object with a few fields and methods.

```
literals/without-enhanced-object-literals.js
const createPerson = function(name, age, sport, sportFn) {
  const person = {
    name: name,
    age: age,
    toString: function() {
      return this.name + ' ' + this.age;
    }
  };

  person['play' + sport] = sportFn;

  return person;
};

const sam =
  createPerson('Sam', 21, 'Soccer',
    function() { console.log(`${this.name}, kick, don't touch`); });
```

```
console.log(sam.name);
console.log(sam.toString());
sam.playSoccer();
```

The createPerson() function receives a few parameters and creates an object using them. It assigns the value of name to a property with the same name and likewise assigns age to age. Finally, it creates a computed property whose name is based on the value of the sport parameter. This last step had to be done outside of the initialization in the past—computed properties were not allowed in the object initialization list. The code works, as we see in the following output:

```
Sam
Sam 21
Sam, kick, don't touch
```

But that's some noisy code; let's see how we can make it concise.

The object literals syntax makes it possible to assign values to fields and create functions within an object. It is the colon notation in { field: value, func: function() {...} }. Enhanced object literal enhances that notation by removing some noise and making a few things implicit.

Shorthand Assignment Notation

If the name of a field is the same as a variable in the lexical scope, for example, name: name, then we can remove the colon and what follows after the colon. In other words, within an object literal, name means name: name.

Let's rewrite the part of the previous code where we are assigning values to the fields:

literals/using-enhanced-object-literals.js
```
const createPerson = function(name, age, sport, sportFn) {
  return {
    name,
    age,
```

We remove the temporary variable person; now we're directly returning the object being created. The value of the name field is set to the value of the parameter with the same name. Likewise, the value of age is set to the value of the parameter with the same name. The variable with the same name may come from the parameter, from a local variable within the function, or even from outside of the function—as long as the variable is in the lexical scope and has the same name as the field of the object we're creating, enhanced object literal can be used.

Shorthand Method Notation

To create a method in an object, we no longer have to use the colon or the function keyword. Drop in the function name followed by the parameter list and write the body of the desired function. Let's change the toString() method to use the enhanced notation.

literals/using-enhanced-object-literals.js
```
toString() {
  return `${this.name} ${this.age}`;
},
```

In addition to using the enhanced object literal notation for the method definition, we improved the implementation by using the template literal instead of using + to concatenate the field values.

The method toString() belongs to the instance—that is, each instance created using the createPerson() function will have its own function. Instead of creating a function internally, we can receive and share a function by storing it into a property, as we did with sportFn assigned to the computed property playSoccer. Speaking of which, next you'll see how to make computed properties a bit easier to create.

Computed Properties in Object Literals

The computed properties, like playSoccer—whose name is computed based on the value of a variable—are no longer forced to be outside of object initialization. Computed properties are first-class citizens and may appear around other members in object initialization, thanks to enhanced object literal. Let's move the initialization of playSoccer property to inside the initialization:

literals/using-enhanced-object-literals.js
```
[`play${sport}`] : sportFn
```

When creating the computed property, we again made use of the template literal syntax instead of using + to append the value of the parameter to the string literal play.

Here's the complete modified code for createPerson() along with the code to exercise that function:

literals/using-enhanced-object-literals.js
```
const createPerson = function(name, age, sport, sportFn) {
  return {
    name,
    age,
    toString() {
      return `${this.name} ${this.age}`;
    },
```

```
    [`play${sport}`] : sportFn
  };
};

const sam =
  createPerson('Sam', 21, 'Soccer',
    function() { console.log(`${this.name}, kick, don't touch`); });

console.log(sam.name);
console.log(sam.toString());
sam.playSoccer();
```

We eliminated the unnecessary local variable and kept all initialization to within the object literal, and that reduced a couple of lines of code. In addition, each line of code also saw some reduction in noise. Less typing, less boilerplate code, for the win.

Destructuring

Destructuring is an elegant way to extract data from arrays and objects. It removes excessive and repetitive use of indexing operators or dots to get to the data within arrays and objects. The notation takes a bit of getting used to, but soon you'll be quite comfortable making use of it in your own code and also recognizing its use in code you read.

Array Destructuring

Functions typically return a single value: a primitive or an object. There is no elegant way to return multiple values other than returning an array. That makes the code within the function easy to write, but it turns the code on the receiving end messy. Let's take a look at an example.

Here's a function that returns an array.

literals/multiple-returns.js
```
const getPresidentName = function(number) {
  //implemented only for number 6
  return ['John', 'Quincy', 'Adams'];
};
```

In the old style, to use the values in the array we would write something like this:

literals/multiple-returns.js
```
const president6 = getPresidentName(6);
const firstName = president6[0];
const lastName = president6[2];
```

The function getPresidentName() returns the first name, the middle name, and the last name for a president at a given number. On the receiving end, we store that into a variable and then extract the parts we desire using the index operator []. The code is neither fluent nor intuitive. It would be nice to assign the result to variables like firstName and lastName without having to use the index operator; destructuring makes that possible.

Extracting Array Values

Let's rewrite the receiving side using destructuring.

```
literals/multiple-returns.js
const [firstName, middleName, lastName] = getPresidentName(6);
```

We declared three variables, firstName, middleName, and lastName, in one shot and initialized them with the three values in the array returned by the getPresident-Name() function, respectively. We did not need the temporary garbage variable president6, and there was no need for the indexing operator.

Instead of const, we may define the variables as let as well.

Ignoring Values

If we cared only about the first name and not the other details, we would gently extract only the first name, like so:

```
literals/multiple-returns.js
const [firstName] = getPresidentName(6);
```

The remaining values in the array would be discarded in this case.

More generally, we can extract only the specific values we care about and ignore the ones in the positions in between using an empty argument. For example, we can ignore the middle name and extract only the first and last names like this:

```
literals/multiple-returns.js
const [firstName,, lastName] = getPresidentName(6);
```

Note that using multiple commas, like ,,,, may make the code hard to read, so do that sparingly.

Extracting More than Available Values

We saw examples of extracting all the values and also extracting fewer values than available. JavaScript does not get angry if we try to extract more than what's available.

```
literals/multiple-returns.js
const [firstName,, lastName, nickName] = getPresidentName(6);
console.log(nickName);
```

The getPresidentName() function is returning an array with only three values. However, in the call we are asking for four values, though we're ignoring the second value. Since there are only three values, the variable nickName is assigned a value of undefined.

Providing a Default Value

We got undefined when we asked for an extra value to be extracted. JavaScript is powerful, but it won't magically create values for positions that don't exist—but you can. Remember, from *Defining Default Values for Parameters*, on page 34, a parameter picks up a default value if the argument is undefined. We can apply that feature here to substitute a default value if a value being extracted is undefined. Let's change the previous code to give a default value for nickName.

```
literals/multiple-returns.js
const [firstName,, lastName, nickName='Old Man Eloquent'] =
  getPresidentName(6);
console.log(nickName);
```

If the getPresidentName() function returned at least four values, then nickName will take the value from the result at the appropriate position. But if the function returned fewer than four values, then nickName will be given the default value assigned, "Old Man Eloquent."

We can provide default values for variables at any position, not just trailing.

Rest Extraction

If we care to give a name for one or more variables but don't want to lose the rest of the values, we can gather them into an array using the ... rest operator.

```
literals/multiple-returns.js
const [firstName, ...otherParts] = getPresidentName(6);
```

The firstName will now contain the string 'John' and the variable otherParts will contain the array ['Quincy', 'Adams'].

Extracting into Existing Variable and Swapping

We can use the destructuring feature to swap two values. This eliminates the need for a temporary variable to store the values while we move them around. It also avoids the extra lines of code often used to swap.

```
literals/multiple-returns.js
let [a, b] = [1, 2];
console.log(`a=${a} b=${b}`);
[a, b] = [b, a];
console.log(`a=${a} b=${b}`);
```

The values in the variables are swapped, and the result is a and b with values 2 and 1, respectively.

This example also illustrated how to extract values into existing variables. We don't have to include let or const. Existing variables may be assigned values from extraction using the same syntax of destructuring.

Extracting Parameter Values

So far you've seen how to extract values from an array created in place or returned from a function. We can also extract values in the parameter list from the arguments passed to a function.

```
literals/multiple-returns.js
const printFirstAndLastOnly = function([first,, last]) {
  console.log(`first ${first} last ${last}`);
};

printFirstAndLastOnly(['John', 'Q', 'Adams']);
```

By using destructuring, we avoided the index operator within the function and also the need for additional variables. Less noise, more elegant.

Destructuring is one of the most powerful features of modern JavaScript. Its power extends beyond arrays. We can use destructuring to extract properties of objects too, as you'll see next.

Object Destructuring

Enhanced object literals that we saw earlier in this chapter provided a nice way to create an object using values from variables in lexical scope. Object destructuring is the opposite—it provides an elegant way to extract data from objects into variables in local or lexical scope.

Let's extract the data from an object using the hard way first and then see how object destructuring helps. Suppose we have an object that holds the details of a person.

```
literals/object-destructuring.js
const weight = 'WeightKG';

const sam = {
  name: 'Sam',
  age: 2,
  height: 110,
  address: { street: '404 Missing St.'},
  shipping: { street: '500 NoName St.'},
  [weight]: 15,
  [Symbol.for('favoriteColor')]: 'Orange',
};
```

Flexible Trailing Commas

A quick digression to celebrate a nice feature in JavaScript. The object property list ends with a comma. This was not allowed in the past, but it's now permitted. In the past, to add a new property to an object or a new element to an array, we had to first locate the current last item and place a comma before entering the new item, possibly on a new line. Now, with the ability to end the last item with a comma, we can jump right into the next line and key in the next new item. This removes the minor annoyance of having to place a comma before an item—it's natural for us to place a comma, as we type, at the end of the current item. JavaScript now allows arrays, object literals, parameter lists, and argument lists to end with comma. A small feature for the language—a lot of joy for the programmers!

Now, let's examine the code to extract the values for the properties. If we want to get only some of the properties, here's a piece of code to achieve this, using the old techniques.

literals/object-destructuring.js
```
const firstName = sam.name;
const theAge = sam.age;
```

We wanted to extract the value of the name property and the age property into the variables firstName and theAge, respectively. But that took a couple of lines and an invocation of the dot notation—that's rather verbose and it can get tiring. Destructuring can reduce a lot of that cruft.

Destructuring Objects

The destructuring syntax for objects is a bit different from the one we used for arrays; after all, the properties of objects are not positional but referenced using property names. Furthermore, a few other restrictions kick in, as we'll see soon. Let's use object destructuring to extract the desired properties.

literals/object-destructuring.js
```
const { name: firstName, age: theAge } = sam;
```

This extracts the value in the name property into firstName and the value in the age property into the theAge variable. If the syntax looks a bit strange, be assured it is. Here's a way to make sense of it. Instead of thinking of it as extraction, think of it as pattern matching.

Suppose we say { a: 1, b: X, c: 3 } = { a: 1, b: 22, c: 3 } and ask the value of X; in a snap, the response will be 22. For every property with the same name on both sides, we compare the values and determine that the variable X should be the value for b on the right side. Now, let's look at the previous code in the same light, with the actual object substituted for the reference sam:

```
const { name: firstName, age: theAge } = { name: 'Sam', age: 2, height: 110 };
```

The property name is mapped to the variable firstName on the left side and the value Sam on the right side. As a result, firstName is given the value Sam. Likewise, age, which is mapped to theAge, is given the value 2. Since we're not using height on the left side, it's ignored.

Extracting to Variables with the Same Name

In the previous example, we extracted name into firstName. If the name of the local variable is the same name as the property, then we can remove the colon and the part to the right, like so:

literals/object-destructuring.js
```
const { name, age: theAge } = sam;
```

Using this syntax, now we created local variables named name and theAge. name is shortcut for name: name. The name variable is initialized with the value Sam of the name property whereas the theAge variable is initialized with the value of the age property.

Extracting Computed Properties

In addition to the simple property names like name, age, and height, the object we created also has computed properties: [weight] and [Symbol.for('favoriteColor')]. Let's see how to extract the computed properties of an object.

literals/object-destructuring.js
```
const { [weight]: wt, [Symbol.for('favoriteColor')]: favColor } = sam;
```

To extract the computed properties, we use the [] notation and to the right of the colon provide a local variable name. In the example, wt is assigned the value of the computed property [weight] and favColor is assigned the value of the Symbol property, respectively.

Assigning Default Values

When extracting, if a property we ask for is not present, we can assign a default value for the missing property.

Next, we're asking for a favorite property that is not present in the object being extracted from. If the value is not present, the default value assigned to the property on the left-hand side kicks in.

literals/object-destructuring.js
```
const { lat, lon, favorite = true} = {lat: 84.45, lon: -114.12};
```

The values for lat and lon are assigned the appropriate value. The favorite variable takes on a value of true.

In the previous example, the name of the local variable is expected to be the same as the name of the property favorite, whether or not that property is present. When using default values, we can also provide a different name for the local variable—for example, liked, using the syntax favorite: liked = true.

Extracting When Passing to a Function

Let's create a function that receives the sam object and prints the name and age.

literals/object-destructuring.js
```
const printInfo = function(person) {
  console.log(`${person.name} is ${person.age} years old`);
};

printInfo(sam);
```

This is a traditional way of writing—we receive the entire object and use the dot notation to access the properties we are interested in. If, for instance, we wanted to access the age property multiple times in the function, then we would either have to use person.age each time or assign the value of the property to a temporary local variable, such as age, and use that instead of the dot notation each time.

Using the object destructuring syntax, we can combine parameter declaration with object value extraction. Let's reimplement the printInfo() function to use object destructuring.

literals/object-destructuring.js
```
const printInfo = function({name: theName, age: theAge}) {
  console.log(`${theName} is ${theAge} years old`);
};

printInfo(sam);
```

There is no difference in calling the function; we still pass the entire object. However, during the invocation of the function, the two desired properties name and age are extracted into the variables theName and theAge.

Of course, if we want to keep the local variable names/parameters the same name as the properties, we can use the shorthand notation, like so:

literals/object-destructuring.js
```
const printInfo = function({name, age}) {
  console.log(`${name} is ${age} years old`);
};
```

Deep Destructuring

So far in the examples we extracted the top-level properties of objects. The destructuring syntax makes it easy to extract properties in lower levels or embedded objects as well. Let's extract the street property of the address embedded object in sam.

literals/object-destructuring.js
```
const { name, address: { street } } = sam;
```

As we saw before, the name property, which is a top-level property, is extracted. In addition, the street property that is nested within the address property is extracted. Use caution; this syntax defines only two variables, name and street. It does not define the address variable. After these changes, we can access name and street, but any attempt to access address will result in a "variable not defined" error.

Dealing with Collisions

We managed to extract the street property from address, but what if we wanted to extract the street properties from both address and shipping? The problem is not the extraction part, but that it will not make sense to assign two values simultaneously to a single variable. Thus we have to provide two different local variable names. We can keep the variable the same as the property for one of the properties and assign a different name for the other. Alternatively, we can provide a different variable name than the property name for both properties.

Let's rewrite the previous code to extract both the street properties:

literals/object-destructuring.js
```
const { name, address: { street }, shipping: { street: shipStreet } } = sam;
```

Again, address and shipping are not defined as variables; only name, street, and shipStreet are defined and the values extracted into them.

Extracting into Existing Variables

In the examples so far, we've extracted properties from objects into new variables, defined using const or possibly let. We are not limited to extracting into new variables. We can extract and assign to existing variables in local or lexical scope.

In *Extracting into Existing Variable and Swapping*, on page 102, we extracted values from an array into existing variables simply using the [existingVariable] = array syntax. So, we may be tempted to try something like this:

```
let theName = '--';
{ name: theName } = sam;
```

The problem here is that we are expecting things to be consistent, but that's too much to expect in our field. The previous code will result in a grim message:

```
{ name: theName } = sam;
                  ^

SyntaxError: Unexpected token =
```

JavaScript does not understand the sudden appearance of the assignment operator after what appears either like a block of code with a label or a JavaScript object.

No worries; all we have to do is whisper into JavaScript's ear that we're not defining a block of code or a new object but extracting into an existing variable, like so:

```
literals/object-destructuring.js
let theName = '--';
({ name: theName } = sam);
```

All we had to do was wrap the extraction code inside a pair of ()—it did not take a whole lot to please the interpreter. The semicolon should be outside the ().

Extracting with …

In the examples so far, we have extracted part of the object, leaving behind some properties. Sometimes we want to copy the whole object, and at the same time, maybe add new properties, or change the values of existing properties. Destructuring can do this quite well.

As an example, the popular JavaScript state container library Redux[1] is based on immutable state. Instead of modifying existing objects, it transforms them into new objects. Typically a transformation may change one or two property values or add a new property while copying the bulk of the existing object's properties.

Let's take a look at a poor approach to copying first and see why this should be avoided, especially when using libraries like Redux.

```
const addAge = function(person, theAge) {
  return {first: person.first, last: person.last, age: theAge };
};

const parker = { first: 'Peter', last: 'Parker' };

console.log(addAge(parker, 15));
```

The addAge() function creates a new object and copies over the first and last properties—currently that's all the properties in the given object. In addition,

---

1. https://redux.js.org/

it adds a new age property and assigns the given value of theAge. If the given person object already has an age property, the copy will have a different value.

The output of the code shows that things are working as expected:

```
{ first: 'Peter', last: 'Parker', age: 15 }
```

But there's a catch. The intent of the addAge() function was to either add or replace the age property in the copy while retaining all the other properties. The code, as written, is not extensible. If we add another property—for example, email—to the person, the addAge() function will not bring that over. Also, if we remove an existing property, the code will produce an unintended result—the copied object will have an undesirable value of undefined for the removed property.

Let's modify the person instance before sending it to addAge, like so:

```
const parker = { first: 'Peter', last: 'Parker',
  email: 'spiderman@superheroes.example.com' };

console.log(addAge(parker, 15));
```

The output shows that the new property added to the person is missing from the copy.

```
{ first: 'Peter', last: 'Parker', age: 15 }
```

The spread operator ... in the destructuring syntax saves the day, as we'd expect from a superhero, and makes the code extensible. Let's rewrite the previous code to use the spread operator with destructuring.

```
literals/extensible-copy.js
const addAge = function(person, theAge) {
  return {...person, last: person.last.toUpperCase(), age: theAge };
}

const parker = { first: 'Peter', last: 'Parker',
  email: 'spiderman@superheroes.example.com' };

console.log(addAge(parker, 15));
```

To make a copy of the object, we use the spread operator ... and then list the new properties and/or properties we'd like to replace. In this example, we replace the last property and at the same time add a new age property.

Let's quickly take a look at the output:

```
{ first: 'Peter',
  last: 'PARKER',
  email: 'spiderman@superheroes.example.com',
  age: 15 }
```

The output shows that the last property has been given a new value in the copy; the age property has been added; and the other properties, though not mentioned explicitly during copying, were kept intact.

If the intent is to keep all the current properties of an object while replacing the values of some and optionally adding a few new properties, then rely on the spread operator instead of specifying each property by name. This is critical from the extensibility point of view and will minimize the need to track down bugs later on.

Wrapping Up

Template literals and destructuring greatly reduce the noise in code and are among the most charming features in modern JavaScript. Thanks to template literals, we'll have no more clutter from multiple lines of +s to concatenate string expressions. Furthermore, tagged templates offer the ability to process literals to implement custom logic. Object literals reduce the ceremony around creating objects, and powerful destructuring makes extracting data from arrays and objects pretty darn easy. Furthermore, mixing destructuring with the rest operator makes the code for copying objects extensible to adding and removing properties.

In the next chapter, you'll learn about all the improvements in JavaScript to do OO programming.

Exercises

Literals and destructuring are some of the most powerful features of Java-Script, but they come with some idiosyncrasies. The following practice exercises will help you hone the concepts. You can find answers to these exercises on page 237.

Exercise 1

Let's implement the greet() method, using template literals, to return the expected string result.

```
'use strict';

const greet = function(name, gender) {
  //Your code goes here
}

console.log(greet('Sara', Symbol.for('female'))); //Hello, Ms. Sara
console.log(greet('Tom', Symbol.for('male'))); //Hello, Mr. Tom
```

Exercise 2

Let's implement a tagged template named stripMargin that removes all leading spaces and all indentations on the new lines. Also, the tagged template should convert all expressions to uppercase.

```
'use strict';
//Your code goes here

const name = 'Jane';

const processed = stripMargin` This is for
  ${name} and it needs to be
        delivered by December 24th.`

console.log(processed);
//This is for JANE and it needs to be delivered by December 24th.
```

Exercise 3

Let's receive the values returned by the given function in discrete variables. If a value is not returned, let's use the value 0 instead.

```
'use strict';

const beforeAndAfter = function(number) {
  if(number < 0) return [];
  if(number === 0) return [1];

  return [number - 1, number + 1];
}

let before = 0;
let after = 0;

//Your code goes here
 = beforeAndAfter(7);
console.log(`${before} and ${after}`); //6 and 8

//Your code goes here
 = beforeAndAfter(9);
console.log(`${before} and ${after}`); //8 and 10

//Your code goes here
 = beforeAndAfter(0);
console.log(`${before} and ${after}`); //0 and 1

//Your code goes here
 = beforeAndAfter(-1);
console.log(`${before} and ${after}`); //0 and 0
```

Exercise 4

Let's invoke the purchaseItems() function in a way that it prints the desired result.

```
'use strict';

const purchaseItems = function(essential1, essential2, ...optionals) {
  console.log(`${essential1}, ${essential2}, ${optionals.join(', ')}`);
}

const mustHaves = ['bread', 'milk'];
const also = ['eggs', 'donuts'];
const andAlso = ['juice', 'tea'];

//call purchaseItems so it prints
//bread, milk, eggs, donuts, coffee, juice, tea
//Your code goes here
```

Exercise 5

Let's use destructuring on parameters to implement the getDetails() function.

```
'use strict';
//Your code goes here

const details =
  getDetails({name: 'Sara',
    born: { month: 1, day: 1, year: 2000 },
    graduated: { month: 5, day: 31, year: 2018 }});

console.log(details);
//Sara born in the year 2000, graduated in 2018.
```

Part III

OO and Modular Code

The facilities used to create classes and to use inheritance have significantly improved in JavaScript. In addition to working with functions, you can reach for the full power of object-oriented programming when you need it. Also, modules provide a nice way to divide the code into files with cohesive code and then intermix them in a logical and meaningful fashion. In this part you'll learn to use classes, benefit from inheritance, and use modern JavaScript modules.

CHAPTER 7

Working with Classes

Older versions of JavaScript supported classes but without using the class keyword. In the past, you may have found object-oriented (OO) programming in JavaScript rather primitive, especially if you were familiar with other mainstream languages. Even today, many programmers still think that JavaScript has little to do with OO programming. One of the main reasons for that is that the old syntax and semantics of working with classes were very confusing and error-prone. Modern JavaScript puts an end to that misery; now it is possible to create beautiful OO code with JavaScript.

In this chapter you'll learn all about creating classes and defining both instance and static members. You'll quickly find that the new syntax is more intuitive, easier to write, easier to maintain, and less error prone than the old syntax. In addition to learning about classes, you'll explore the semantic differences from classes in other languages, how to examine properties, and how to make use of new built-in collection classes in JavaScript.

By the end of this chapter you will be able to not only freely use classes, but also mix the functional programming style from Chapter 5, *Arrow Functions and Functional Style*, on page 69 with the OO style we focus on here.

Creating a Class

Classes are the most fundamental part of OO programming, and yet, in the earlier versions, JavaScript did not have an explicit keyword to define classes. It was never clear if we were working with a class or a function. Serious OO programming requires more rigorous syntax and a clearer specification for creating and using classes. Modern JavaScript delivers that quite well, fortunately.

We'll quickly revisit the classes of the past, which were masquerading as functions, so we can have a greater appreciation for the updated OO features that are now available in the language. Then we'll dive into the facilities to create classes—language capabilities that are bound to please the OO programmer in you.

Out with the Old Way

To create a class, we used to write a constructor function. The constructor looked much like any other function in syntax. To tell the difference between a regular function and a constructor, we relied on programmers following the convention to capitalize the function name. While function car() is considered a function, function Car() is considered a constructor. That's just the beginning of confusion. Let's take a look at how members of a class were defined.

It was not clear how to define the members of a class. Should we write

```
function Car() {
  this.turn = function(direction) { console.log('...turning...'); }
}
```

or

```
function Car() {}

Car.prototype.turn = function(direction) { console.log('...turning...'); }
```

or

```
function Car() {}

Car.turn = function(direction) { console.log('...turning...'); }
```

Each of these has consequences, and having different ways to define functions placed a burden on programmers and resulted in errors.

Another problem was that there was nothing to stop someone from placing a new before a function, like new car(), or invoking a constructor as a function, like Car(). Accidentally using a piece of code in ways other than it was intended is a source of error and a huge time sink.

What about inheritance? And how do we override a method? Do we use

```
this.__proto__.foo.apply(this, arguments);
```

to call the method of the base class? Coding that is a form of cruel and unusual punishment. Not only was the syntax unclear, the approach was verbose and highly error prone.

Enough of that—out with the horrific old, in with the new, enriched, pleasant syntax.

In with the New Way

JavaScript has streamlined the syntax to create classes. The keyword class makes the intent obvious and unambiguous—you don't have to wonder anymore if the programmer meant a function or a constructor. Let's define a class named Car:

```
classes/define-class.js
class Car {}

console.log(Car);
```

The keyword class followed by an optional name of the class and an empty {} is the minimum syntax to define a class. It's that simple—no fuss, no confusion.

Even though we used the class syntax, we're actually creating a function, one that can only be used with new. The output from the code shows this:

```
[Function: Car]
```

In spite of the fact that the class syntax defines a function—albeit reserved for creating an object—if we invoke the class as if it were a regular function, we'll get an error:

```
Car(); //BROKEN CODE
^

TypeError: Class constructor Car cannot be invoked without 'new'
```

Furthermore, unlike the function Car() syntax, class Car does not hoist the definition of Car—that is, the definition of the class is not moved to the top of the file or function. The class is available for use only after the point of definition in the execution flow. Thus, the following code is not valid:

```
classes/no-hoisting.js
new Car(); //BROKEN CODE

class Car {}
```

If we refer to Car before we define it, we'll get an error, like so:

```
ReferenceError: Car is not defined
```

However, if the definition comes to life before the point of reference in the flow of execution, as in the following example, then it's all good:

```
classes/ok-use.js
const createCar = function() {
  return new Car();
};

class Car {}

console.log(createCar());
```

In short, the new syntax makes defining a class a pleasant and effortless experience, removes the issues with incorrect use, and at the same time, keeps the semantics of defining a class the same as before.

Implementing a Constructor

You know how to create a class, but you haven't seen how to define the body of the constructor. Creating a class defines a no-parameter default constructor, which appears to be empty bodied. But you may want to execute some code as part of object construction. For that we need to define an explicit constructor. That's exactly what we'll do next.

Let's first examine the default constructor that is automatically created when you define a class.

classes/default-constructor.js
```
class Car {}

console.log(Reflect.ownKeys(Car.prototype));
```

We created a class named Car, with a default constructor. Then, using the Reflect class's ownKeys() method, we examine the properties of the Car's prototype—you'll learn about Reflect in Chapter 12, *Deep Dive into Metaprogramming*, on page 201. This reveals the default constructor that JavaScript quietly created for us:

```
[ 'constructor' ]
```

We may provide an implementation or body for the constructor if we like. For that, we'll implement a special method named constructor in the class, like so:

classes/constructor.js
```
class Car {
  constructor(year) {
    this.year = year;
  }
}
console.log(new Car(2018));
```

The constructor may take zero, one, two, or any number of parameters, including default and rest parameters. The body of the constructor may initialize fields, like this.year in the example, and may perform actions. The output of the previous code shows that the constructor initialized the this.year field:

```
Car { year: 2018 }
```

A constructor is called when an instance is created using the new keyword. The constructor can't be called directly without new, as we saw earlier. If you do not have anything useful to do when an object is created, then do not implement a constructor—the default constructor is sufficient. If you want to initialize some fields or perform some actions when an instance is created, then write a constructor. However, keep the constructor short and the execution fast—you don't want to slow down during creation of objects.

Defining a Method

Methods are an integral part of classes. They exhibit behavior and are often used to perform some action, and possibly to effect state change.

To define a method, place the function body within the {} of the class definition—but without the function keyword. Let's rewrite the Car class, this time adding another field and a method.

```
classes/create-method.js
class Car {
  constructor(year) {
    this.year = year;
    this.miles = 0;
  }

  drive(distance) {
    this.miles += distance;
  }
}
```

In the constructor we initialized this.year to the value received in the year parameter and initialized this.miles to a value of 0. In the drive() method we increase the this.miles value by the value received in the distance parameter.

A method may take zero, one, or more parameters, including default and rest parameters. Methods may access and modify any fields of the class and may perform actions. They may also access any variable in their scope and invoke functions in their scope, including other methods of the instance. However, unlike in languages like Java and C#, we have to use this. to refer to other methods of the instance. For example, use this.turn() to invoke a hypothetical turn() method of the instance. Without the this., JavaScript will look for a turn() function in the lexical scope of the class definition and not an instance method. If such a method does not exist in the lexical scope, then we'll get a runtime error.

JavaScript restricts the characters that can make a field or a method name. However, it provides an easy way to work around its own restriction, as we'll see next.

Defining Computed Members

Sometimes we like to give dynamic names to members of a class—that is, to fields, properties, and methods. The approach to achieve this is also useful as a workaround to provide arbitrary names for members, bypassing the language's restriction on making the members with only alphanumeric characters.

Recall using special method names like Symbol.search and Symbol.iterator in Chapter 4, *Iterators and Symbols*, on page 47. Writing a method named Symbol.iterator() {} will result in an unexpected token error. We had to place it within [], like so: [Symbol.iterator]() {}.

To create a computed property, we place a variable containing the name of the property as the value in []. Alternatively, we can place a string or a template literal within [] as well. Let's explore this with an example.

```
classes/computed-members.js
const NYD = `New Year's Day`;

class Holidays {
  constructor() {
    this[NYD] = 'January 1';
    this["Valentine's Day"] = 'February 14';
  }

  ['list holidays']() {
    return Object.keys(this);
  }
}
```

NYD is a variable that contains the value evaluated from a template literal. In essence, it contains the string "New Year's Day" as its value. Within the constructor of the Holidays class, we use the variable NYD to create a computed field with the contained string as field name.

Instead of using a variable, we may also embed a string or template literal directly within the [], like we do for the field named "Valentine's Day" or the method named 'list holidays'.

In addition to defining computed fields and methods within the class, we can add them to an instance, like so:

```
classes/computed-members.js
const usHolidays = new Holidays();
usHolidays['4th of July'] = 'July 4';
```

The object usHolidays is an instance of the Holidays class but has an additional computed field named 4th of July.

To access a computed field, place its computed name within []. If that expression appears on the left side of an assignment, the value on the right side of the assignment is assigned to that field. For example, the string 'July 4' is assigned to the computed field '4th of July' in the previous code. Let's access the value of a computed field and also invoke a computed method.

classes/computed-members.js

```
console.log(usHolidays[`Valentine's Day`]);
const methodName = 'list holidays';
console.log(usHolidays[methodName]());
```

Even though we defined the field Valentine's Day using a string, we are referring to it using a template literal—that's no problem as the template literal evaluates to the same string. To invoke the method named list holidays, we either place that string, or a variable containing that string, inside [], like methodName, which contains that string as value. The () after the [] tells JavaScript to invoke as a method instead of accessing the computed name as a field.

Creating Properties

JavaScript now supports C#-style properties. From the caller point of view, a property gives an illusion of a field but works as a method. Let's revisit the Car class we created earlier and introduce another method that returns a value and then turn that into a property.

Suppose we want to know how old a car is. The year of make is provided when an instance is created. We use the getAge() method to find the age of the car, like so:

```
getAge() {
  return new Date().getFullYear() - this.year;
}
```

The method subtracts the year of make from the current year. We invoke this method using the familiar method call syntax:

```
const car = new Car(2007);
```

```
console.log(car.getAge());
```

That works, but getAge() is a Java-style getter. C# developers write properties instead of getter methods, and JavaScript now provides the same capability. A property may have a getter, a setter, or both. If a property has only a getter, it becomes a read-only property. We'll take a look at setters later, but for now let's keep our focus on the getter.

If a method merely acts as a getter—that is, it returns directly the value of a field or a computed result—then implement it as a read-only property instead of as a method. Let's now turn the getAge() method of Car into a property.

```
get age() {
  return new Date().getFullYear() - this.year;
}
```

The property getter uses the get keyword followed by the name of the property—age in this example. Ignoring the word get for a moment, the code is no different from writing a method named age(). Placing get in front of the method turns the method name into a property. We can't call getAge() anymore—there's no such method. We can't call age() either since it's really not a method. We have to use the property name directly to refer to it, like so:

```
console.log(car.age);
car.age = 7;
```

When car.age is used as an expression, JavaScript will quietly call the body of code attached to get age().

If we place car.age on the left side of an assignment, then JavaScript will look for a set age(value), where value may be replaced by any name for the parameter. Since we do not have a setter for this property, JavaScript will quietly ignore the assignment. If we use 'use strict';—and we should; see *Making Objects const*, on page 21—then the assignment will result in an error: Cannot set property age of #<Car> which has only a getter.

Let's create a read-write property in Car.

```
get distanceTraveled() { return this.miles; }

set distanceTraveled(value) {
  if(value < this.miles) {
    throw new Error(
      `Sorry, can't set value to less than current distance traveled.`);
  }
  this.miles = value;
}
```

Although getters for properties are not allowed to take any parameters, the setters are required to take exactly one parameter.

The getter for the distanceTraveled property merely returns the value in the this.miles field. The setter for the property, however, throws an exception if the value provided is less than the current value in this.miles; otherwise, it sets the value of this.miles to the given value.

Let's exercise this property's getter and setter:

```
const car = new Car(2007);
car.drive(10);

console.log(car.distanceTraveled);

car.distanceTraveled = 14;
console.log(car.distanceTraveled);

try {
  car.distanceTraveled = 1;
} catch(ex) {
  console.log(ex.message);
}
```

We first call drive(10)—that will increase the value of this.miles from the initial value of 0 to 10. Then we access the property distanceTraveled to get the current value of this.miles. Next we place the property distanceTraveled on the left-hand side of an assignment, thus passing the value of 14 to the property's setter. Once again we access the property to get its current value of 14. Finally, within the safety net of the try-catch block, we set a value of 1 for the property. Since this value is less than the current value in this.miles, the call will result in an exception. Here's the output from the code:

```
10
14
Sorry, can't set value to less than current distance traveled.
```

A property setter is useful to perform some checks and verifications before a field is modified. Keep in mind, though, that JavaScript does not provide a way to encapsulate fields—there's no concept of private as in other languages. You may try to hide fields from access using some tricks, but there's really no elegant, effective way to encapsulate. If you don't want the users of your class to use a field directly, then don't document it and hope they're good citizens who will not touch what hasn't been publicized.

We've seen how to define instance members. Next we'll see how to define class members.

Defining Class Members

When creating abstractions, we often arrive at methods that may not be specific to any particular instance. Sometimes they are general and sometimes they may deal with multiple instances. A class method, instead of an instance method, is used to design these.

JavaScript makes it easy to define static methods and static properties. It does not, however, provide an elegant way to define static fields. Let's continue with our Car class to add a few static members.

First, let's add a static field to the class. For this, we have to step out of the class definition, like so:

```
Car.distanceFactor = 0.01; //This goes outside class Car {...}
```

We may also define property getters (and setters if we like), and those go within the class with the static prefix. For example, let's define an ageFactor property as a class member:

```
static get ageFactor() { return 0.1; }
```

Except for the static prefix, there's no difference between how we define an instance property getter and a class property getter. Of course, the class property getters and setters will not have implicit access to any instance properties, fields, or methods.

The keyword this within static getters, static setters, and static methods is dynamically scoped—it does not refer to the instance of the class. When a static member is called on a class, this refers to the class, but if this is bound to some other object by the caller, then this may refer to something other than the class.

Finally, let's define a static method in the Car class:

```
static pickBetter(carA, carB) {
  const computeScore = car =>
    car.age * Car.ageFactor + car.distanceTraveled * Car.distanceFactor;

  return computeScore(carA) < computeScore(carB) ? carA : carB;
}
```

The pickBetter() method is marked as static but it looks much like an instance method otherwise. While we may use this to refer to the static members, it is safer to use the class name, like Car.ageFactor, instead of this.ageFactor—this will prevent us from issues with this referring to something other than the class at runtime due to dynamic scoping.

Let's take a look at calling the static method of the class.

```
const car1 = new Car(2007);
car1.drive(150000);

const car2 = new Car(2010);
car2.drive(175000);

console.log(Car.pickBetter(car1, car2));
```

Instead of calling on any particular instance, we call pickBetter() using the class name. Instance methods can't be called using the class reference and static methods can't be called using an instance reference.

Class Expressions

Class expressions are useful to create dynamic classes at runtime based on, for example, properties you read from a file, database, or user-provided input. Imagine creating a class factory function that will create and return a class—that's a good place to use a class expression.

JavaScript supports both a class statement—which you use to define a class—and a class expression. The two key differences between a class expression and a class statement are

- The class name is optional for class expressions but required for class statements.

- The class expression should be treated as an expression—that is, it should be returned, passed to another function, or be stored in a variable.

Class statements are more common than class expressions, but the latter is useful to create classes dynamically.

Let's create a function that acts as a class factory—that is, it dynamically creates and returns a class with fields provided as parameters to the call.

```
classes/class-expressions.js
const createClass = function(...fields) {
  return class {
    constructor(...values) {
      fields.forEach((field, index) => this[field] = values[index]);
    }
  };
};
```

The createClass() function takes a rest parameter, fields, to hold the names of the fields of the class to be created. Within the body of the function, we use a class expression to create and return a class with no explicit name—this feature enables us to create C#-like anonymous classes in JavaScript. Within the anonymous class, we create a constructor, which also takes a rest parameter of values to be assigned to the fields. Since the field names are not known at code writing time, we use the [] notation to access the fields based on their names contained in the fields array.

The class created from a call to this function is anonymous, but we can assign any name to it on the receiving end, like Book or Actor, for example:

classes/class-expressions.js
```
const Book = createClass('title', 'subtitle', 'pages');
const Actor = createClass('firstName', 'lastName', 'yearStarted');
```

Once we obtain a reference to classes created using class expressions, we can use them like classes defined using the class statement. Let's create an instance of the Actor class we created using class expression.

classes/class-expressions.js
```
const fisher = new Actor('Carrie', 'Fisher', 1969);
console.log(fisher);
```

To the constructor we passed values for each field of the class. These correspond to the field names we provided in the second call to the createClass() function. Here's the output of this code, showing the details of the instance created.

```
{ firstName: 'Carrie', lastName: 'Fisher', yearStarted: 1969 }
```

Since our class was not given a name during creation, the output shows the instance like it's a JavaScript object—there's no class name prefix in the output.

In rare situations, you may find it useful to give a name for a class defined using a class expression. For example:

classes/class-expression-named.js
```
const Movie = class Show {
  constructor() {
    console.log('creating instance...');
    console.log(Show);
  }
};

console.log('Movie is the class name');
console.log(Movie);
const classic = new Movie('Gone with the Wind');

try {
  console.log('however...');
  console.log(Show);
} catch(ex) {
  console.log(ex.message);
}
```

The name Show is visible only within the class. Outside, the class is known only by the name to which the expression was assigned—Movie in this example. If we try to refer to it using the internal name Show, we will run into a runtime exception, as we see in the output:

```
Movie is the class name
[Function: Show]
creating instance...
```

```
[Function: Show]
however...
Show is not defined
```

The internal name is useful to call a static method of the class that is defined using class expression from within an instance method or another static method of the class.

Although two classes can't have the same name, multiple classes defined using class expression can have the same internal name.

You've learned how to create classes with the updated syntax. Next let's take a look at some built-in classes available in modern JavaScript.

New Built-in Classes: Set, Map, WeakSet, and WeakMap

We often use collections of objects when programming. In other languages, you may have used arrays, lists, sets, associative maps, or dictionaries. Sadly, JavaScript offered only arrays in the past.

When programmers needed a set or a map, they resorted to workarounds. These workarounds made the code hard to maintain, and when the code resulted in unintended behavior, we had more errors to deal with.

JavaScript now offers built-in classes for sets and maps as first-class citizens in the language. We will take a look at sets first and then maps. We will wrap up by looking at some special variations of these two classes for better memory use.

Using Set

The Array class that has been available in JavaScript from the beginning is sufficient to deal with an ordered collection of data. However, what if you wanted to create an unordered collection? What if you needed values held in the collection to be unique? Say you want to keep a collection of credit cards that belong to a user. You may want to query whether a particular credit card exists in your collection. Array is a poor choice for such operations; we really need a Set. JavaScript has finally agreed with that sentiment.

A set is a unique collection of primitives and objects—duplicates are not allowed. We can create an empty set and add objects to it, or initialize a set with the contents of an iterable, like an array.

Here's a set of names with five values, but one of the values presented during construction is not included in the set due to duplication.

classes/creating-set.js
```
const names = new Set(['Jack', 'Jill', 'Jake', 'Jack', 'Sara']);
```

Use the property size to get the current number of elements in the set.

```
classes/creating-set.js
console.log(names.size);
```

This will return a value of 4 for the given set. Whether we created an empty set or a set with values as we did in the previous example, we can add elements to an existing set. For example, let's add a new value to an existing set.

```
classes/creating-set.js
names.add('Mike');
```

One nice feature of the add() method is that it returns the current Set—that makes it convenient to chain operations, like more calls to add() or other methods of Set, like so:

```
classes/creating-set.js
names.add('Kate')
  .add('Kara');
```

We can use the has() method to check whether a set has a particular element. Likewise, we can empty out an existing set using the clear() method or remove an existing element using the delete() method.

To get all the values from a Set, use either keys() or values(). Thanks to the presence of the entries() method, we can also iterate over a Set using the enhanced for loop, like so:

```
classes/creating-set.js
for(const name of names) {
  console.log(name);
}
```

If you prefer the functional style internal iterator instead, Set has you covered with forEach:

```
classes/creating-set.js
names.forEach(name => console.log(name));
```

Talking about functional style, you may be wondering about methods like filter() and map(). Sadly, Set does not offer these methods, but there's a workaround. We can create an array from the set, as we concatenated arrays in *The Spread Operator*, on page 31, and then use the functional style methods on the array. For example, let's use filter(), map(), and forEach() to pick only names that start with 'J', transform to uppercase, and print.

```
classes/creating-set.js
[...names].filter(name => name.startsWith('J'))
  .map(name => name.toUpperCase())
  .forEach(name => console.log(name));
```

Use Array to create an ordered collection of values and Set for a collection of distinct values. Besides a collection of values, JavaScript now offers a way to create a dictionary of keys and values, as we'll see next.

Using Map

Associative maps or dictionaries are significant data structures in programming. You may have used Map in Java or Dictionary in C#, for example. Suppose you want to keep track of teams and scores during the sports season. A map will make it easy to create and update the score values and also to look up the scores based on a team's name. It's hard to believe that we can seriously program without maps—we can't.

Since an object in JavaScript has keys and values, and since there was no special Map type, in the past programmers often used simple objects to represent maps. Unfortunately, this resulted in a few problems. For one, there was no foolproof way to iterate over the keys—the keys() method converted fields to strings and that resulted in the accidental collision of keys. Also, there was no easy way to add new keys and values; in short, using a generic object to represent a map was not intuitive or elegant. The new Map type in JavaScript fixes that issue.

A Map is an associative collection of keys and values where the keys are distinct. Keys and values may be any primitive or object. We can create an empty map and then add values to it, or we can create it with some initial values.

Let's create a Map of names as the key and some scores as values.

```
classes/creating-map.js
const scores =
  new Map([['Sara', 12], ['Bob', 11], ['Jill', 15], ['Bruce', 14]]);

scores.set('Jake', 14);

console.log(scores.size);
```

The scores Map has been initialized with a collection of names and scores—the initial data for the map may be any iterable with a pair of keys and values. After creation we added another key and value to the Map using the set() method. To find out the number of keys currently in the Map, we use the size property.

To iterate over the collection of keys and values, we use the entries() method. Since it returns an iterable, we can use the enhanced for loop along with destructuring. For example, let's extract the name and score for each key-value pair and print:

classes/creating-map.js
```
for(const [name, score] of scores.entries()) {
  console.log(`${name} : ${score}`);
}
```

Instead of using the external iterator, we can also use the internal iterator, forEach(), to iterate over the keys and values, but the sequence of parameters provided to the function passed to forEach() is rather odd. Let's take a look at an example to iterate and then discuss the parameters.

classes/creating-map.js
```
scores.forEach((score, name) => console.log(`${name} : ${score}`));
```

The first parameter received by the function is the value for a key that appears as the second parameter. It is more natural to think of receiving key and value instead of value and key, but the reason for this sequence is that the same forEach() method may be used to iterate over only the values:

classes/creating-map.js
```
scores.forEach(score => console.log(score));
```

If you receive only one parameter, that ends up being the value; if you receive two parameters, then they stand for value and key for each key-value pair in the Map.

If you like to iterate over only the keys, then use the keys() method, and to get an iterable of only the values use the values() method. Finally, to query whether a key exists, use the has() method.

WeakSet and WeakMap

Suppose you added an object as a value to a Set or as a key to a Map. If that object is no longer needed in your application, it can't be garbage collected. The Set or the Map that holds on to the object will prevent it from being cleaned up. This is not very gentle on memory usage and may be an issue in some applications that use a large amount of data. WeakSet, a counterpart of Set, and WeakMap, a counterpart of Map, can be used to solve this issue, since both have a minimal impact on memory usage.

The word *weak* refers to coupling, as in weak coupling. A Set, for example, tightly holds on to the data that is added. However, a WeakSet will hold on only weakly and will not prevent the object from being released. Let's discuss why we may need a weak collection before looking at the built-in weak collections in JavaScript.

Suppose you have an application where information about various vehicles based on vehicle identification number (VIN) is obtained from a database.

Each time you need that information, you may not want to perform a fetch. It may be far more efficient to cache that information, for example, in a Map. However, if the number of vehicles the application deals with becomes large, and as time goes on, some of the vehicles are no longer being processed, then you'd have to explicitly remove those vehicle details from the cache. Otherwise, the application may suffer from excessive memory usage.

This is where a WeakMap can help. Now suppose, instead of using Map for the cache we used a WeakMap. When a VIN is discarded, the data associated with that VIN as key within the WeakMap becomes stale and becomes a candidate for garbage collection. When the memory demand increases, the runtime may perform an automatic cleanup of these stale objects without any explicit programming effort on our part. A big win for less code and efficient memory usage at the same time.

Another scenario where a weak collection is useful is in GUI programming. A UI control may be added to a collection so that events can be sent to it. However, if the UI control is no longer needed, we would not want it to be held in the collection. If we used a Set, for example, we will have to do an explicit delete. A WeakSet can release the object automatically when it is no longer needed in the program.

The values stored in a WeakSet and the keys in a WeakMap may be garbage collected if they're not otherwise needed in the application. Thus, these objects may go away at any time without notice. To avoid any surprises, WeakSet and WeakMap have some restrictions on how we can access the elements:

- While the values stored in a Set and the keys placed into a Map may be primitive or objects, the values in a WeakSet and keys in a WeakMap are required to be objects, not primitives.

- The weak collections are not enumerable. The reason for this is while in the middle of enumeration, if it were possible, an object held in the collection may be garbage collected and that would throw a wrench into the iteration.

The WeakSet provides only the methods add(), delete(), and has() to work on the elements in the collection. The WeakMap provides the get(), delete(), set(), and has() methods. Just as we can't enumerate on a weak collection, we can't query for its size either—there's no size property.

Let's compare the behavior of Map and WeakMap. Here's an example that puts a lot of elements into an instance of Map:

```
memory/memory-usage-map.js
const MAX = 100000000;
const map = new Map();

for(let i = 0; i <= MAX; i++) {
  const key = {index: i};
  map.set(key, i);
}

console.log("DONE");
```

Through each iteration a new object is created on the heap and then inserted as a key into the map with a primitive value as the value for the key. Each key that is created on the heap during an iteration may be garbage collected at the end of that iteration; however, the Map will keep them alive. The result of this code is an error due to excessive memory usage:

```
...
FATAL ERROR: invalid table size Allocation failed -
JavaScript heap out of memory
```

If on your system you do not get an out-of-memory error, try increasing the value of MAX in the previous code by an order of magnitude until you get the error—and congratulations on having a machine with a lot of memory.

Let's change new Map() in the previous code to new WeakMap():

```
//...
const map = new WeakMap();
//...
```

Now, let's run the code. It may take a while to complete, but it eventually will without any errors:

```
DONE
```

The example shows that while Map prevents objects, which are otherwise not needed, from being garbage collected, the WeakMap doesn't cling on to the objects. sIf the objects gotta go, they gotta go—weak collections don't prevent that.

Wrapping Up

The syntax for creating classes in modern JavaScript is on par with many other languages that support the object-oriented paradigm. A number of traps that troubled programmers in the past have been closed with the updated syntax and behavior of classes. It is less noisy and less error prone to define classes, define methods and properties, and define getters and setters. In addition to creating classes, we can create dynamic anonymous classes using class expressions. In this chapter, after learning how to create your own classes, you also learned how to use the new Set, Map, and their weak reference alternatives that are kind to memory usage.

JavaScript has also significantly improved inheritance, and we'll focus on that in the next chapter.

Exercises

These exercises will help you practice the rich JavaScript syntax for creating classes. You can find answers to these exercises on page 239.

Exercise 1

Implement a class that produces the expected result.

```
'use strict';

//Your code does here

const book = new Book('Who Moved My Cheese?', 'Spencer Johnson', 96);
console.log(book.title); //Who Moved My Cheese
console.log(book.pages); //96

try {
  book.pages = 96;
} catch(ex) {
  console.log(ex.message);
  //Cannot set property pages of #<Book> which has only a getter
}
console.log(book.copiesSold); //0
book.copiesSold = 1;
console.log(book.copiesSold); //1

try {
  book.copiesSold = -2;
} catch(ex) {
  console.log(ex.message);//Value can't be negative
}
console.log(book.copiesSold); //1
```

Exercise 2

Let's play with some static members in this exercise.

```
'use strict';

//Your code goes here

console.log(Tax.stateRate); //0.08
console.log(Tax.forAmount(100)); // 8

const forAmount = Tax.forAmount;
this.stateRate = 0.01;
console.log(forAmount.call(this, 100)); //8
```

Exercise 3

We'll use some computed properties in this exercise.

```
'use strict';

//Your code goes here

const todo = new Todo();
console.log(todo['learn JavaScript']); //'done'
console.log(todo['write elegant code']);//'work-in-progress'
console.log(todo['automate tests']);//'work-in-progress'
console.log(todo.completedCount); //1
```

Exercise 4

Let's use Map instead of the handcrafted Todo class.

```
'use strict';

//Your code goes here

const todo = createTodo(); //Returns a Map
console.log(todo.get('learn JavaScript')); //'done'
console.log(todo.get('write elegant code'));//'work-in-progress'
console.log(todo.get('automate tests'));//'work-in-progress'
console.log(completedCount(todo)); //1
```

Exercise 5

In this exercise we will create a Set and process the elements in it.

```
'use strict';

//Your code goes here

const sports = create(['Soccer', 'Football', 'Cricket', 'Tennis', 'soccer']);

console.log(sports.has('FOOTBALL')); //true
console.log(sports.has('Football')); //false
console.log(sports.size); //4

const inLowerCase = toLowerCase(sports);
console.log(inLowerCase.has('football'));
console.log(inLowerCase.size); //4
```

CHAPTER 8

Using Inheritance

JavaScript's original implementation of inheritance was different from other mainstream languages in two ways. Although most mainstream languages provided class-based inheritance, JavaScript implemented prototypal inheritance. Furthermore, for the vast majority of programmers it was not clear how to effectively use inheritance in JavaScript. The syntax was confusing, error prone, and hard to maintain. Thankfully, the language has evolved and the syntax for inheritance is now much easier to use and understand.

The updated syntax is akin to Java and that may lead us to believe that the inheritance model of JavaScript is similar to that of Java—but that's not true. JavaScript has always provided prototypal inheritance and that has not changed with the new syntax.

In this chapter we'll start with a quick introduction to prototypal inheritance. Then you'll learn the updated syntax for inheriting from existing classes. Along the way we'll explore how to control the instance that is created when working with a class hierarchy.

Understanding Prototypal Inheritance

Unlike class-based inheritance, prototypal inheritance is implemented using delegation. Remember the sage advice from good design books: delegation is better than inheritance. Prototype-based languages like JavaScript take that advice to heart. Although languages like Java, C#, C++, Ruby, and a number of other OO languages provide class-based inheritance, prototype-based languages use an object chain to delegate calls. Instead of relying on a base class or superclass, prototypal inheritance relies on an object next in the chain to serve as its base. Class-based inheritance is rather inflexible—once you inherit your class from another class, it's stuck to the parent. In prototype-based languages, inheritance is dynamic; you may alter the object that serves as the base at runtime. That base object is called the object's prototype.

Prototype Chain

Since inheritance is implemented using an object chain, and not using a class hierarchy, to understand prototypal inheritance we have to know how object chaining behaves. An example will help.

```
classes/examine-prototype.js
class Counter {}

const counter1 = new Counter();
const counter2 = new Counter();

const counter1Prototype = Reflect.getPrototypeOf(counter1);
const counter2Prototype = Reflect.getPrototypeOf(counter2);

console.log(counter1 === counter2); //false
console.log(counter1Prototype === counter2Prototype); //true
```

We created a class Counter, then two instances of the class, and compared their identity and the identity of their prototypes. The instances are different, but they share their prototypes.

JavaScript forms a prototype chain. For example, we can obtain the prototype of counter1 by calling Reflect.getPrototypeOf(counter1). In turn, we can obtain the prototype of the prototype, and so on. What we'll find from that exercise is the following:

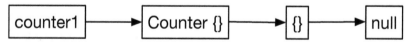

The instance counter1 of Counter has a prototype Counter {}, which in turn has a prototype {}, which has null as its prototype, thus ending the prototype chain. The instance counter2 has the exact chain as counter1.

Although two objects of the same class in class-based inheritance share the same class hierarchy, two objects of the same class in prototypal inheritance share the same object chain. At least that's the default behavior. As you'll soon see, we can dynamically alter that chain—such dynamic capability is hard to imagine in class-based inheritance.

Behavior of Get vs. Set

The purpose of inheritance is to reuse the methods and properties. In class-based inheritance, the instances of a class reuse the members of the class's base class. In prototypal inheritance, the prototype is reused. When a property or a method is accessed on an object, the object may reuse the members in its prototype by delegating calls to its prototype. However, the behavior is widely different when getting a property compared to setting it. Knowing this is critical to effectively use inheritance in JavaScript, so let's dig in.

We'll modify the code to change the members of the prototype so we can see how the reuse works in prototypal inheritance.

```
class Counter {}

Counter.prototype.count = 0;
Counter.prototype.increment = function() { this.count += 1; };

const counter1 = new Counter();
const counter2 = new Counter();

console.log(counter1.count);
console.log(counter2.count);

counter1.increment();
console.log(counter1.count);
console.log(counter2.count);
```

We added and initialized a field, count, to the prototype. Then we added a method, increment(), to the prototype as well. The method, when called, will add 1 to this.count. We then created two instances of Counter—counter1 and counter2—and displayed the value of count. The count field does not exist directly in these instances, but JavaScript will get the values from the prototype. Earlier we verified that the instances share a prototype. Both the lines will display the value of 0.

We then called the increment() method on counter1. Once again, increment() is reused from the prototype and it increments the value of this.count. We then asked for the value of count again on the two instances.

A part of our brain may say that the output of the last two lines will be 1 and 0, respectively. But maybe another logical part of our brain questions that thinking. Hmm...

The instances of Counter share the prototype, but changing one object should not affect another. When we run the code, we get the output that confirms the isolation of the instances:

```
0
0
1
0
```

That's great, but what's the magic? The reason for this behavior is how JavaScript uses prototypes:

Gets search deep, but sets are always shallow.

When we access—that is, get—a member on an instance, if the instance has that member the value is immediately returned. If the member is missing, then JavaScript quietly forwards the request for the member to the instance's prototype. The steps for lookup are then carried out through the prototype chain until either the member is found or the search reaches the end of the chain. On the other hand, when a field is set on an instance, the set happens on that instance. JavaScript does not perform any lookup to see if the member being set is present. If it is present, the value gets overwritten. If the member does not exist, then it is created with the value given.

In the example, when increment() calls this.count, even though the method is part of the prototype, this refers to the counter1 instance. Thus, after the call to increment(), counter1 acquires the count field. We can verify this quickly with a small change to the code:

```
const counter1 = new Counter();

console.log(
  `Prototype has: ${Object.keys(Reflect.getPrototypeOf(counter1))}`);

console.log(`Before increment instance has: ${Object.keys(counter1)}`);
counter1.increment();
console.log(`After increment instance has: ${Object.keys(counter1)}`);
```

In this modified version, we create an instance of Counter and display the members (keys) of the prototype. Then we display the members of the counter1 instance. After calling the increment() method, we again display the members of the instance. The output confirms that the instance acquired a field after the call to increment().

```
Prototype has: count,increment
Before increment instance has:
After increment instance has: count
```

When increment() is called for the first time on an instance, the value of count is obtained from the prototype, and the incremented value is then set on the instance instead of on the prototype.

We have seen how JavaScript uses its prototype chain to implement prototypal inheritance. Next we will see how this relates to the updated syntax for inheritance.

Inheriting from a Class

In the past, to implement prototypal inheritance you had to literally change the prototype on the constructor function. This was rather inconvenient, error prone, and not intuitive. Also, there was no clear way to override methods.

This was so hard that most programmers either got it wrong or relied on libraries to do it for them.

The updated syntax for inheritance greatly simplifies the task of creating proto-typal inheritance. There is also a clear and elegant way to override methods. The syntax for inheritance is much like the one used by other mainstream languages, especially Java—that's good news and bad news.

The good news is that programming inheritance is now very easy and approach-able, and the code is easier to understand and maintain.

The bad news, however, is that the syntax is so much like class-based inheri-tance. That may lead you to believe that JavaScript supports class-based inher-itance. But although the syntax looks like class-based inheritance, semantically, under the hood, JavaScript still uses prototypal inheritance, as we discussed in the previous section. *Be warned.*

To understand how the new inheritance syntax relates to prototypal inheri-tance, let's look at some examples.

Extending a Class

In the past we created constructor functions to represent classes and modified their prototype to implement prototypal inheritance. Now, in modern Java-Script, we create classes using the class keyword. Likewise, we implement prototypal inheritance using a different keyword as well.

We need a base class to serve as the prototype and a derived class to reuse the prototype. In short, we need a simple inheritance hierarchy. For that, let's first create a class that will serve as the base. Let's start with a class, Person:

```
classes/inheritance.js
class Person {
  constructor(firstName, lastName) {
    console.log('initializing Person fields');
    this.firstName = firstName;
    this.lastName = lastName;
  }

  toString() {
    return `Name: ${this.firstName} ${this.lastName}`;
  }

  get fullName() { return `${this.firstName} ${this.lastName}`; }

  get surname() { return this.lastName; }
}
```

Now let's inherit from the Person class a ReputablePerson class.

```
classes/inheritance.js
class ReputablePerson extends Person {
  constructor(firstName, lastName, rating) {
    console.log('creating a ReputablePerson');
    super(firstName, lastName);
    this.rating = rating;
  }
}
```

Use extends to inherit a class from another class. In the constructor, a call to super() is required and should appear before accessing this. The call to super() will invoke the constructor of the base class, and JavaScript insists that the state of the base part of the instance is initialized before the state of the derived part. Swapping the last two lines in the constructor of ReputablePerson will result in a runtime error.

Overriding Methods

Although we can reuse the properties and methods of a base class, from the extensibility point of view, in the derived class you may want to provide an alternative implementation for a method or a property that is in the base. To override a method of the base class, write a method in the derived class with the same method name as in the base class. Likewise, to override a property in the derived, define a property with the same name as in the base class.

Let's override the toString() method and the firstName property of Person in the ReputablePerson class:

```
classes/inheritance.js
toString() {
  return `${super.toString()} Rating: ${this.rating}`;
}

get fullName() {
  return `Reputed ${this.surname}, ${super.fullName} `;
}
```

Since a field, method, or a property may be in the base class, in the derived class, or in the instance itself, we have to be careful to use the proper syntax to access the appropriate thing. Here are the rules you need to follow:

- To access the member in the instance or in the derived class instead of the one in the base class, use this—remember that this is dynamically scoped.

- If a member does not exist in the instance or in the derived class but exists in the base class, use this. If in the future you override this member in the derived class, then it will take precedence—this is most likely what you'd want.

- To bypass the member of the derived class and access the one in the base class, use super().

In the overriding toString() method, we called the toString() method of the base class using the super. notation. Likewise, in the overriding property getter we access the fullName property of the base class by using the super. prefix. However, to access the surname getter, we did not use the super. notation. That's because there is no member with that name in the derived class that shadows a member in the base class. It is safe to use this. here for two reasons:

- When a field or property is not present in an object, JavaScript will search for it in the prototype chain—that is, it will automatically look it up in the base class.

- If we override the field or property in the derived class, then we will correctly use the overridden field or property in the instance and not the one in the base class.

In general, the only time we should use the super. prefix is

- to access a member of the base class from within an overriding member of the derived class with the same name

- from any other member when we intentionally want to bypass a member in the derived class and access the one in the base class

Let's use the derived class we created to see the overriding method and property in action.

```
classes/inheritance.js
const alan = new ReputablePerson('Alan', 'Turing', 5);
console.log(alan.toString());
console.log(alan.fullName);
```

The output from the code shows the constructor call sequence. The overriding method and property was called, and the overriding members collaborated with the base members:

```
creating a ReputablePerson
initializing Person fields
Name: Alan Turing Rating: 5
Reputed Turing, Alan Turing
```

extends Implies Prototypal Inheritance

Even though JavaScript uses the extends keyword, which is popular for inheritance in Java, it's important to remember that the inheritance is prototype based and not class based. Let's verify this key design for inheritance in Java-Script with an example.

We'll continue with the Person and ReputablePerson classes we've been using. We can obtain the prototype of an object using the Reflect.getPrototypeOf() method. Since prototypes form a chain, we can repeatedly or recursively use this method to walk the inheritance hierarchy—that is, the prototype chain.

Let's write a function that, given an object, will print it and then print the object's prototype chain.

```
classes/prototypal.js
const printPrototypeHierarchy = function(instance) {
  if(instance !== null) {
    console.log(instance);
    printPrototypeHierarchy(Reflect.getPrototypeOf(instance));
  }
};
```

The method prints the given object and recursively calls itself, passing the prototype of the object at hand, until it reaches the end of the prototype chain. Let's call it on an instance of ReputablePerson:

```
classes/prototypal.js
const alan = new ReputablePerson('Alan', 'Turing', 5);

printPrototypeHierarchy(alan);
```

The excerpt of the output from this call to printPrototypeHierarchy is shown next:

```
ReputablePerson { firstName: 'Alan', lastName: 'Turing', rating: 5 }
ReputablePerson {}
Person {}
{}
```

The first line of the output shows the details of the first instance passed to printPrototypeHierarchy; the second line shows the prototype of that instance. The third line shows the prototype of the prototype, and the fourth line shows the terminal prototype.

Changing the Prototype Chain

Unlike class-based inheritance hierarchy, the prototype chain is not frozen in time. We can change the prototype chain—cautiously—if we desire. We'll see many reasons to change the prototype in Chapter 11, *Exploring Metaprogramming*, on page 187.

Let's alter the inheritance hierarchy we saw in the previous output to include a new object—for example, the prototype of a ComputerWiz class—in the chain. Here's the code for that:

```
classes/prototypal.js
class ComputerWiz {}

Reflect.setPrototypeOf(Reflect.getPrototypeOf(alan), ComputerWiz.prototype);

console.log('...after change of prototype...');

printPrototypeHierarchy(alan);
```

Instead of altering the prototype of the instance alan, we're altering the prototype of the prototype of alan. Let's take a look at the excerpt from the output after this change:

```
...after change of prototype...
ReputablePerson { firstName: 'Alan', lastName: 'Turing', rating: 5 }
ReputablePerson {}
ComputerWiz {}
{}
```

Compare this output with the one we saw before the change to the prototype hierarchy. From the prototype chain, everything below and including Person has been replaced with a new chain starting with ComputerWiz.

We modified the prototype of prototype of alan—remember that instances of a class share prototypes. Thus, if we create another object of ReputablePerson, then its prototype chain will be the same as the modified prototype chain of alan. Let's verify that:

```
classes/prototypal.js
const ada = new ReputablePerson('Ada', 'Lovelace', 5);
printPrototypeHierarchy(ada);
```

Here's the output for this part of the code:

```
ReputablePerson { firstName: 'Ada', lastName: 'Lovelace', rating: 5 }
ReputablePerson {}
ComputerWiz {}
{}
```

Not only does ada, which was created after alan, share the prototype chain with alan, any object of ReputablePerson that may have been created before alan was created also shares the same prototype chain.

We have to be very careful when changing the prototype chains—we'll see use cases for this in Chapter 11, *Exploring Metaprogramming*, on page 187—if the change is drastic and unintended, it may result in unexpected, hard-to-debug behavior.

Using Default Constructors

Recall that if you do not write a constructor, JavaScript provides a default constructor for the class. The same rule applies to derived classes, with one bonus—the default constructor automatically calls super to pass any arguments to the base class. This feature is nice and removes the need to write silly constructors that do not do anything except pass data to the base class. Once you get used to it, you may wish languages like Java and C# had this feature.

Let's extend an AwesomePerson class from the Person class we wrote earlier. Our AwesomePerson class is not going to introduce any new fields; it will only override a property of the base class. If we were forced to write a constructor, that would be pure noise to merely forward the parameters to the base class. The default constructor thankfully acts as a nice quiet passthrough constructor, as we see here:

```
class AwesomePerson extends Person {
  get fullName() {
    return `Awesome ${super.fullName}`;
  }
}
```

Let's create an object of this new class to see how awesome the default constructor is:

```
const ball = new AwesomePerson('Lucille', 'Ball');
console.log(ball.fullName);
```

We passed the first and last names to the constructor when creating the instance ball, even though we did not write a constructor for the AwesomePerson class. Let's take a look at the output to see how this decision turned out:

```
initializing Person fields
Awesome Lucille Ball
```

Quite well, as we can see; the constructor of the Person base class was called when the instance of AwesomePerson was created and the fields on the base class were properly initialized.

Extending Legacy Classes

In the examples so far, we've inherited from a class created using the class keyword. However, we can inherit from a class created using the old function keyword as well—this is necessary for backward compatibility—classes defined using the old syntax can be used as a base class with the new extends keyword.

Here's a short example of a class created using the legacy approach and a derived class created using the newer syntax:

```
classes/inherit-from-function.js
function LegacyClass(value) {
  this.value = value;
}

class NewClass extends LegacyClass {}

console.log(new NewClass(1));
```

Even though the base class is created using the legacy approach, the derived class plays by the new rules—the default constructor performs the automatic passthrough of the arguments.

You've learned how to extend from classes and to build a class hierarchy—that is, how to implement prototypal inheritance using the updated syntax for classes and inheritance. There's one gotcha, however, when working with a hierarchy of classes—deciding the type of instance to create from within methods. Next, we'll see what JavaScript provides to address that question.

Managing Instance Types with species

Suppose a method—for example, clone()—of your class creates and returns an instance of its own type. Now, suppose you inherit from this class. Automatically a user of your derived class can reuse the clone() method defined in its base class. But when called on an instance of the derived class, should clone() return an object of the base type or the derived type?

In general, when using inheritance, if a method in the base class creates an instance, should that instance be of the base type or the derived type? It's a mark of an educated mind to say "It depends!"

Sure, it may depend on the context, the application, and maybe several other things. But at the programming level we need to have a way to manage the type of the instance that's created. We will first take a look at how some built-in classes deal with this and then focus on creating similar behavior for our own code.

Two Built-in Classes, Different Behaviors

Let's take a look at two classes in JavaScript that implement the same method but with two different behaviors.

```
classes/array-vs-string.js
class MyString extends String {}
class MyArray extends Array {}

const concString = new MyString().concat(new MyString());
const concArray = new MyArray().concat(new MyArray());

console.log(`instanceof MyString?: ${concString instanceof MyString}`);
console.log(`instanceof MyArray?: ${concArray instanceof MyArray}`);
```

We took two well-known built-in classes in JavaScript and extended from each one of them. The instance concString is an instance obtained by calling the concat() method on an instance of the specialized class MyString. Likewise, the instance concArray is an instance obtained by calling the same method but on the specialized class MyArray. Finally, we examine if these two instances are of the same type as the instance on which the concat() method was called. Here's the result of that check:

```
instanceof MyString?: false
instanceof MyArray?: true
```

The concat() method of the String class decided to keep the instance it returns as its own type even though the method was called on a derived instance—how rude. The Array class, on the other hand, is playing nice, making the returned instance the same type as the instance on which the method concat() is called. Curious—how can we implement the behavior like Array's in our own code? You'll see how next.

When implementing a method in a base class, we can

- make the returned instance the same type as the base class
- make the returned instance the same type as the derived class
- let the derived class tell us what the type should be

In the code we saw examples of the first two options, with String disregarding the derived type and Array creating an instance of the derived type. Although Array appears to use the second option, in reality it uses the third option. Our derived class MyArray can tell its base class Array what type of instance concat() or other methods of Array should create. You'll soon learn how to specify the type of instance to use, but first, let's dig in further to learn how to implement each one of these options.

Sticking to the Base Type

We'll create a base class and a derived class and learn ways to manage the types of instances the base methods create. Let's start with a class named Names and a derived SpecializedNames class.

```
classes/managing-instances.js
class Names {
  constructor(...names) {
    this.names = names;
  }
}

class SpecializedNames extends Names {
}
```

The base class constructor receives a rest parameter of names and stores that into a field named names. The derived class does not have any methods, and its default constructor will faithfully pass parameters to its base class.

Let's implement a filter1() method in the Names class that will return an instance with only selected names.

```
classes/managing-instances.js
filter1(selector) {
  return new Names(...this.names.filter(selector));
}
```

The filter1() method receives a function reference, selector, as a parameter; passes that to the filter() method of the names array; and finally creates an instance of Names using the result of the call to filter(). The filter1() method hardcoded the class name in new Names(), and so the instance returned by filter1() will be an instance of Names even if the method is called on the derived instance. Let's verify this.

```
classes/managing-instances.js
const specializedNames = new SpecializedNames('Java', 'C#', 'JavaScript');

console.log(specializedNames.filter1(name => name.startsWith('Java')));
```

We created an instance specializedNames of SpecializedNames, invoked the filter1() method on that instance, and printed the response from that method. The method of the base class is executed in the context of the derived class. Nevertheless, the instance is of the base type since filter1() hardcoded the type. Let's verify that's true from the output:

```
Names { names: [ 'Java', 'JavaScript' ] }
```

The output reveals the type of the instance along with the data it contains. The filter1() method behaves like the concat() method of String—rather inconsiderate of the derived class. It decided to create only an object of the base type, regardless of the runtime type of the instance on which the method is called.

Choosing Based on the Runtime Type

Let's see how we can play as a good citizen and create an instance based on the runtime type of the object on which a method is called. We'll do that by implementing a filter2() method.

At runtime, rather than hardcoding the class name, if we want to invoke the constructor of the actual type of this, we have to obtain a reference to the constructor. Thankfully, that's pretty easy. We already saw how to do that in *Implementing a Constructor*, on page 118—when we examined the prototype it showed a property named constructor. To get access to the constructor of an object, fetch its prototype and query for its constructor property. Let's do that in the filter2() method.

```
classes/managing-instances.js
filter2(selector) {
  const constructor = Reflect.getPrototypeOf(this).constructor;

  return new constructor(...this.names.filter(selector));
}
```

Unlike the filter1() method that hardcoded the class name, filter2() gets the constructor of this and then does a new on it, passing the filtered data. Even though filter2() is in the Names class, the instance created using this approach will be of the actual context object on which the method is called. Let's use this method on the instance of specializedNames:

```
classes/managing-instances.js
console.log(specializedNames.filter2(name => name.startsWith('Java')));
```

Since the instance on which filter2() is called is of the derived type, the instance returned from filter2() is also of the derived type. Here's the output to confirm that:

```
SpecializedNames { names: [ 'Java', 'JavaScript' ] }
```

While filter1() assumed the instance should be of a specific type, filter2() is assuming it should be the same type as the context object. A better approach, we may argue, is where the method asks the context object what type the new instance should be. That's what we'll do in a filter3() method next.

Configuring the Type

Once we obtain a constructor—remember a class is actually a constructor in JavaScript—we can get static methods and properties from it. We will use a static property named kindHint, a made-up name, to give us a hint for the type of instance to create. If this kindHint property is not in a class, we'll fall back to use the constructor.

Here's our filter3() method, which instead of arbitrarily deciding the type of instance to create, will be highly considerate and ask the class for its choice.

```
classes/managing-instances.js
filter3(selector) {
  const constructor =
    Reflect.getPrototypeOf(this).constructor.kindHint ||
      Reflect.getPrototypeOf(this).constructor;

  return new constructor(...this.names.filter(selector));
}
```

The method navigates from the context object this to its prototype, then to the constructor, and asks for the kindHint property. In other words, the method is asking for a static property on the context object's class. The constructor reference then refers to the value returned by the kindHint property if that property is found and the value is not undefined; otherwise, the constructor reference refers to the constructor of the context object. The filter3() method then uses the constructor reference to create an instance.

Let's use the new filter3() method on the specializedNames instance:

```
classes/managing-instances.js
console.log(specializedNames.filter3(name => name.startsWith('Java')));
```

Since we have not implemented the kindHint property in the SpecializedNames class yet, the filter3() method returns an instance of SpecializedNames, as we see here:

```
SpecializedNames { names: [ 'Java', 'JavaScript' ] }
```

Let's now implement the kindHint property in SpecializedNames.

```
classes/managing-instances.js
class SpecializedNames extends Names {
  static get kindHint() {
    return Names;
  }
}
```

The static getter for the property kindHint in SpecializedNames returns the constructor for Names; it may return any constructor, including SpecializedNames. Now let's rerun the code and see what filter3() returns:

```
Names { names: [ 'Java', 'JavaScript' ] }
```

The filter3() method asked the kindHint property of SpecializedNames what type of object it should create. The SpecializedName class decided to hide its details and let the instance created by filter3() be an instance of the base type Names.

That worked, but there's a catch. The name kindHint is quite arbitrary and not unique. What if a class already has a kindHint method for some other purpose or intent and we decide to extend that class from Names? Interfaces would have solved this issue, but JavaScript doesn't have interfaces. Recall that Symbol solves issues with a lack of interfaces and uniqueness. Let's see how Symbol helps here.

Using species

We may create our own symbol, for example, Symbol.for("KINDHINT"), but there's already a predefined symbol for this purpose in JavaScript—Symbol.species.

Symbol.species is used to convey the constructor to be used to create derived objects. Let's modify the SpecializedName class to use species instead of kindHint:

```
class SpecializedNames extends Names {
  static get [Symbol.species]() {
    return Names;
  }
}
```

We replaced kindHint with [Symbol.species] and all else is the same in the class. Now, instead of looking for kindHint in the filter3() method, we should look for this special symbol.

```
filter3(selector) {
  const constructor =
    Reflect.getPrototypeOf(this).constructor[Symbol.species] ||
      Reflect.getPrototypeOf(this).constructor;

  return new constructor(...this.names.filter(selector));
}
```

Here again, the only change we made was to modify constructor.kindHint as constructor[Symbol.species]—all else is the same as before. The output of the code, for a call to filter3() after this change is the same as when we used kindHint.

The Array class uses Symbol.species in a similar way. We saw earlier how the concat() method of Array when called on the instance of the derived class MyArray resulted in an instance of MyArray. We can change that behavior by implementing the Symbol.species property getter in MyArray, like so:

```
class MyArray extends Array {
  static get [Symbol.species]() { return Array; }
}

const concArray = new MyArray().concat(new MyArray());
console.log(`instanceof MyArray?: ${concArray instanceof MyArray}`);
```

Before we implemented this property getter, the concat() method of Array when called on an instance of MyArray resulted in an instance of MyArray. Now, since the derived class MyArray has a different wish, the instance is different accordingly, as we see from the output:

```
instanceof MyArray?: false
```

When designing a base class, if you like to decide which instance of derived class to create, then use the Symbol.species to query for that intent. When writing a derived class, if you want to control the type of instance your base class will create, refer to the base class's documentation to see if it provides a way.

Wrapping Up

JavaScript supports object-oriented programming, but unlike most of the other mainstream languages, it offers prototypal inheritance instead of class-based inheritance. The updated syntax for inheritance is similar to the one in Java, but the semantics remain true to the roots of JavaScript. It is much easier now to use inheritance and to override methods. The code is easier to understand and to maintain, and it is not prone to errors as it was in the past. Furthermore, you can directly and comfortably use inheritance instead of relying on libraries to do it for you. In addition to supporting inheritance, JavaScript provides a special symbol, species, that can be used to control the type of instance that's created when working with inheritance.

In the next chapter we will explore the new modules capability in JavaScript that helps to split up large projects into cohesive multiple files.

Exercises

These exercises will help you practice inheriting from built-in classes and to extend their capabilities. You can find answers to these exercises on page 241.

Exercise 1

The Set class provided in JavaScript can use some extensions. Let's create FunctionalSet to provide filter(), map(), and reduce().

```
'use strict';

//Your code goes here

const set = new FunctionalSet(['Jack', 'Jill', 'Tom', 'Jerry']);

const jSet = set.filter(name => name.startsWith('J'));
const allCaps = set.map(name => name.toUpperCase());

const totalLengthOfJWords =
  set.filter(name => name.startsWith('J'))
    .reduce((total, word) => total + word.length, 0);
```

```
console.log(jSet); //FunctionalSet { 'Jack', 'Jill', 'Jerry' }
console.log(allCaps); //FunctionalSet { 'JACK', 'JILL', 'TOM', 'JERRY' }
console.log(totalLengthOfJWords); //13
```

Exercise 2

The add() method of Set returns the instance of Set with the added element. In the previous exercise we inherited from Set and our FunctionalSet provided three extra functions. However, we never called add(). Let's change

```
const set = new FunctionalSet(['Jack', 'Jill', 'Tom', 'Jerry']);
```

to

```
const set = new FunctionalSet(['Jack', 'Jill', 'Tom', 'Jerry'])
  .add('Bill');
```

What change do you have to make for your solution in Exercise 1 to work for this modified code?

Exercise 3

Implement a BoundedSet that inherits from Set to provide the desired behavior shown in the code:

```
'use strict';

//Your code goes here

const set = new BoundedSet(5, ['Apple', 'Banana', 'Grape', 'Mangoe']);

set.add('Orange');
set.add('Apple');

try {
  set.add('Tangerine');
} catch(ex) {
  console.log(ex.message); //exceeded capacity of 5 elements
}

set.delete('Grape');
set.add('Peach');
console.log(set.size); //5

const set2 = new BoundedSet(2, ['Apple', 'Banana', 'Grape']);
console.log(set2.size); //0
console.log(set2); //BoundedSet { capacity: 2 }
```

Exercise 4

Complete the code so it produces the desired result, using the modern Java-Script conventions:

```
'use strict';

class Base {
```

```
  copy() {
    //Your code goes here
  }
}

class Derived1 extends Base {
      //Your code goes here
}

class Derived2 extends Base {
      //Your code goes here
}

const derived1 = new Derived1();
const derived2 = new Derived2();

console.log(derived1.copy()); //Base {}
console.log(derived2.copy()); //Derived2 {}
```

Exercise 5

We will combine two classes that inherit from a class in this exercise to produce the desired result:

```
'use strict';

class SpecialWordChecker {
  isSpecial(word) { return word !== word; }
}

class PalindromeChecker extends SpecialWordChecker {
      //Your code goes here
}

class AlphabeticalChecker extends SpecialWordChecker {
      //Your code goes here
}

const checkIfSpecial = function(specialWordChecker, word) {
  const result = specialWordChecker.isSpecial(word) ? 'is' : 'is not';
  console.log(`${word} ${result} special`);
};

const palindromeChecker = new PalindromeChecker();
checkIfSpecial(palindromeChecker, 'mom'); //mom is special
checkIfSpecial(palindromeChecker, 'abe'); //abe is not special

const alphabeticalChecker = new AlphabeticalChecker();
checkIfSpecial(alphabeticalChecker, 'mom'); //mom is not special
checkIfSpecial(alphabeticalChecker, 'abe'); //abe is special

//Combine PalindromeChecker and AlphabeticalChecker here
const alphabeticalAndPalindromeChecker = //Your code goes here

checkIfSpecial(alphabeticalAndPalindromeChecker, 'mom'); //mom is special
checkIfSpecial(alphabeticalAndPalindromeChecker, 'abe'); //abe is special
```

CHAPTER 9

Using Modules

Well-designed software is *cohesive*. Cohesion is when a piece of code is narrow, focused, and does one thing well. A good designer strives to achieve cohesion at all levels: functions, classes, and especially files.

A well-designed file should contain only things closely related to each other. Like things should be together in one file, and unlike things should be apart from each other in different files. In addition to making the code cohesive, small files focused on one particular concern also promote better reuse.

Nontrivial applications need many functions and multiple classes with intricate dependencies. Having the ability to access everything from everywhere leads to chaos, confusion, and errors. A piece of code should be well contained; programmers should be able to clearly specify what is available for others to use and intentionally declare things they need from the outside. This is where JavaScript modules come in.

JavaScript modules are used to modularize code—that is, to divide code into parts that have different concerns, but they may need to depend on one another. For example, each component and service class you create in, say, React and Angular will belong to separate modules. Each group of functions related to a common set of operations may belong to a module. In modern JavaScript, any nontrivial application will be made up of modules. Use modules to define clear boundaries in code and to specify what's internal to your file and what may be used from the outside.

A JavaScript module is a well-encapsulated file. As a creator of a module, you're responsible for clearly specifying what you need—the imports—and what you provide for others to use—the exports. Within a module, you can't use what you haven't imported. Likewise, the users of your module can't use what you haven't exported. This prevents accidental and unintentional dependencies in code and thus reduces errors.

By learning about modules, you will be able to understand how they're used in code that use libraries and frameworks, like React and Angular. Furthermore, you will be able to decide how to break your large applications into well-structured parts. In this chapter you'll learn how to create modules, export code from modules, and import code into other modules. Along the way you'll examine the consequences of the decisions you make.

Creating a Module

Simply put, in JavaScript, a module is an individual file that contains variables, constants, functions, and classes. Modules follow the Vegas theme: "What happens in Vegas stays in Vegas." Code within a module is executed in strict mode—you don't need to specify 'use strict';—so the variables within a module do not accidentally spillover to global scope.

The author of a module has to carefully choose what to export from the file to the outside world. All else is invisible and unreachable directly from the outside. Likewise, for a module to use something that's not part of it, it first has to import it. Once imported, the reference becomes part of the current module's scope.

Support for Modules

NodeJS, starting in version 8.5, provides experimental support for modules, with the --experimental-modules command-line flag. NodeJS requires files that use modules to be named with the .mjs extension instead of .js.

The browser support for modules varies across browsers and versions. Tools like Babel may be used to transpile code with modules into traditional JavaScript code for execution on old browsers that don't support modules.

Let's create a few modules and learn how dependencies are loaded and executed. Here's a module named right in a file named right.mjs:

modules/right.mjs
```
console.log('executing right module');

const message = 'right called';

export const right = function() {
  console.log(message);
};
```

Unlike languages like Java, there is no module keyword in JavaScript, there is no ceremony to create a module—simply define a file with imports and exports to convey what you want to use and what you want to make available for outside your module, respectively.

The contents of this entire file are part of the right module. The constant message is internal to the module; it isn't exported and so won't be visible outside of this module. Using the export keyword, the module exports a variable named right, which refers to a function. This function may be used by the users of the right module through the reference named right. The reference right is the only thing this module makes visible for the outside world to use. At the top of the file, we put an informational print statement to signal when the code within the file is executed. This will help us to clearly see how JavaScript manages loading of files.

Now, let's create a second module named middle that loads the previous module:

modules/middle.mjs

```
import { right } from './right';

console.log('executing middle module');

export const middle = function() {
  console.log('middle called');
};
```

It's customary to place all the imports needed for a file at the top—imports are not allowed in nested code; they're required to be in the top level of a file. The middle module imports the right variable from the right module, prints an informational message that this module's file is loaded and executed, and exports a variable named middle.

Finally, let's create a module named left that loads both right and middle modules, like so:

modules/left.mjs

```
import { right } from './right';
import { middle } from './middle';

middle();
right();
```

The left module loads the two modules, right and middle, and imports the variables right and middle from the right and middle modules, respectively. Finally, the left module calls the two functions referenced by the middle and right variables.

Let's focus on who loads the right module in this example. First, when the file containing the left module is executed, it appears to load the right module. Then when the left module loads middle, the middle module in turn appears to load the right module on its first line. You may wonder if that means the right module file will be loaded twice. Thankfully, *no*. JavaScript modules are managed smartly—a module is loaded only once when the first import is seen in the execution control flow. If a module has already been loaded, a request to load it is skipped, but any variables we import are assigned to the proper references. To verify this behavior, run the left module; remember to include the necessary command-line option.

```
node --experimental-modules left.mjs
```

The output from the code is

```
(node:78813) ExperimentalWarning: The ESM module loader is experimental.
executing right module
executing middle module
middle called
right called
```

The example shows that when working with modules, you may freely import modules without worry about repetitive or redundant executions of any imported code.

We know how to define modules and tie them together. Next, let's explore the various options to export and import.

Exporting from a Module

Primitives, functions, objects, and classes defined within a module are visible to the outside only if exported. JavaScript offers several options for exporting; choose the simplest option that meets your needs in a given situation.

Inlining Exports

You may declare a reference or a class and at the same time export it—that is, inline the export keyword in the declaration. This approach is the easiest and least noisy approach to exporting. To inline an export, prefix a declaration with the export keyword, which makes the declared reference available outside the module. The name of the declared reference becomes the name that is exported—this is called a *named export*.

For example, the following code exports a primitive, a function, an object, and a class, with their respective names. The primitive referenced by the variable FREEZINGPOINT_IN_F is not exported and is visible only within the module/file.

modules/temperature.mjs
```
export const FREEZING_POINT = 0;

export function f2c(fahrenheit) {
  return (fahrenheit - 32) / 1.8;
}
```

```
export const temperaturePoints = { freezing: 0, boiling: 100 };

export class Thermostat {
  constructor() {
    //...initialization sequence
  }
}

const FREEZINGPOINT_IN_F = 32;
```

Marking references with export at the point of declaration makes the code transparent—we can readily see if a reference has been exported or not. However, since the exports are spread out in the file, it may make it hard to quickly get a glimpse of everything exported from a module. This is generally not a huge concern if the files are relatively small.

Exporting Explicitly

You're not forced to export at the point of declaration. You can export an existing function, object, and so forth at any time by explicitly declaring an export. Although inlining exports is less noisy and avoids an extra line for export, explicitly exporting is necessary when we want to export select names when using multiple declarations.

In the following code, we explicitly export the c2f function, which we could have exported inline as well. However, we want to export only FREEZINGPOINT_IN_K, from the multiple declarations, and not export BOILINGPOINT_IN_K. Explicit export is a good choice for this.

modules/temperature.mjs
```
function c2f(celsius) {
  return celsius * 1.8 + 32;
}

const FREEZINGPOINT_IN_K = 273.15, BOILINGPOINT_IN_K = 373.15;

export { c2f, FREEZINGPOINT_IN_K };
```

Prefer inline exports over explicit exports, and in general, use explicit exports only when an inline export is not suitable.

Exporting with a Different Name

So far we've exported the declarations with their name. However, we can export them with a different name if we desire. This is useful, for example, if we decide to give a more descriptive name for a function for the outside world to use but keep a shorter name for internal use.

Here's an example to illustrate exporting with a different name:

modules/temperature.mjs
```
function c2k(celsius) {
  return celsius + 273.15;
}

export { c2k as celsiusToKelvin };
```

The name c2k is only visible within the module—kind of like nicknames used within families. However, outside the module this function is known by the name celsiusToKelvin and can be called only with that name.

Default Exports

A default export may signify a major, the most significant, or the only export a module may like to expose. Although a module can have zero or more named exports, it can have at most one default export. Use a default export if you have only one reference or class to export. Even when you have multiple things to export, you may use a default export if most users of your module will use a particular reference more frequently than other exported references.

To mark an export as default, follow the export keyword with the default keyword. Default exports have one restriction, however; export default is not permitted in front of the keywords const and let while export without default is allowed. In short, inlining of default exports is permitted for functions and classes, but not for variables and constants. You may explicitly export variables and constants as default. Let's export as default a function from our module.

modules/temperature.mjs
```
export default function unitsOfMeasures() {
  return ['Celsius', 'Delisle scale', 'Fahrenheit', 'Kelvin', /*...*/];
}
```

The unitsOfMeasures() function is exported as default. Instead of exporting a function as default, we can similarly export a class as default.

In the previous code we used an inline default export on the function. We can also perform an explicit default export at a later time after declaring the function with no export, like so: export default unitsOfMeasures. As we discussed before, this approach is especially useful to export a variable that was declared using const or let; that's because default can't be followed by const or let.

When we create a named export, the name of the reference used in the file becomes the exported name. When we create a named export with a different name, that new name we provide becomes the name visible outside the module. When we create a default export, however, the name visible outside the module becomes default and the importing module may bind the name default to whatever name it likes. We'll see this later when we explore imports.

If you mark an export as default when declaring a function or a class, the name you provide for the function or class is not visible outside the module. If you have no use for that name internally in your module, then you can omit the name entirely. So, for instance, instead of exporting a function like this:

```
export default function unitsOfMeasures() {
  return ['Celsius', 'Delisle scale', 'Fahrenheit', 'Kelvin', /*...*/];
}
```

if you have no use for that function within your module, then you may omit the name of the function, like so:

```
export default function() {
  return ['Celsius', 'Delisle scale', 'Fahrenheit', 'Kelvin', /*...*/];
}
```

Likewise, we can omit the name of a class, if we like, when creating an inline default export for a class. For example, export default class { /*...*/ } will work instead of export default class SomeNameNoOneCares { /*...*/ } as well.

Reexporting from Another Module

You can reexport modules to reduce the number of imports and to make dependencies transitive. Occasionally you may want to make available to the users of your module some references that are contained in other modules.

For example, let's say we create a weather module but we want to expose functions from the temperature module we created previously and also another hypothetical pressure module. The weather module may itself expose some references that it contains. Now suppose a module wants to use the references in the weather, temperature, and pressure modules. That user does not need three imports. Instead, by importing the weather module, thanks to reexport, the user will have access to references exported by all the three modules: weather, temperature, and pressure.

Here's a way to reexport all exported references, except default, from temperature:

```
export * from './temperature';
```

Now, the modules that import weather can use all references exported by temperature as if they were exported by weather.

You can export select references from other modules instead of reexporting everything that's exported. For example, the following reexport will export only Thermostat and celsiusToKelvin from temperature.

```
export { Thermostat, celsiusToKelvin } from './temperature';
```

An importer of the module that does this reexport will not have access to references like f2c in temperature unless it directly imports the temperature module.

Reexport all—that is, export *—does not reexport a default export. A module can reexport any reference, or the default, from another module as its own default if it chooses. Likewise, it may rename a reference from another module while exporting. This can be achieved using the facility to export with a different name we saw in *Exporting with a Different Name,* on page 159. Here's an example with export...as to reexport.

```
export { Thermostat as Thermo, default as default } from './temperature';
```

Here the weather module is reexporting the Thermostat class from temperature with a new name, Thermo. The user of the reexporting module will know Thermostat of temperature as Thermo. Likewise, it takes the default export of temperature—that is, the function unitsOfMeasures()—and exports as its own default.

Instead of reexporting another modules default as your own module's default, you can use any exported reference from another module as your default, like so:

```
export { Thermostat as Thermo, f2c as default } from './temperature';
```

Here the function f2c, which is a named export and not a default export in temperature, is reexported from this module as its own default. In the same vein, your module can reexport the default from another module with a different name:

```
export { Thermostat as Thermo, default as uom } from './temperature';
```

The function unitsOfMeasures exported as default from temperature is now reexported as uom. This technique, renaming a default from another module, is useful when a module reexports multiple modules and wants to make the defaults from more than one module available to the user.

Importing from a Module

A module must import references it wants to use, such as primitives, functions, objects, or classes exported by other modules. The import directive should specify the location of the module or file to load. The path may be a relative path, an absolute path, or the name of the module file. In the last case, the location is decided based on the runtime environment and configuration; for example, Node may pick the module from the node_modules directory. The path in general does not include the file extension. JavaScript offers a variety of import options—choose the one that best meets your needs.

Importing Named Exports

There are two rules to bring in named exports from another module. First, the name specified in the import for the reference should match the exported name. Second, the names have to be specified within a {} block. Let's create a module that imports some references from the temperature module.

modules/temperature-operations.mjs
```
import { FREEZING_POINT, celsiusToKelvin } from './temperature';

const fpInK = celsiusToKelvin(FREEZING_POINT);
```

The temperature-operations module currently imports only two of the different exports from the temperature module. It imports the inlined export of FREEZING_POINT and the given name celsiusToKelvin for c2k. The reference name c2k is not visible outside of the temperature module and so that reference can't be imported. Once we import the desired references, we can access them as shown in the last line. The list of names within {} can include any of the named exports from the module specified at the tail end of the import directive.

Resolving Conflicts

Conflicts may occur in one of two ways. A name exported by a module may collide with a name used within the module that is importing that reference. Or a module may be importing two references with the same name from two different modules and those names collide. Thankfully, there are a few workarounds.

Suppose we have a home module with a Thermostat class, as well as a temperature module with a Thermostat class, and a module imports Thermostat from both the temperature module and the home module, like so:

```
import { Thermostat } from './temperature';
import { Thermostat } from './home';
```

This will result in a fatal error:

```
import { Thermostat } from './home';
         ^^^^^^^^^^
SyntaxError: Identifier 'Thermostat' has already been declared
```

One approach to resolve this is to import at least one of the references as a different name.

```
import { Thermostat } from './temperature';
import { Thermostat as HomeThermostat } from './home';
```

Alternatively, you can import the exports from one of the modules into a namespace object, like so:

```
import { Thermostat } from './temperature';
import * as home from './home';
```

```
console.log(Thermostat);
console.log(home.Thermostat);
```

All the exports from the home module are imported into a namespace object, home, in this example. In the module with the previous imports, Thermostat refers to the variable in the temperature module. To access the Thermostat in the home module, an explicit namespace resolution, home.Thermostat, is needed. We'll delve more into importing into namespaces soon, but first let's look at importing defaults.

Importing a Default Export

Unlike named exports, default exports do not have a name other than default. Here's a rather odd but legal way to import the default export from the temperature module.

```
import { default as uom } from './temperature';
```

The import is mapping the default exported name from the temperature module to the name uom for use within the imported module. We can reduce some noise by replacing { default as uom } with uom, like so:

```
import uom from './temperature';
```

On the importing side, default exports may be given any name that the importing modules desire, like uom in this example.

Importing Both Default and Named Exports

The {} syntax gives access to named exports while the syntax without {} surrounding a name indicates an import of default export. In one import directive we can bring in both the default export, if present, and any of the named exports.

```
import uom, { celsiusToKelvin, FREEZING_POINT as brrr } from './temperature';
```

Here uom stands for the imported name of the default export. The names in the {} should match the exported names; you can also use as to give a different name, like brrr in the example.

Importing Everything into a Namespace

If a module will use a number of exports from a module, it can be tedious to mention the name of each one of the desired references within {}. You can ask JavaScript to bring over all of them using the wildcard.

Let's invite all named exports from the temperature module to the party:

```
import * as heat from './temperature';

const fpInK = heat.celsiusToKelvin(heat.FREEZING_POINT);
```

When using wildcards, the exports are imported into a namespace object, heat in this case. The name of the namespace object is at the discretion of the importing module, but the properties imported into the namespace have their respective exported names from the exporting modules.

A wildcard brings over all exports from the specified module, except the default export. If you don't want the default export to feel left out of the party, do it a favor and send an invite, like so:

```
import uom, * as heat from './temperature';
```

While the exported references from the temperature module can be accessed by reaching into the namespace heat, the default export of that module can be accessed using the given uom name.

Importing for Side Effects

On rare occasions we may not need anything to be imported from a module, but we may want to run the code contained in a module for its side effects. A module, when executed, can place some classes into the window object in a browser, for example. The file may not really export any references, or even if it does, we may not care about them at that point. In that case, to have the module file executed without really importing anything, we can use an import followed by the module filename. For example:

```
import 'some-side-effect-causing-module'
```

will run the specified module without importing anything.

Even though this feature exists, avoid creating modules that cause side effects. Generally, such code becomes hard to maintain and to test, and is error-prone.

Wrapping Up

JavaScript now provides an effective way to split functions and classes into files or modules. Modules are essential to manage the complexity of large applications and to keep code cohesive and make it easier to reuse. Code within modules run in strict mode. You can be very deliberate about what's internal to a module and what should be exported. JavaScript offers a variety of options to import classes, functions, variables, and primitives from modules.

In the next chapter we'll look at promises and the new asynchronous programming features of JavaScript.

Exercises

The imports and exports have some moving parts that can get a bit challenging. Use these exercises to hone in on your understanding. You can find answers to these exercises on page 244.

Exercise 1

State true or false for each of the following:

1. In the execution flow, the code within a module is loaded as many times as it is imported.

2. An inlined export—that is, placing `export` when defining a variable—turns the variable into the default export for that module.

3. If two imported modules have default exports, we will get an error in the importing module.

4. We should use inline exports where possible instead of explicit exports.

5. A module can have either a single default export or any number of nondefault exports, but not both.

Exercise 2

When would you use an explicit export instead of an implicit export?

Exercise 3

When a module imports a default export, what name does it see?

Exercise 4

What does the following syntax mean?

```
export * from 'some-module';
```

Exercise 5

A module named fasttrack has many exports, including one default. How can we import all the items exported by that module, including the default one?

Part IV

Going Meta

Buckle up; we're kicking things up a notch in this part. You'll learn about promises and the asynchronous programming facility of JavaScript. Then you'll dive into metaprogramming and explore ways to write a program that dynamically writes parts of itself, and learn about injection versus synthesis using proxies. Get ready—here comes some advanced features of JavaScript.

CHAPTER 10

Keeping Your Promises

Asynchronous programming is a way of life in JavaScript. Unless a method returns instantaneously, we should never call it with the intention of waiting for a response. Most functions in JavaScript libraries and frameworks are asynchronous. Although making a call and getting the results later is not new in JavaScript, the mechanics of this have evolved over the past few years.

The traditional approach to asynchronous programming was to use callbacks. Unfortunately, as we'll soon discuss, there are many issues with callbacks. In modern JavaScript, promises replace callbacks for asynchronous programming. A code that returns a promise is nonblocking and will eventually return a result or an error to the caller through the promise.

Although legacy libraries still use callbacks, that approach is the least desirable. As we'll see, there are libraries to convert callbacks into promises.

Newer functions rely on promises, which are easier to work with compared to callbacks; their structure is a lot like the structure in the functional style of programming. Promises are much better not only for propagating errors, but in recovering from them as well. We'll explore various ways to work with promises in this chapter.

Promises are arguably better than callbacks, but there's a bit of ceremony in using them. When compared to the structure of synchronous imperative style code, they are different and require some planning. There are benefits to keeping the code structure the same for both synchronous and asynchronous programming—that's where async and await come in. By the end of this chapter, you'll know how promises can be extended to use the new async and await.

No Thanks to Callback Hell

Any method that does not return instantaneously should be asynchronous. The traditional approach to designing asynchronous functions relied on callbacks. Let's take a look at a small example and discuss the issues with this approach.

```
promises/readfile.js
const fs = require('fs');

const displayFileContent = function(pathToFile) {
  const handleFile = function(err, contents) {
    if(err) {
      console.log(err.message);
    } else {
      console.log(contents.toString());
    }
  };

  try {
    fs.readFile(pathToFile, handleFile);
  } catch(ex) {
    console.log(ex.message);
  }
};
```

We first bring in the fs library that provides both synchronous and asynchronous functions to read files. In the displayFileContent() function, we create a callback handler named handleFile. This callback function takes two parameters: err and contents. That's the location of the first issue—is it error and data, or data and then error? There is no standardized order of the parameters; some functions may send an error first whereas others may send data as the first argument.

Within the callback handler we either print the error details or process the response and print some result. Therein lies the second issue—since we print the result right here in this handler, this function is hard to reuse. If we wanted to perform some other operations on the response before printing it, it is quite hard to extend this code to achieve that. The callback will require a callback to receive the data—this leads to what's called *callback hell*. In other words, callbacks don't compose well when a series of callbacks are necessary.

There's a third issue with the way errors are handled. The callback handler dealt with the situation when there was an error with the file. However, read-File(), which is an asynchronous method of fs, may also blow up at the call site if the first argument is undefined or null. Again, there's a lack of consistency in how errors are handled in callbacks. Furthermore, instead of printing the error, if we want to propagate the error to the caller, we have to deal with that in multiple places, within the callback and also in the catch block—messy.

To summarize, callback hell comes from the fact that callbacks

- don't compose easily for multiple levels of callbacks
- lead to code that is hard to extend
- have no consistency between order of parameters
- have no consistent way to handle errors

Let's explore how promises solve these issues elegantly.

Promises to the Rescue

Newer asynchronous functions in JavaScript are designed to return a promise instead of taking a callback. A promise is an object through which a function may propagate an error or result sometime in the future. At any time, a promise is in one of three states: pending, resolved, or rejected.

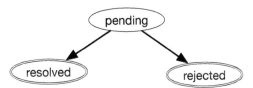

If an asynchronous function has not completed its task, the promise it returned will be in the pending state. Whenever the asynchronous function completes successfully, it will set the promise into the resolved state. At this time, the promise generates or emits the result passed through it—we refer to this as the *promise resolves*. If an asynchronous function finishes with an error, then it sets the promise into the rejected state. At this time, the promise generates or emits the error passed through it—we refer to this as the *promise rejects*.

A promise may be created in one of these three states; however, resolved and rejected are end states. Once a promise ends in either of these states, it will never change to another state. Also, a promise may be in the pending state for an unknown period of time or forever—that is, as long as the asynchronous function that returned the promise has not completed its task.

Let's discuss how promises solve the issues that make callbacks undesirable.

We often pass the result of one synchronous function as an argument to another synchronous function. When working with asynchronous functions, likewise, we often want to pass the result of one function to another. If the asynchronous functions use callbacks, it is extremely hard to achieve this—code becomes clumsy and unwieldy. At the same time, passing results from one function to another is very easy if the asynchronous functions use promises. That's because promises may form a chain and, as a result, compose really well to pass data from one function to another.

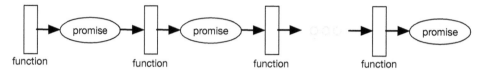

Upon receiving a promise from an asynchronous function, we can either discard that promise or propagate another promise for further handling. Thus, code can form a chain where each function in the chain performs one cohesive operation and leaves it to the next function in the chain to either complete the operation or extend the task for further processing.

Extending the chain of promises is natural and effortless. For this, a function in the chain, as we'll see, may return a promise or simply return a primitive, an object, or throw an exception—JavaScript will quietly wrap these into a promise to extend the chain.

Promises consistently and clearly discern data from errors by providing two separate channels of communication: the data channel used with then() and the error channel used with catch(). Unlike callbacks, there is no confusion related to parameter ordering or about which is data versus error. Let's discuss this further with the following illustration.

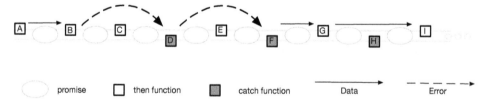

Two kinds of functions may be part of a promises chain—the then() functions and the catch() functions. A then() function is used to receive and process data. A catch() function is used to receive and process an error. Depending on what's returned by each of these functions, the next step in the process is decided.

For example, in the figure the then() functions A and B are followed by an alternating series of then() and catch() function pairs. The then() function A returns a piece of data, and that's wrapped into a resolving promise. The then() function B receives the resolved data in this promise for processing. This then() function, B, throws an exception, and that's wrapped into a rejecting promise by JavaScript. Since the result of the then() function, B, is a rejection, the then() function, C, in the chain is skipped and the promise arrives at the following catch() function, D.

This catch() function, D, also throws an exception and as a result that exception is passed to the subsequent catch() function, F, skipping the then() function, E. The catch() function, F, returns a piece of data, which is wrapped by JavaScript into a promise, and that arrives into the next then() function, G, in the series. In short, a resolved promise finds the next then() function in the chain while a rejected promise seeks the next catch() function in the chain.

Think of the promises chain as two tracks, top and bottom. When things go well, you stay or move over to the top track. When things blow up or a promise is rejected, you move over or stay on the bottom track.

We discussed the behavior of promises. Let's dive into code and see how to create and use promises.

Ways to Create a Promise

In order to return a promise, asynchronous functions have to first create a promise. If the asynchronous function finds that the task at hand is time consuming, it will internally hold a reference to the promise it creates and return the promise instantaneously to its caller. Once the task is completed, it will pass the result or the error through that promise. However, if the asynchronous function can quickly complete the task at hand, then it can return the promise in the resolved state instead of the pending state, making the result available to the caller right away through the promise. Likewise, if the asynchronous function finds an error in the input parameters given to it, or decides to return an error for any reason, it can return a promise in the rejected state instead of the pending state, passing the error details through the promise it returns.

When writing an asynchronous function, you may create a promise in a resolved state, a rejected state, or a pending state with the intent to resolve or reject later. Let's use all these three approaches in one small example.

```
promises/create-promise.js
const computeSqrtAsync = function(number) {
  if(number < 0) {
    return Promise.reject('no negative number, please.');
  }

  if(number === 0) {
    return Promise.resolve(0);
  }

  return new Promise(function(resolve, reject) {
    setTimeout(() => resolve(Math.sqrt(number)), 1000);
  });
};
```

The computeSqrtAsync() function returns an instance of promise, but in one of three different states depending on what's passed in as a parameter.

If the number passed in is less than 0, it returns a promise in the rejected state, created using the reject() static method of Promise.

If it is 0, then the promise returned is in the resolved state, created using the resolve() static method of Promise.

For any parameter value greater than 0, the returned promise is in a pending state, created using new. The constructor of Promise takes a function as its parameter. This function accepts two function references—resolve and reject—which are used to resolve or reject the promise, respectively. JavaScript will call the function attached to the constructor, and the caller of the original function receives the created promise.

In the function passed to the constructor of Promise, we can reject or resolve right away, or call other asynchronous functions to eventually resolve or reject. In this example, we called setTimeout() to create a delayed evaluation. After a second delay, we resolve the promise by calling the resolve function reference. Instead, we may have rejected the promise, if we like, using the reject function reference.

Let's take a peek at the state of the promise instances returned by the function computeSqrtAsync().

```
promises/create-promise.js
const forNegative1 = computeSqrtAsync(-1);
const forZero = computeSqrtAsync(0);
const forSixteen = computeSqrtAsync(16);

console.log(forNegative1);
console.log(forZero);
console.log(forSixteen);
```

We save the promises returned for each of the three calls into variables and print them out. When you run the code right now, in addition to printing the states of the promises, node.js may complain that the rejection of one or more promises has not been handled. Ignore that warning for now; it will go away once we extend the code further, after we discuss the output.

The output from running the code shows the different states in addition to the value of rejection or resolution, if available:

```
Promise { <rejected> 'no negative number, please.' }
Promise { 0 }
Promise { <pending> }
```

We can infer the state of the promises from the output. However, there's really no way to explicitly query a promise for its state—that's due to a good design decision, since the state may change by the time we use the returned information if such a query method were present.

Calls to functions that return promises are nonblocking. The control will immediately flow to the next statement or expression that's after the function call.

Whether a promise rejects or resolves immediately or at a later time, the way to handle the response is just the same. To receive the successful response if and when a promise resolves, use the then() function on the promise. To receive the error details from a promise if and when it rejects, use the catch() function. Let's write a function that takes a promise and prints the result if the given promise resolves and the error if it rejects.

promises/create-promise.js
```
const reportOnPromise = function(promise) {
  promise
    .then(result => console.log(`result is ${result}.`))
    .catch(error => console.log(`ERROR: ${error}`));
};
```

The reportOnPromise() function works with any promise. Both then() and catch() are instance methods on the promise. They both return another instance of the promise; the state of each depends on what's returned by the respective functions passed to then() and catch(). Both the functions passed to then() and catch() in this example print the details of what they receive. Let's call the reportOnPromise() function with each one of the promises we have received from the three calls.

promises/create-promise.js
```
reportOnPromise(forNegative1);
reportOnPromise(forZero);
reportOnPromise(forSixteen);
```

Here's the output from these calls:
```
result is 0.
ERROR: no negative number, please.
result is 4.
```

Since the calls are asynchronous, there is no guarantee of order in the printed messages. As we see from the output, the then() function is called if the promise passed in resolves; otherwise, the catch() function is called if the promise is rejected. If the promise continues to be in the pending state, then neither the then() function nor the catch() function will be called.

In this example, the chain had only two functions: then() and catch(). Let's explore a longer chain next.

Chaining Promises

One elegant feature of promises is that they form a pipeline like in the functional composition we saw in *Arrow Functions and Functional Style*, on page 85. Since both then() and catch() return a promise, calls to these functions may be chained to apply a series of filtering and transformations. An example will help you appreciate this elegance.

In the example in *No Thanks to Callback Hell*, on page 170 we used the fs library's readFile() asynchronous method that relied on callback. The fs-extra library provides a wrapper around the functions of the fs library. We will use that to read the contents of a file asynchronously, but this time using promises instead of callbacks.

Wrapping Callbacks into Promises

fs-extra is a library that wraps the callback-taking fs library of functions into Promise-returning functions. This library works with only methods of fs, but what about your own legacy code or any third-party functions?

The bluebird[a] library was designed for this purpose. You can create a wrapper around any callback taking function using this library. Although you can design new asynchronous functions to work with Promise's, use a library like bluebird to alleviate the pain of using legacy asynchronous functions.

---

a.   http://bluebirdjs.com/docs/getting-started.html

First, we need to install the fs-extra package. To do that, run the following command at your command prompt:

```
npm install fs-extra
```

This will install the package into your current project. Now that the package is ready for use, let's make use of it.

promises/readfile-with-promises.js
```
const fs = require('fs-extra');

const countLinesWithText = function(pathToFile) {
  fs.readFile(pathToFile)
    .then(content => content.toString())
    .then(content => content.split('\n'))
    .then(lines => lines.filter(line => line.includes('THIS LINE')))
    .then(lines => lines.length)
```

```
    .then(count => checkLineExists(count))
    .then(count => console.log(`Number of lines with THIS LINE is ${count}`))
    .catch(error => console.log(`ERROR: ${pathToFile}, ${error.message}`));
};

const checkLineExists = function(count) {
  if(count === 0) {
    throw new Error('text does not exist in file');
  }

  return count;
};
```

In the countLinesWithText() function, we call the readFile() method from the fs-extra library. This function returns a promise, which will either resolve with the content of the given file or reject with an error if something goes wrong. We apply a series of then() calls to the result of readFile().

The action performed by each of the then() calls is cohesive—small and focused: converting content to strings, splitting into an array along the line breaks, picking only lines with the words 'THIS LINE', counting the number of lines, and finally printing the result. You may combine a few of these functions, like for example, contents.toString().split('\n'), if you prefer.

All the then() sequence of calls will be evaluated only if the promise returned by readFile() resolves and there are no exceptions anywhere in this chain. However, if the promise returned by readFile() was rejected or if there was any exception along the way in the pipeline, then the function passed to the catch() method will be triggered.

The checkLineExists() function throws an exception if count is 0; otherwise it returns the value of count. Since this function is called from one of the functions passed to then(), that call to then() will either return a promise that resolves or rejects, depending on whether checkLineExists() returns or blows up with an exception, respectively.

Let's exercise the countLinesWithText() function with a few different arguments.

promises/readfile-with-promises.js
```
countLinesWithText('readfile-with-promises.js');
countLinesWithText('readfile.js');
countLinesWithText('invalid');
countLinesWithText();
```

In the first call, we pass the name of the file that contains this code. In the second call, we pass the readfile.js file, which does not contain the expected text. Then, in the last two calls, we pass a nonexistent filename and nothing—the parameter becomes undefined in this case. Recall that the errors from the last two calls were not handled the same way by the readFile() method of the fs library. But since promises deal with errors in a consistent manner, the behavior of the code is much easier to predict and deal with when the readFile() of fs-extra is used.

Each of the calls to countLinesWithText() is asynchronous, and the order of the output is not predictable. Let's take a look at the output of running the previous code.

```
ERROR: undefined, path must be a string or Buffer
ERROR: invalid, ENOENT: no such file or directory, open 'invalid'
Number of lines with THIS LINE is 2
ERROR: readfile.js, text does not exist in file
```

The output shows the result of data or errors progressing through the pipeline. When readfile-with-promises.js was passed as an argument, all the then() functions were executed and the catch() function was totally skipped. When readfile.js was passed, the series of then() functions, except the last one, were executed. Since the call to checkLineExists() throws an exception for this case, the last then() is skipped and the catch() is executed. When the argument is 'invalid' or missing, the readFile() function rejects the promise and all the then() functions in the pipeline are skipped. The final catch() is executed in these two cases.

Working with Multiple Promises

In the examples so far, promises were used to implement a single asynchronous task. In nontrivial scenarios, we may need multiple asynchronous tasks to be executed to solve a problem. For example, a currency exchange broker may want to pick the best price quote from more than one provider. A promise carries the response for a single asynchronous task, but when dealing with multiple tasks, we need to combine data from multiple asynchronous functions, each returning a promise.

JavaScript provides two options to deal with multiple asynchronous tasks:

- Let the tasks race and pick the first promise that resolves or rejects.
- Wait for all the tasks to resolve or for any one of them to reject.

Let's explore each of these options with examples.

Racing Promises

The race() static method of Promise takes an array of promises and returns the first one to resolve or reject. Let's create two promises, one that resolves after a delay and the other that rejects after a timeout has expired.

promises/race.js
```
const createPromise = function(timeInMillis) {
  return new Promise(function(resolve, reject) {
    setTimeout(() => resolve(timeInMillis), timeInMillis);
  });
};

const createTimeout = function(timeInMillis) {
  return new Promise(function(resolve, reject) {
    setTimeout(() => reject(`timeout after ${timeInMillis} MS`), timeInMillis);
  });
};
```

The createPromise() function returns a promise that resolves after the time given as a parameter. The createTimeout() function returns a promise that rejects after the time given as a parameter. Let's create a few promises using these functions and let them compete with each other.

promises/race.js
```
Promise.race([createPromise(1000), createPromise(2000), createTimeout(3000)])
  .then(result => console.log(`completed after ${result} MS`))
  .catch(error => console.log(`ERROR: ${error}`));

Promise.race([createPromise(3500), createPromise(4000), createTimeout(2000)])
  .then(result => console.log(`completed after ${result} MS`))
  .catch(error => console.log(`ERROR: ${error}`));
```

To the first call to race(), we pass three promises: one that will finish in one second, the second that will finish in two seconds, and the third that will time out after three seconds. Since the first will finish first, the result reported within then() will be the result of this promise.

To the second call to race() we pass three promises as well, but in this case the timeout will occur before the other two promises complete. The catch() function will be used in this case instead of the then() function.

Let's confirm this behavior from the output:

```
completed after 1000 MS
ERROR: timeout after 2000 MS
```

There are times when we may want to pick among multiple solutions to a given problem. For example, in optimization problems, there may be multiple optimal solutions and any one of them may be acceptable. In these cases we don't have to wait for the completion of all solutions—the first one to finish is adequate. Use the race() function to pick one among multiple asynchronous tasks that return promises.

Gathering All Promises

The all() static method of promise takes an array of promises and passes an array of resolved results to the then() function when all promises resolve. If any one of the given promises is rejected, then the then() function is not called; the catch() function is used instead.

We will soon use the all() function to work with multiple asynchronous tasks. But before we get to the code that uses the all() function, we need to create a small program that will execute calls concurrently. This will help us to see the power of the all() method when run asynchronously and concurrently.

service/count-prime-service.js

```js
'use strict';

const cluster = require('cluster');
const http = require('http');
const url = require('url');
const querystring = require('querystring');
const port = 8084;
const number_of_processes = 8;

const isPrime = function(number) {
  for(let i = 2; i < number; i++) {
    if (number % i === 0) {
      return false;
    }
  }

  return number > 1;
};

const countNumberOfPrimes = function(number) {
  let count = 0;

  for(let i = 1; i <= number; i++) {
    if(isPrime(i)) {
      count++;
    }
  }

  return count;
};

const handler = function(request, response) {
  const params = querystring.parse(url.parse(request.url).query);

  const number = parseInt(params.number);

  const count = countNumberOfPrimes(number);

  response.writeHead(200, { 'Content-Type': 'text/plain' });
  return response.end(`${count}`);
};
```

```
if(cluster.isMaster) {
  for(let i = 0; i < number_of_processes; i++) {
    cluster.fork();
  }
} else {
  http.createServer(handler).listen(port);
}
```

This example shows a small HTTP server that runs in node.js. The isPrime() function returns a boolean result of true or false depending on whether or not the given number is a prime number. It has been written intentionally to be slow or time consuming. The countNumberOfPrimes() function returns the number of prime numbers between 1 and the given number. The handler() function parses the query string from an HTTP request, extracts the number parameter, computes the number of primes in the range 1 to that number, and sends the result via the HTTP response. The code, when started, runs a cluster of eight processes that can process the incoming requests concurrently.

Let's now work on the code that will use this service. First, we need to install both the fs-extra and the request-promise packages using the following command:

```
npm install fs-extra request request-promise
```

We included request in that list of packages since request-promise needs it.

Now, let's write the code to use the service.

promises/all.js
```
const fs = require('fs-extra');
const request = require('request-promise');

const countPrimes = function(number) {
  if(isNaN(number)) {
    return Promise.reject(`'${number}' is not a number`);
  }

  return request(`http://localhost:8084?number=${number}`)
    .then(count => `Number of primes from 1 to ${number} is ${count}`);
};
```

The countPrimes() method receives a number and returns a promise. If the given parameter is not a number, it immediately returns a promise in the rejected state. On the other hand, if the given parameter is a number, then it makes an asynchronous call to the service that computes the number of primes.

Suppose we have a file where each line is a number and we want to determine the number of primes for the numbers on each line. We can compute the values for each line at the same time, asynchronously. Using the readFile() methods of fs-extra, we may asynchronously process the contents of an input file. Then, for each line we can invoke the countPrimes() method. We can use the map() method of the array to transform the array of lines to an array of promises. Then, using the all() method we can wait for the completion of the asynchronous calls. The countPrimesForEachLine() function takes the path to a file and prints the details of the count.

promises/all.js

```
const countPrimesForEachLine = function(pathToFile) {
  fs.readFile(pathToFile)
    .then(content => content.toString())
    .then(content =>content.split('\n'))
    .then(lines => Promise.all(lines.map(countPrimes)))
    .then(counts => console.log(counts))
    .catch(error => console.log(error));
};
```

The call to the catch() function will kick in if there was a failure in processing the file or any of the lines in the file.

Let's create two files. The first file, numbers.txt, has lines with valid numbers:

promises/numbers.txt

```
100
1000
5000
```

The second file, numbers-with-error.txt, has a line of text that is not a number:

promises/numbers-with-error.txt

```
100
invalid text
5000
```

Let's invoke countPrimesForEachLine(), passing the names of these two files.

promises/all.js

```
countPrimesForEachLine('numbers.txt');
countPrimesForEachLine('numbers-with-error.txt');
```

For the file with valid numbers in it, the result will be the number of primes for each line. However, when the second file with invalid input is passed, the output shows the processing error—all() fails fast when any of the promises provided to it fail.

```
'invalid text' is not a number
[ 'Number of primes from 1 to 100 is 25',
  'Number of primes from 1 to 1000 is 168',
  'Number of primes from 1 to 5000 is 669' ]
```

One caveat with all() is that if computations were to take an indefinitely long amount of time, then it might lead to starvation. To avoid this concern, we can use a timeout promise, like the one we created earlier using the createTime-out() function. We can then combine the race() function and the all() function to achieve timeout if the task takes too long. We will explore this approach as part of the exercises at the end of this chapter.

Async and Await

We saw how promises are superior to callbacks, but there's one drawback to using promises. The structure of synchronous imperative code is drastically different from the structure of asynchronous code that uses promises. Unlike the sequential code that flows naturally from one statement or expression to the next, we have to get our head wrapped around the then() and the catch() sequence.

The async and await feature was introduced to keep the code structure identical between synchronous and asynchronous code. This does not affect the way we write asynchronous functions, but it largely changes the way we use them.

There are two rules to using this feature:

- To be able to use an asynchronous function as if it were a synchronous function, *optionally* mark the promise-returning asynchronous function with the async keyword.

- To call the asynchronous function as if it were a synchronous function, place the await keyword right in front of a call. The await keyword may be used only within functions marked async.

Let's explore this feature by first comparing synchronous to asynchronous code structure. Then we'll look at how async and await help.

Let's create two functions—one synchronous and one asynchronous—they both take a number and return the double of the number.

promises/async-await.js
```
const computeSync = function(number) {
  if(number < 0) {
    throw new Error('no negative, please');
  }
  return number * 2;
};

const computeAsync = function(number) {
  if(number < 0) {
    return Promise.reject('no negative, please');
  }
  return Promise.resolve(number * 2);
};
```

computeAsync() is the asynchronous counterpart to the synchronous computeSync(). If the given parameter is negative, the synchronous function throws an exception while the asynchronous function returns a promise that rejects.

Here are two functions that call the previous two functions. The first function, callComputeSync, makes synchronous calls to computeSync(). The second function, callComputeAsync(), makes asynchronous calls to computeAsync().

```
promises/async-await.js
const callComputeSync = function(number) {
  try {
    const result = computeSync(number);
    console.log(`Result is ${result}`);
  } catch(ex) {
    console.log(ex.message);
  }
}

const callComputeAsync = function(number) {
  computeAsync(number)
    .then(result => console.log(`Result is ${result}`))
    .catch(err => console.log(err));
}
```

The code structure is quite different between the synchronous version and the asynchronous version. We can make the code structure look the same by using async and await.

Let's see how to make the asynchronous call structurally look like a synchronous call—it will run like the second call but look and feel like the first one. Let's copy over the callComputeSync() function to a new function, callCompute(), and make two changes like so:

```
promises/async-await.js
const callCompute = async function(number) {
  try {
    const result = await computeAsync(number);
    console.log(`Result is ${result}`);
  } catch(ex) {
    console.log(ex);
  }
}
```

The only difference between callComputeSync() and callCompute() is that the second function is marked as async and, where the first function called computeSync(), the second calls computeAsync() with the keyword await prefixed.

When an asynchronous function call is prefixed with await, JavaScript will make the call to the function and suspend execution of the current function flow, to wait for the promise to resolve or reject. If the promise resolves, then it moves forward. If the promise rejects, then it jumps into the catch block of the surrounding try-catch block. The suspension of execution upon reaching an await is much like the suspension of execution when execution reaches the yield keyword we saw in *Using Yield*, on page 61.

While the promise is a surefire replacement for callbacks, async-await is not a replacement but an enhancement. Here are some things to consider when deciding to use then-catch compared to async-await:

- If the code is not in an async function, then you can't use await; prefer then-catch in this case.

- If you are converting a legacy synchronous code to make it asynchronous, await will preserve the code structure, compared to then-catch, which will totally change the code structure.

- It is often easier to prototype a synchronous version of a function and then convert it to the asynchronous version when needed. In this case again, async-await shines compared to then-catch.

- Then then-catch syntax may be more suitable when creating functional style code and the async-await more suitable when writing imperative style code. At the same time, use caution—async-await may be error prone if the function that we are waiting for completion modifies a shared state; such state change may make the suspended code vulnerable.

Use promises to create asynchronous functions and then pick between then-catch and async-await for calling asynchronous functions.

Wrapping Up

JavaScript programs traditionally used callbacks, but that made the code complex and hard to maintain. The promise is an alternative that provides a data channel and an error channel and can be easily composed into a chain of operations. That gives a functional style flavor to code—elegant and easy to work with. The newly introduced async and await builds on promises to bring back familiar imperative code structure while keeping the execution asynchronous.

Exercises

Here are some exercises for you to practice and improve your understanding of promises. You can find answers to these exercises on page 245.

Exercise 1

Will Promise.race() wait for at least one of the candidate promises to resolve?

Exercise 2

Will Promise.all() wait for all candidate promises to either resolve or reject?

Exercise 3

Write a program, using promises, that will print the program's source code. The current filename can be obtained using the variable __filename.

Exercise 4

In *Gathering All Promises*, on page 180 the numbers.txt file had a few small numbers. Change that file to hold the values 100000 and 500000 on two separate lines. Now, when the program all.js is run, it takes a long time to complete. Modify the code such that if the execution takes more than 1 second the program will time out and exit. Use the createTimeout() function we created in your solution. Remember to leave the count-prime-service.js program running to serve the http call.

Exercise 5

The previous exercise uses promises. Convert the code to use async and await.

CHAPTER 11

Exploring Metaprogramming

Metaprogramming is a way to extend a program at runtime—it's the ability to write code that writes code. It's one of the most complex and yet one of the newest and most powerful features of JavaScript. You may use metaprogramming to dynamically extend code where you feel fit.

JavaScript classes are open—that is, you can extend them without using inheritance, which means you're not limited to using the facilities provided by the author of the class. You can add your own convenience methods and properties to classes so that the code may be easier and more fluent to use, to meet your own style or preferences. And you can add these behaviors dynamically at runtime, anytime.

Inheritance forces you to create a new class to extend the behavior of a class. Metaprogramming permits you to extend a class in place. That is, when you extend a class using inheritance, the added features are available only in the instance of the derived class and not in the instances of the base class. However, when you extend a class with metaprogramming you enhance an existing class without creating any additional classes.

Several JavaScript libraries and frameworks, like React and Angular, make extensive use of metaprogramming to pull metadata from code, to take special actions or implement special behaviors. Knowing metaprogramming greatly demystifies the code you write to use these libraries or frameworks. Furthermore, it helps you approach testing such code with greater confidence. Metaprogramming is like a smartphone; once you get hooked, you wonder how anyone survived without one.

Metaprogramming comes in two flavors: member injection and member synthesis. Injection, which we discuss in this chapter, is useful to add well-known methods to existing classes. Synthesis, which the next chapter dives into, is useful to dynamically create methods and properties based on the current state of objects.

Metaprogramming is quite powerful, but we have to be very careful when using it. In this chapter we'll start with a short discussion of the capabilities of metaprogramming and the cautions we should take in using it. Then we'll look at various techniques to inject members into existing classes.

Now is a good time to refill your favorite beverage—we've got some serious coding ahead of us.

The Power and Perils of Metaprogramming

Metaprogramming is writing code that writes code. When using a third-party class, if you've ever said, "It would be really great to have this particular method in the class at hand," you can use metaprogramming to make that wish come true.

Metaprogramming is not practically approachable for most developers unless the language lends itself for extension using hygienic syntax native to the language. In general, dynamically typed languages, due to their ability to dispatch method calls without rigorous type verification, offer better metaprogramming facilities than statically typed languages.

Just because a language is dynamically typed, however, does not make it automatically suitable for metaprogramming. The language has to offer specific tools for that. A good example of this is JavaScript. Even though the language has been dynamically typed from its inception, until recently it lacked the necessary tools to do full-fledged metaprogramming.

Injection vs. Synthesis

Metaprogramming comes in two flavors: *injection* and *synthesis*. The former is relatively simple and JavaScript has had this capability from the beginning. The latter is more complex and powerful, and has been possible only recently in JavaScript.

Injection is a technique where we can add, or replace, specific methods or properties into a class. The names of these members are known at code writing time. Suppose you want to know if a particular date is in a leap year. You can extract the year from the date object at hand and pass that to a utility method that may tell whether the given year is a leap year. But it would be really convenient if we could do givenDate.isInLeapYear(). The ability to make that possible, even though we don't have access to the source code for the Date class, is metaprogramming and, more specifically, member injection.

Synthesis is more dynamic than injection—I call it adult metaprogramming—it needs more maturity and practice than injection. Suppose Employee is a class that represents employee data that's in a database. The data that goes into a database may be highly fluid. For example, every employee may have properties like firstName, lastName, corporateCreditCard, and so on. At code writing time we may not know what properties exist. Some properties may disappear and new ones may emerge in these databases as the system evolves. However, a programmer using our Employee class may want to write something like Employee.findThoseWithFirstName('Sara') or Employee.findThoseWithCorporateCreditCard('xxxx-xxxx-xxxx-1234'). In the future, when a new property named costCenter is added, the user of the Employee class may want to write Employee.findThoseWithCostCenter(...).

None of these findThose... methods may actually exist in the Employee class at any time. But when the call is made to a method that starts with findThoseWith, as a convention, then we may want to synthesize or dynamically create the code to query for data with a property whose name follows findThoseWith. That's also metaprogramming but, more specifically, method synthesis. Examples of such approaches are the popular ActiveRecords library in Ruby on Rails and Grails Object Relational Mapping (GORM) in Grails.

Risks of Metaprogramming

Metaprogramming has the unrelenting power to alter the structure of objects and classes, so you have to be careful when using it. It can be frustrating and hard to work with code if you find several new and unclear method calls on instances of, for example, the class 'Date', in arbitrary places in code because of metaprogramming. Furthermore, metaprogramming may introduce dynamic behavior, and that may introduce bugs in code. Imagine how many more bugs we could introduce by writing code that writes code—that can become a meta-problem.

Remember Voltaire's wise words: "With great power comes great responsibility." When using metaprogramming:

- Reach for it sparingly and only when it is absolutely necessary. When you feel the urge to create dynamic behaviors, ask for a second opinion.

- Do not inject or synthesize methods in arbitrary places in code. Structure the application so that developers can go to a single location—a directory, for example—where all the code related to injection and synthesis is placed. When developers find an unfamiliar method call, they can more easily locate the code that does related metaprogramming in a project that is better structured.

- Ask for extensive, thorough code reviews. Find a colleague you respect and ask him or her to examine the code, its implications, and the use cases. Having more pairs of eyes on the code can reduce the risk.

- Write rigorous automated tests. Tests do not prevent errors from ever occurring, but they prevent them from recurring. Good tests can improve confidence by keeping an eye on metaprogramming as the code evolves. This is one of the great ways to reduce the risks of metaprogramming.

Let's dive into metaprogramming. We'll see what JavaScript makes possible—you're in for a treat.

Dynamic Access

To access a field, a property, or a method, we use the dot notation in JavaScript much like in languages like Java, C#, and many other languages. However, in addition, we can access a member of an instance using the [] operator—we'll look at yet another alternative to this in *Getting and Setting Properties*, on page 203.

Use the dot notation, like sam.age or sam.play(), if you know the member name at code writing time. If the member name is not known until runtime, then use the [] notation. Suppose variables named fieldName and methodName contain the name of a field and a method—for example, "age" and "play", respectively. Then sam[fieldName] is equivalent to writing sam.age and sam[methodName]() is like writing sam.play().

If you're curious to find all the members in an instance named instance, use the Object.keys(instance) method. The reason the method is called keys is that JavaScript considers objects to be like hashmaps, with keys and values. Alternatively, you can iterate over the members using the for member in instance {} form. Let's try out these facilities with an example.

```
metaprogramming/dynamic-access.js
class Person {
  constructor(age) {
    this.age = age;
  }

  play() { console.log(`The ${this.age} year old is playing`); }

  get years() { return this.age; }
}

const sam = new Person(2);

console.log(sam.age);
sam.play();
```

```
const fieldName = 'age';
const methodName = 'play';

console.log(sam[fieldName]);
sam[methodName]();

console.log(`Members of sam: ${Object.keys(sam)}`);

for(const property in sam) {
  console.log(`Property: ${property} value: ${sam[property]}`);
}
```

We access the field and the method using both the dot notation and the []
notation. We also query for the keys and iterate over the keys. Let's take a
look at the output:

```
2
The 2 year old is playing
2
The 2 year old is playing
Members of sam: age
Property: age value: 2
```

> ## Use Caution Embedding Member Names in Strings
>
> When using the [] notation, we use variables that contain member names. It is fine
> if you fill those variables dynamically based on the members present in an object at
> runtime. However, if you're hardcoding the names as strings, use caution.
>
> Transpilation tools and uglification tools, which are used to shorten JavaScript code
> for efficient transmission over the wire, may rename member names to shorter names.
> If the tools used during development and testing are different from the ones used in
> production, you may run into errors that appear only in production.

The code behaved as expected for the most part. While the age field showed
up in the keys and the iteration of keys, the constructor, the play() method,
and the years property went AWOL. That's because these are not directly part
of the object but are kept in the object's prototype. Let's query the prototype
using the getOwnPropertyName() method of Object, like so:

metaprogramming/dynamic-access.js
```
console.log(Object.getOwnPropertyNames(Reflect.getPrototypeOf(sam)));
```

The getOwnPropertyName() method gets the properties and fields of a given object.
The constructor, the properties, and the methods defined in a class are stored
as properties in its prototype. Let's examine the output of this last code
snippet to see evidence of this:

```
[ 'constructor', 'play', 'years' ]
```

With the ability to dynamically access members and to iterate over the keys, we can explore any object at runtime, much like how we use reflection in languages like Java and C#.

Member Injection

Querying an object to find out what it contains is like asking a restaurant what's on their menu. The best kind of restaurants I like to frequent are the ones willing to make what I like, off the menu, within reason, of course. In other words, you may want to make up stuff in a class that's not already there—enter member injection.

You can use member injection to introduce brand-new methods into an object or into the prototype of a class. The member you add to an object is then available for use on that particular object. The member you inject into a prototype of a class becomes available on all the instances of that class.

Use member injection to add convenience methods or properties that you feel should be in a class. These may be members that are general in nature but were not added by the author of the class. These members may also be specific to your domain, and having them on the class may make your code more fluent and easy to work with.

We'll first look at injecting a member into an instance and then explore how to inject a member into a class.

Injecting a Method into an Instance

Let's explore injection with an instance of the String class. In general, we should not use new to create a string; we should write const text = 'live'; to create a primitive instead of const text = new String('live');, which will result in an object. However, the primitive string does not permit injecting a property on that instance. So, for the sake of this example we will create an object using new. Later you'll learn how to inject a method so it's available on primitive strings.

Suppose we want to reverse a string—for instance, to check whether a given string is a palindrome. Let's try calling a reverse() method and see how that goes.

metaprogramming/inject-into-string-instance.js
```
const text = new String('live');

try {
  text.reverse();
} catch(ex) {
  console.log(ex.message);
}
```

We called the reverse() method defensively for a good reason. There's no reverse() method and the call will blow up:

```
text.reverse is not a function
```

But you don't have to take "no" for an answer; if you want a reverse() method on the instance, you should have it and no one has the right to deny that. Injecting a method into an instance is straightforward—create the function you desire and set it into a field for the method name you want. Remember the function will run in the context of the instance, so this within the function refers to the instance. Let's inject a reverse() method into the text instance and then call the method:

metaprogramming/inject-into-string-instance.js
```
text.reverse = function() { return this.split('').reverse().join(''); };

console.log(text.reverse());
```

In the newly added reverse() method, we convert the string to an array using the split() method, reverse the array, and put it back together into a string using the join() method. Let's take a look at the result of the call to reverse():

```
evil
```

It took no effort at all to inject a new method into the string object—that's wicked.

The steps to inject a field, instead of a method, into an instance is the same. Instead of assigning a function to the name, assign a value to the name. The name then can be used as a field instead of a method.

In this example, we injected a new reverse() method into an instance. If the method were already there, then the new implementation would quietly replace the existing one. Yes, that's truly wicked; use caution.

The effort was minimal, but we only added the method to that particular instance. If we call the reverse() method on another instance of String, it will fail. Here's a piece of code to verify that:

metaprogramming/inject-into-string-instance.js
```
const anotherText = new String('rats');

try {
  console.log(anotherText.reverse());
} catch(ex) {
  console.log(ex.message);
}
```

The result of this call is

```
anotherText.reverse is not a function
```

Before you see how to make the method available on all instances of String, let's discuss whether that's a good idea. You know the answer already: It depends!

In general, injecting or replacing a method on an instance is less risky than doing so on an entire class. When writing automated tests, you may like to stub or mock a method to facilitate testing of other methods that depend on the stubbed or mocked method. In this case, it's much safer to use injection on an instance rather than on a class—this will keep tests isolated from each other; see *Test-Driving JavaScript Applications [Sub16]* to learn how to automate tests for JavaScript and the role metaprogramming plays in testing. Also, in a web application, you may want to inject some behavior into an instance when processing a request. In this scenario, if this method is really intended for the current call, injecting the method into a class may not be prudent as it will have a global effect instead of being restricted to one particular call.

However, if we are creating a method that will truly benefit users of all instances of a class, then inject the method into the class's prototype. Let's see how to do that next.

Injecting a Method into a Class's Prototype

We injected the reverse() method into one single instance. Let's make that method available in all instances. It's not much effort—the key is to inject the method into the class's prototype instead of into the class itself. That's because instances of a class share a common prototype and JavaScript uses an object's prototype chain to look for properties—see *Understanding Prototypal Inheritance*, on page 135.

Let's create a few instances of String, one using new and the others without it. When we inject a method into the String class's prototype, all these instances will have it.

```
metaprogramming/inject-into-string-class.js
'use strict';

const text = new String('live');
const anotherText = 'rats';
const primitiveText = 'part';

String.prototype.reverse =
  function() { return this.split('').reverse().join(''); };

console.log(text.reverse());
console.log(anotherText.reverse());
console.log(primitiveText.reverse());
```

We can see the reach of method injection into the class's prototype in the output:

```
evil
star
trap
```

Again, remember that, if the instance method was already present in the class—that is, in the prototype—then injection will replace it for all instances. However, if we inject a method into only one instance, then the method is replaced only on that instance and other instances of the class will continue to use the original method.

Injecting a Property

Injecting fields and methods was straightforward—you assign to the name you desire either a value or a function. Properties are a different story.

When authoring a class we write properties like they're methods but mark them with get for getters and set for setters. Thus, you may be tempted to inject a property in the same way you injected a method, with an additional get or a set somewhere in the code; unfortunately, that will not work.

To inject a property, use a special defineProperty() method. The method takes three parameters: the object on which to inject the property, the name of the property as a string, and an object with get and/or set each referring to a function. Let's take a look at the syntax with an example.

Here's an example that injects an isInLeapYear property into an instance of the Date class.

```
metaprogramming/inject-a-property.js
const today = new Date();

Object.defineProperty(today, 'isInLeapYear', {
  get: function() {
    const year = this.getFullYear();
    return (year % 4 === 0 && year % 100 !== 0) || (year % 400 === 0);
  }
});

console.log(`${today.getFullYear()} is a leap year?: ${today.isInLeapYear}`);
```

The property is a read-only property since we provided a getter but not a setter. We can optionally add a setter where it makes sense—we'll use a setter in an example later.

Let's run the code and observe the output:

```
2018 is a leap year?: false
```

The first argument passed to defineProperty() is the instance to which the property should be added. The method faithfully implemented its intended task. However, the isInLeapYear property is available only on that one instance. How do we make it available on all instances of Date?

Yep, instead of today pass Date.prototype for that. Let's give that a try:

```
metaprogramming/inject-a-property.js
Object.defineProperty(Date.prototype, 'isInLeapYear', {
  get: function() {
    const year = this.getFullYear();
    return (year % 4 === 0 && year % 100 !== 0) || (year % 400 === 0);
  }
});

for(const year of [2018, 2019, 2020, 2021]) {
  const yayOrNay = new Date(year, 1, 1).isInLeapYear ? '' : 'not ';
  console.log(`${year} is ${yayOrNay}a leap year`);
}
```

Except for passing Date.prototype instead of an instance reference, the injection code is no different from the previous version. We created a few instances of Date and tried accessing the injected property on them. Let's glance at the output:

```
2018 is not a leap year
2019 is not a leap year
2020 is a leap year
2021 is not a leap year
```

Injecting a property took a bit more effort than injecting a field or a method. We saw how to inject a single property using defineProperty(). If you want to inject multiple properties, you can use that method, but repetitive calls to defineProperty() will make the code verbose and hard to maintain. The method defineProperties() will ease that pain, as you'll see next.

Injecting Multiple Properties

Instead of adding one property at a time, we can add multiple properties in one shot—let's explore how. Along the way, you'll see how to inject read-write properties. The properties we injected so far were read-only since we created only getters. Next we'll create setters as well so the properties may not only be read but also modified.

First, let's think of a couple of useful properties to add to an existing class. The Array class in JavaScript provides a number of nice methods, but there's no elegant way to access the first or last element. We will inject a first and a last property into the Array class. For this example, let's start with an array of language names:

metaprogramming/array-fluency.js
```
const langs = ['JavaScript', 'Ruby', 'Python', 'Clojure'];
```

Here's a snippet of code to get some elements from the langs array:

metaprogramming/array-fluency.js
```
const firstElement = langs[0];
const lastElement = langs[langs.length - 1]; //eh?
```

The code to access the first element is marginally bearable, but the effort to get the last element is inhumane. Why not use a property called first to get or set the first element and a property named last for the last element? Well, that would be nice, but these properties are not already defined and any effort to use them will result in undefined on get. The set will result in creating a new field with those names—not what we want.

We want to define two properties, both first and last. We want them to be available on all instances of Array, so we'll inject them into Array.prototype. Furthermore, we want to be able to both read and update the values at those positions, so we'll write both get and set for the properties. Let's get that working. Add the following code before the definition of const firstElement.

metaprogramming/array-fluency.js
```
Object.defineProperties(Array.prototype, {
  first: {
    get: function() { return this[0]; },
    set: function(value) { this[0] = value; }
  },
  last: {
    get: function() { return this[this.length - 1]; },
    set: function(value) { this[Math.max(this.length - 1, 0)] = value; }
  }
});
```

Unlike defineProperty(), which took three arguments, defineProperties() takes only two: the candidate object for injection and an object with properties as the key. For each property, provide a getter and/or a setter. Within the functions for the properties, we can use existing ways to access the appropriate elements.

Let's modify the lines with const firstElement and const lastElement to use the new properties and then print the values received. We'll use the properties to set the values to new values as well.

```
metaprogramming/array-fluency.js
const firstElement = langs.first;
const lastElement = langs.last;

console.log(firstElement);
console.log(lastElement);

langs.first = 'Modern JavaScript';
langs.last = 'ClojureScript';

console.log(langs);
```

Let's examine the output to verify the code's behavior.

```
JavaScript
Clojure
[ 'Modern JavaScript', 'Ruby', 'Python', 'ClojureScript' ]
```

Once these properties are injected into the Array prototype, we can enjoy their fluency on any instance of Array.

We injected properties in a way that makes them available on instances of a class. Likewise, we can inject static properties that will be available at a class level instead of on any instances of the class. As we saw in *Defining Class Members*, on page 123, to add a static property at the time of creating a class we used static get... for the getter and static set... for the setter. However, to inject a static property from outside the class, don't use the static keyword. Instead, use the defineProperty() or defineProperties() method, but inject the property into the class instead of the prototype of the class.

You've learned how to perform member injection. That's one flavor of metaprogramming. In the next chapter, we will dive into the other flavor: the powerful method synthesis.

Wrapping Up

Metaprogramming is an advanced concept that provides the ability to extend a program at runtime. It is used extensively by libraries and frameworks, but you can also cautiously use it to extend third-party classes in order to make code fluent, less noisy, and easier to use. Member injection is useful to add a known method, field, or property into a class without inheriting from it. To add a method to a class, inject it into the class's prototype. To inject properties, use the defineProperty() or defineProperties() method.

Exercises

The following exercises will help you strengthen your metaprogramming skills to query objects and inject members. You can find answers to these exercises on page 248.

Exercise 1

Complete the following code to print the properties of the given object.

```
'use strict';

const printProperties = function(obj) {
  //Your code goes here
};

printProperties({language: 'JavaScript', typing: 'dynamic'});
printProperties(
{tool: 'Redux', language: 'JavaScript', purpose: 'transpiler', });

/*
language is JavaScript
typing is dynamic
tool is Redux
language is JavaScript
purpose is transpiler
*/
```

Exercise 2

Implement a percent() method to produce the desired result shown in the following code.

```
'use strict';

//Your code goes here

const value1 = 0.35;
const value2 = 0.91;

console.log(value1.percent()); //35%
console.log(value2.percent()); //91%

try {
  const value3 = 44;
  console.log(value3.percent());
} catch(ex) {
  console.log(ex.message); // value should be less than 1
}
```

Exercise 3

In the following code, create custom properties to extract the integer part and the fractional part from a number.

```
'use strict';

//Your code goes here

const printParts = function(number) {
  console.log(
    `whole: ${number.integerPart} decimal: ${number.fractionalPart}`);
};

printParts(22.12);     //whole: 22 decimal: 12
printParts(.14);       //whole: 0 decimal: 14
printParts(-23.19);    //whole: -23 decimal: 19
printParts(42);        //whole: 42 decimal: 0
```

Exercise 4

Let's enhance the Set class with a combine() instance method.

```
'use strict';

//Your code goes here

const names1 = new Set(['Tom', 'Sara', 'Brad', 'Kim']);
const names2 = new Set(['Mike', 'Kate']);

const combinedNames = names1.combine(names2);

console.log(names1.size);        //4
console.log(names2.size);        //2
console.log(combinedNames.size); //6
console.log(combinedNames);
  //Set { 'Tom', 'Sara', 'Brad', 'Kim', 'Mike', 'Kate' }
```

Exercise 5

How would you add a method to an instance instead of to all the instances of a class? When would you prefer doing that instead of adding the method so it is available on all instances of a class?

CHAPTER 12

Deep Dive into Metaprogramming

Method synthesis is the most powerful form of metaprogramming. You can alter the API and the behavior of objects based on the runtime context and state of the objects. You can take existing classes and twist and turn them, the way it make sense to meet your needs, far beyond what was intended by the author of a class.

Method synthesis was not possible until very recently in JavaScript. All you could do in the past was method injection, which you saw in the previous chapter. With the introduction of method synthesis and two new classes—Reflect and Proxy—you can intercept method invocations right in the middle of their execution and change the fate of the calls, the way you like.

With the ability to synthesize members at runtime, different objects of a class may entertain different methods and behavior. While this is highly complex programming, it provides phenomenal flexibility to alter the behavior of objects, and it makes the code incredibly extensible.

The Reflect class is a gateway interface to query for and access properties, methods, and metadata of objects. Whenever you want to get some details about an object's metadata—for example, access the prototype of an object—Reflect is your go-to interface for such operations.

Proxy is the ninja of metaprogramming. It can wrap around objects and serve as an interceptor. You can configure a proxy to simply route a call to the actual method of the wrapped object or to an alternative implementation that you choose dynamically at runtime. This way, you can selectively alter the behavior of existing classes, without physically changing their source code.

While Proxy is the way to synthesize your own custom behavior, the state-of-the-art decorator is the way to synthesize predefined behaviors. In other words, to cook up your own dynamic methods, use Proxy. To inject a recipe of methods, created by a third party, use decorators. Although decorators are not currently supported natively by JavaScript runtimes, we'll see how to make use of them with transpilers.

Take a deep breath; you're about to dive into one of the most exhilarating capabilities of JavaScript. By far, I'd say, this is the most exciting part of both the language and this book.

Purpose of Reflect

We've used a few methods of Reflect so far in this book. It's time to step back and take a fresh look at this class. Reflect has two main purposes:

- It's a go-to place for various meta-operations on objects. For example, Reflect provides methods to get and set the prototype of an object and to check whether a property exists in an object, just to mention a couple.

- The Proxy class, which we'll see soon, by default routes its methods to methods of Reflect. Then when using a proxy we can override only select operations and conveniently leave the rest to the default implementations.

There are about two dozen methods in Reflect; let's sample a few interesting and often used methods of this class.

Invoking a Function Through Reflect

In traditional JavaScript there were three different ways to invoke a function: using (), call(), or apply(). Suppose we have a function named greet:

```
const greet = function(msg, name) {
  const pleasantry = typeof(this) === 'string' ? this : 'have a nice day';
  console.log(`${msg} ${name}, ${pleasantry}`);
};
```

We can invoke the greet() function, for example, with arguments 'Howdy' and 'Jane', in one of the following ways:

- greet('Howdy', 'Jane'); is the most common way to invoke, with no implicit context object attached to the call. Each of the arguments provided was able to bind, based on the position, to the corresponding parameters of the function.

- greet.call('how are you?', 'Howdy', 'Jane');, where the first argument binds to this—the context object—and the remaining arguments bind to the parameters of the function.

- greet.apply('how are you?', ['Howdy', 'Jane']);, where the first argument binds to this and each element in the second array argument binds to the parameters of the function.

Although these methods are still available in modern JavaScript, if a context object needs to be passed in, Reflect's apply() function is now the preferred alternative to using call() or apply() directly on the function. Here's the rewrite of the last invocation to greet(), using Reflect's apply():

```
Reflect.apply(greet, 'how are you?', ['Howdy', 'Jane']);
```

It may appear to be redundant at first, but Reflect's apply() function is quite useful when altering behavior of method calls, as you'll see in *Intercepting Function Calls Using Proxy*, on page 211.

Accessing the Prototype

JavaScript now has a elegant way to get and change the prototype of an object. Let's access the prototype of an instance of Date to learn about the new methods of Reflect.

```
metaprogramming/get-set-prototype.js
const today = new Date();
console.log(Reflect.getPrototypeOf(today));

const myPrototype = {};
Reflect.setPrototypeOf(today, myPrototype);

console.log(Reflect.getPrototypeOf(today));
```

We obtained the prototype of the today instance using the getPrototypeOf() method—this returns the Date class's prototype, as we see in the output shown next. Then, using the setPrototypeOf() we modify the prototype of the today instance. We then verify that the change took effect by fetching the prototype of the instance yet again.

```
Date {}
{}
```

We saw the power and purpose of prototypes in *Understanding Prototypal Inheritance*, on page 135. Modifying the prototype of an object is a risky business—it alters the inheritance hierarchy of instances—so use it judiciously and sparingly.

Getting and Setting Properties

In *Dynamic Access*, on page 190 we explored ways to dynamically access properties. Reflect provides alternatives to both get and set properties. Let's revisit the example where we used [] to access properties. Here's the Person class we created earlier, repeated for convenience:

metaprogramming/reflect-get-set.js
```
class Person {
  constructor(age) {
    this.age = age;
  }

  play() { console.log(`The ${this.age} year old is playing`); }

  get years() { return this.age; }
}
```

To access the age property, for example, on an instance sam of Person, we can perform sam.age. However, if we don't know the name of the property at code writing time, we can pass the property name as string to Reflect's get() method. To set a value for the property, we can use the set() method. Let's see how:

metaprogramming/reflect-get-set.js
```
const sam = new Person(2);

const propertyName = 'age';

Reflect.set(sam, propertyName, 3);
console.log(Reflect.get(sam, propertyName));
```

The call to set() changes the initial value of age from 2 to 3. The call to get() returns the current value of the property.

It may appear that there's no real benefit to using Reflect's get() or set() to access a property dynamically instead of using []. If at all, the code is more verbose in comparison. That's a reasonable assessment, but get() and set() will make more sense when we use the methods in the context of Proxy later in this chapter.

In *Invoking a Function Through Reflect*, on page 202, we used Reflect's apply() to invoke a stand-alone function. We can use apply() to call a method of a class as well. Let's call the play() method using Reflect.apply():

metaprogramming/reflect-get-set.js
```
Reflect.apply(sam.play, sam, []);
Reflect.apply(Person.prototype.play, sam, []);
```

For the first argument, to get a reference to the play() method, we can use either the instance or the class's prototype as reference. The second argument has to be the instance on which we like to invoke the method—that is, the context this object. The third argument is the array of arguments—an empty array since play does not have any parameters. The output from these two calls is

```
The 3 year old is playing
The 3 year old is playing
```

Exploring Properties Through Reflect

Reflect has methods to iterate over the keys of an object and to check whether a property exists in an object. Here's an example to get an array of all the keys in an object and to check if the object has a property named age:

metaprogramming/reflect-get-set.js

```
console.log(Reflect.ownKeys(sam));
console.log(Reflect.has(sam, 'age'));
```

The ownKeys() method of Reflect takes an instance as a parameter and returns an array of all the key names—properties, fields, and methods. The has() method will return true if the instance passed for the first parameter contains a property named in the second parameter; it will return false otherwise.

Here's the output from this snippet of code:

```
[ 'age' ]
true
```

In addition to providing a way to access various metadata of an object, Reflect serves as a conduit for default implementation of methods in Proxy. Metaprogramming, especially method synthesis, relies on Proxy. Let's dive into that topic next and learn how to dynamically introduce methods into classes.

Metaprogramming with Proxy

In an earlier example, in *Injecting Multiple Properties*, on page 196, we introduced a few missing properties like first and last into arrays. That's member injection—we knew what to introduce or inject at code writing time. While that's fun and useful, member synthesis ups the challenge and the resulting benefits by a few notches. With synthesis we can bring on board new members into a class based on runtime context. We can also alter the behavior of existing methods or properties dynamically based on the current state at runtime. To achieve this, we need the help of the Proxy class. We'll first explore this newly added class in JavaScript and then employ it for method synthesis.

The Proxy Class

An instance of the Proxy class stands in for another object or a function—also known as *target*—and can intercept or trap calls to fields, methods, and properties on its target.

To create a proxy, provide two things:

- a target—the proxy stands in for this
- a handler—this traps and intercepts calls on the target

Use the handler to trap any operation that may be performed on an object or a function. By default, if you don't trap a call it defaults to a method on Reflect, as illustrated in the figure, so that the calls are forwarded to the target.

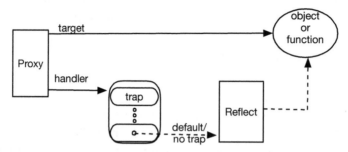

We can use Proxy to synthesize behavior on a class, but before we get to that, let's see how to use a Proxy.

Creating a Dummy Proxy

A proxy with no handler acts like a dummy, merely forwarding all calls, through Reflect, to its target. Creating a dummy is a good starting point before breathing life into a proxy, so let's start with that. But first, we need a class to play with. Here's an Employee class with some fields and properties:

```
metaprogramming/creating-proxy.js
class Employee {
  constructor(firstName, lastName, yearOfBirth) {
    this.firstName = firstName;
    this.lastName = lastName;
    this.yearOfBirth = yearOfBirth;
  }

  get fullname() { return `${this.firstName} ${this.lastName}`; }
  get age() { return new Date().getFullYear() - this.yearOfBirth; }
}

const printInfo = function(employee) {
  console.log(`First name: ${employee.firstName}`);
  console.log(`Fullname: ${employee.fullname}`);
  console.log(`Age: ${employee.age}`);
};

const john = new Employee('John', 'Doe', 2010);
```

The Employee class has a constructor to initialize a few fields and has two properties. The function printInfo() displays the firstName field, with the fullname and age properties of the object given as parameters. Finally, john is an instance of Employee that we'll use to create proxies for.

Let's create a dummy proxy for the john instance.

```
metaprogramming/creating-proxy.js
const handler = {};
const proxyDoe = new Proxy(john, handler);
printInfo(proxyDoe);
```

We created an instance of Proxy using new, and we provided the target john as the first argument to the constructor and an empty handler as the second argument. Since there are no traps in the handler, the Proxy will route all calls on the proxy to the underlying target. We can see this behavior from the output of calling printInfo() with the dummy proxy as the argument:

```
First name: John
Fullname: John Doe
Age: 8
```

Let's continue to keep the proxy as dummy for a little longer but quietly spy on property access next.

Creating a Trap to Spy

The dummy proxy we created has no traps in its handler. For each method that's available on Reflect, we can optionally create a trap in the handler. To create a trap to be used when reading an object's property, provide a get() function in the handler.

The trap function for get() takes three arguments:

- target: This is same as the first argument we passed to the constructor of Proxy.

- propertyName: This is the property we are trying to get. For example, if we called proxy.foo, then propertyName has the value "foo".

- receiver: This is the proxy that receives the call.

Let's spy on the call to read a property and report what we observe. After reporting the details, we'll forward the call to the target via Reflect. That is, we'll manually do what the Proxy does by default if we do not provide a trap.

```
const handler = {
  get: function(target, propertyName, receiver) {
    if(propertyName === 'firstName') {
      console.log(`target is john? ${john === target}`);
      console.log(`propertyName is ${propertyName}`);
      console.log(`receiver is proxyDoe? ${proxyDoe === receiver}`);
    }

    return Reflect.get(target, propertyName);
  }
};
```

We only updated the handler; the rest of the code to create the proxy proxyDoe and to pass it to printInfo() remains unchanged. In the updated handler, we added a trap for the get() function—a handler is an object with trap names as keys and the corresponding intercepting functions as values. Within this trap, we verify that the three parameters passed to the function are the target, the name of the property being requested, and the proxy that receives the request, respectively. Finally, since the trap merely acts as a spy, it passes the property call to the intended target using the get() method of Reflect.

Even though when writing a class we use the get keyword only to define properties, the get() trap of a proxy is called at the time any field, method, or property is accessed. Thus, in the example with the updated handler, the get() trap will intercept calls to the field firstName as well as the properties fullName and age on proxyDoe.

```
target is john? true
propertyName is firstName
receiver is proxyDoe? true
First name: John
Fullname: John Doe
Age: 8
```

The proxy with the updated handler spied on the call, but it's still a dummy; it indiscreetly forwarded each operation to the target. Let's breathe some life into the proxy next, to truly intercept and alter the behavior during calls.

Altering Behavior Using Traps

Instead of forwarding every call to the target, let's modify the behavior of the proxy to take some action. printInfo() is asking for firstName and then fullName. But it then goes on to ask for age—how rude. Let's convey that feeling to the caller by changing the handler again.

```
const handler = {
  get: function(target, propertyName, receiver) {
    if(propertyName === 'age') {
      return `It's not polite to ask that question, dear`;
    }

    return Reflect.get(target, propertyName);
  }
};
```

In this modified version of the trap, we intercept the request for the age property and forward all other read accesses to the target. When age is requested, we return a message of rejection instead of the real value.

```
First name: John
Fullname: John Doe
Age: It's not polite to ask that question, dear
```

The trap may instead return an adjusted value of age (whoever tells their real age anyway?) or throw an exception, or perform any action that may be appropriate for the application at hand.

The above use of proxy, to restrict access to some members of a class, is an example of the *Control Proxy* pattern presented in the popular *Design Patterns: Elements of Reusable Object-Oriented Software [GHJV95]*.

Leasing an Object Using a Revocable Proxy

You've learned to create proxies and write traps; let's move on to applying this knowledge. Our target is method synthesis, but let's explore one other benefit of proxies: the ability to lease an object.

Suppose we want to limit the lifetime of an object. A function that creates an object with new may use it as long as it wants, as long as the instance reference is in scope. If you want to return an object to a caller but withdraw or revoke access to that object either after some time or when some condition is met, use a *revocable* proxy.

Here's a counterFactory() function that creates an instance of a Counter class but returns a revocable proxy to it instead of the original object.

```
metaprogramming/revocable.js
const counterFactory = function() {
  class Counter {
    constructor() { this.value = 0; }
    increment() { this.value += 1; }

    get count() { return this.value; }
  }
  const { proxy: counterProxy, revoke: revokeFunction } =
    Proxy.revocable(new Counter(), {});

  const leaseTime = 100;
  setTimeout(revokeFunction, leaseTime);

  return counterProxy;
};
```

In the function, instead of using new Proxy() we used Proxy.revocable() to create a proxy. Much like Proxy's constructor, the revocable() method takes a target and a handler as parameters. However, unlike a call to new on constructor, which returns a new instance of Proxy, here we get an object with two properties: proxy and revoke. The proxy property refers to the new instance of Proxy created, and the revoke property is a reference to a function that, when called, will revoke the privilege to use the proxy and hence the underlying target.

As the next step, in the counterFactory() function we scheduled a call to the revoke function at the end of an arbitrary lease time. You can revoke based on some other event instead of time as well. Finally we return the proxy to the caller of counterFactory().

Let's take a look at an example of code that calls the counterFactory() method.

metaprogramming/revocable.js

```javascript
const counter = counterFactory();

const incrementAndDisplay = function() {
  try {
    counter.increment();
    console.log(counter.count);
    setTimeout(incrementAndDisplay, 20);
  } catch(ex) {
    console.log(ex.message);
  }
};

incrementAndDisplay();
```

The incrementAndDisplay() function invokes the increment() method on the counter instance that's in the lexical scope, displays the current value of the counter, and schedules another asynchronous call to itself. In case something were to go wrong with these calls, the exception handler will report the error and not schedule any further calls to the function.

Let's run the code and see how it fares.

```
1
2
3
4
5
Cannot perform 'get' on a proxy that has been revoked
```

The incrementAndDisplay() function happily marched along until counterFactory() revoked access; at that point, our effort to invoke increment() on the counter instance met a terrible fate.

The error message says "Cannot perform 'get' on a proxy..." instead of saying it can't invoke 'increment' or something like that. The reason for this is, as you'll recall from *Creating a Trap to Spy*, on page 207, the get() handler on Proxy is called for any field, property, or method.

Before we move on to the next topic, let's do a quick refactoring to reduce some noise in the counterFactory() function. In this function, we have the following code:

```
const { proxy: counterProxy, revoke: revokeFunction } =
  Proxy.revocable(new Counter(), {});
```

That's destructuring, but it's a bit smelly. We can reduce the clutter using the default property mapping capability of destructuring you learned in Chapter 6, *Literals and Destructuring*, on page 91. Before you look at the next piece of code, spend a few minutes refactoring the previous clumsy code. When done, compare the code you created with the following:

```
const { proxy, revoke } = Proxy.revocable(new Counter(), {});

const leaseTime = 100;
setTimeout(revoke, leaseTime);

return proxy;
```

Since the object returned by Proxy.revocable() has properties named proxy and revoke, we can use the same names for our local variables. Thus, instead of revokeFunction now the revoke function is referenced by the variable named revoke. Likewise, instead of the variable counterProxy to hold the proxy, now the proxy resides in the variable named proxy. Less noise leads to better code.

Intercepting Function Calls Using Proxy

Aspect-oriented programming (AOP) is a special case of metaprogramming where function calls may be intercepted with advices. An advice is a piece of code that is exercised in a particular context. In life we often receive three kinds of advices: good, bad, and unsolicited. AOP also has three kinds of advices:

- Before advice: runs before the intended function call
- After advice: runs after the intended function call
- Around advice: runs *instead* of the intended function

Logging is the most infamous example of AOP advices since it's overused by authors. We may inject a call to log parameters passed to a function, for informational or debugging purposes. Or we may log the result of a function call before it's passed back to the caller.

There are many other uses of AOP advices. For instance, we may use them to monitor the context of execution of a function call, to check for authorization or permission to call, to alter arguments passed to a function, or to change a URL from production to test server. There are countless scenarios where we can use AOP. Let's see how to create advices with an example.

Proxy can be used to implement AOP like advices. Recollect the apply() function of Reflect from *Invoking a Function Through Reflect*, on page 202—it's the alternative for apply() on functions. Proxy's handler routes any call to apply on a Proxy, by default, to Reflect. We can override that implementation to inject advices.

Let's start with a function that returns a greeting string given a message and name.

metaprogramming/aop.js
```
const greet = function(message, name) {
  return `${message} ${name}!`;
};

const invokeGreet = function(func, name) {
  console.log(func('hi', name));
};

invokeGreet(greet, 'Bob');
```

The invokeGreet() function receives a function reference as the first parameter and a name as the second argument. It then calls the given function and prints the result. With no AOP advices, let's make a call to the greet function via the invokeGreet() function.

```
hi Bob!
```

Implementing a Before Advice

The message passed as the first argument by invokeGreet() to greet() is a lowercase hi. Let's use AOP before the advice to capitalize that. In this approach, the caller invokeGreet() isn't going to change, nor will the target greet() be altered. We'll intercept and transform the first argument, and then forward the argument to greet().

metaprogramming/aop.js
```
const beforeAdvice = new Proxy(greet, {
  apply: function(target, thisArg, args) {
    const message = args[0];
    const msgInCaps = message[0].toUpperCase() + message.slice(1);

    return Reflect.apply(target, thisArg, [msgInCaps, ...args.slice(1)]);
  }
});

invokeGreet(beforeAdvice, 'Bob');
```

We create a new Proxy with greet as the target. In the handler, we override the apply() function. This function, by default, calls Reflect.apply(). However, in the overridden implementation we intercept and transform the arguments *before* the call goes to the target method.

```
Hi Bob!
```

The before advice may perform any operations it desires, call services, transform arguments, log details about the call—whatever it wants based on the needs of the application.

Implementing an After Advice

Instead of, or in addition to, the before advice, we can perform an after advice, a piece of code that runs after the call. The after advice can optionally transform the result of the function call. In the case of logging, for example, it'll merely note the result and return it to the caller. However, if we like we can transform the output or return a different output, depending on the needs of the application.

Let's write a new before and after advice for the greet() function. In it, we'll alter the message argument before the call and, after the call, transform to uppercase the result of the call before returning the result to the caller.

```
metaprogramming/aop.js
const beforeAndAfterAdvice = new Proxy(greet, {
  apply: function(target, thisArg, args) {
    const newArguments = ['Howdy', ...args.slice(1)];

    const result = Reflect.apply(target, thisArg, newArguments);

    return result.toUpperCase();
  }
});

invokeGreet(beforeAndAfterAdvice, 'Bob');
```

Instead of storing the result in the result variable, we could have called toUpperCase() directly after the closing parenthesis of the Reflect.apply(...) call; introducing that variable makes it clear that we're performing a post-call operation to return the result:

```
HOWDY BOB!
```

In this example, we took the result returned by Reflect.apply() and transformed it before returning. This example assumes that nothing goes wrong. But in general we have to program defensively. Wrap the call to Reflect.apply() in either a try-finally or try-catch-finally. If you like an after advice to run no matter the success or failure of the function, then put the advice in the finally block. If you want an advice to run only upon successful return from the function, then place it after the function call within the try block. If an advice should run only in the case of failure, then place it in the catch block.

Implementing an Around Advice

"Should I take these pills before food or after food?" asked the patient. "I suggest you take it instead of the meal," joked the doctor. That's kind of what an around advice is; it hijacks the call and provides an alternative implementation. The around advice may be selective; it may bypass the call based on some conditions—the values of arguments, some external state or configuration parameter, and so forth.

Let's write an around advice for the greet() function.

```
metaprogramming/aop.js
const aroundAdvice = new Proxy(greet, {
  apply: function(target, thisArg, args) {
    if(args[1] === 'Doc') {
      return "What's up, Doc?";
    }
    else {
      return Reflect.apply(target, thisArg, args);
    }
  }
});

invokeGreet(aroundAdvice, 'Bob');
invokeGreet(aroundAdvice, 'Doc');
```

In the advice, we check if the second argument is equal to 'Doc' and bypass the call to the greet() function and instead return an alternative response. Otherwise, we continue with the call to the original method. Here's the result of making two calls to the invokeGreet() function.

```
hi Bob!
What's up, Doc?
```

We saw the different capabilities of Proxy. One of the most charming facilities it offers is method synthesis. Let's learn how to use that capability next.

Synthesizing Members with Proxy

In *Injecting Multiple Properties*, on page 196 we injected the first and last properties into instances of Array so we could fluently get the first and last elements of an array. We came up with property names like first and last at the time of metaprogramming, but on many occasions we may want to devise property or method names at runtime based on the execution context or state of an object. In other words, we may not know the name of a property to be injected at code writing time—it comes to life at runtime.

To practice method synthesis, let's create an example to use a Map that holds an associative set of keys and values of languages and authors.

```
metaprogramming/fluent-map.js
const langsAndAuthors = new Map([
  ['JavaScript', 'Eich'], ['Java', 'Gosling']]);
```

```
const accessLangsMap = function(map) {
  console.log(`Number of languages: ${map.size}`);
  console.log(`Author of JavaScript: ${map.get('JavaScript')}`);
  console.log(`Asking fluently: ${map.JavaScript}`);
};
```

```
accessLangsMap(langsAndAuthors);
```

The langsAndAuthors map contains the names of two prominent languages as keys and their authors as values.

The accessLangsMap() function receives an instance of Map and prints size—a property—and calls the get() method to get the value for the JavaScript key. It then, in good faith, tries to access the key as if it's a property.

It would be really nice to access the author's name by using the dot notation, but sadly that does not yield the desired result:

```
Number of languages: 2
Author of JavaScript: Eich
Asking fluently: undefined
```

You'll now learn to synthesize dynamic properties on a map—they're dynamic because we may later add other keys like Ruby or Python, for example, to our map. We can't predict their names at the time of metaprogramming to handle the nonexistent property or method.

Member Synthesis for an Instance

Let's synthesize properties on the langsAndAuthors instance of Map. In *Metaprogramming with Proxy*, on page 205 you learned how to trap calls to members using Proxy. We'll use that technique here to create a trap for the missing property.

Recall that the get() trap in a handler of a proxy is called whenever a field, method, or property is invoked. The trap is called for both existing and nonexisting members. When implementing a trap, we must do a few different things depending on whether the request is for a property or a method.

During synthesis, if a call for an existing property is received, we may want to immediately return the property on the target.

If the call, however, is to an existing method, we may want to return the actual method of the target, but we will have to bind it to the target before returning. Let's discuss the reason for binding. When a method is called with the syntax obj.someMethod(); JavaScript automatically binds obj as the context object this within the method. However, if we assign the method to a variable—like const methodRef = obj.someMethod;—then the this context will be unbounded if we call methodRef();. To resolve this, we will have to explicitly bind the context object before making the call.

Finally, if the requested member does not exist on the target object, then we can synthesize the behavior for it.

Let's create a Proxy for the langsAndAuthors object to synthesize dynamic properties.

```
metaprogramming/fluent-map.js
const handler = {
  get: function(target, propertyName, receiver) {
    if(Reflect.has(target, propertyName)) {
      const property = Reflect.get(target, propertyName);

      if(property instanceof Function) { //existing method, bind and return
        return property.bind(target);
      }

      //existing property, return as-is
      return property;
    }

    //synthesize property: we assume it is a key
    return target.get(propertyName);
  }
};

const proxy = new Proxy(langsAndAuthors, handler);

accessLangsMap(proxy);
```

In the handler we create a trap for get(). In the trap we first check if the property with the given name, in the variable propertyName, exists on the target, using the has() method of Reflect. If it exists, we then check if it is an instance of Function. If it is a function, we bind the obtained property to target and return. If it is not a function, we return the property value as is.

If has() returns false, telling us that the property does not exist, then it's time to synthesize a behavior for the call.

Since our objective in this example is to create dynamic properties for keys, in the synthesis part of the trap we assume the given property name is a key and return the value for that key by using the get() method on the target. If the key does not exist, the result will be undefined.

Finally, take a look at the last line, the call to the accessLangsMap() function. Instead of passing langsAndAuthors, we pass the proxy reference that we created. The output from this call is different from when we passed the original map instance:

```
Number of languages: 2
Author of JavaScript: Eich
Asking fluently: Eich
```

The output shows that even though Map instances do not have a property named Eich, the proxy on our langsAndAuthors instance was able to respond to it.

Before we declare this solution a great success, let's discuss one pitfall. A key as a dynamic property is available only when used through a proxy on that one particular instance of Map. It would be nice if the solution worked on all instances as well as directly on the instances of Map instead of a proxy. With some deep understanding of JavaScript and metaprogramming, we can make that happen, as you'll see next.

Synthesizing Members Directly on an Instance

Rather than calling proxy.key, we should be able to perform anyInstanceOfMap.key. To achieve that, we need to bring two different pieces of knowledge together.

First, when a nonexistent property is requested on an object, JavaScript automatically requests it from the object's prototype. If the prototype does not have it, then the search continues through the prototype chain—see *Understanding Prototypal Inheritance*, on page 135.

Second, a proxy can trap requests for properties, fields, and methods, among other things—in essence, the details we have explored in this chapter.

Let's combine these two pieces of knowledge to create a powerful synthesis. If a property or a method exists, then we simply want to use it—there is no need to mess with proxy or traps in that case. Let the proxy step in only if a property or a method does not exist. We know that JavaScript will look to an object's prototype when something does not exist on an object—that's a good spot to synthesize. Thus, we can place the proxy behind an object, as its prototype, instead of what we did in the previous section, to put the proxy in front of the object—ta-da!

We almost have a solution, but we have to be careful when replacing prototypes. An instance of Map gets its instance methods from its prototype—that is, Map.prototype. Replacing the Map instance's prototype will unfortunately get rid of those methods—not a good idea. It turns out that Map.prototype's prototype is an empty object; we can find this by calling

```
console.log(Reflect.getPrototypeOf(Map.prototype));
```

That's a good candidate to replace with a proxy. This design thought is illustrated in the prototype diagram on page 218.

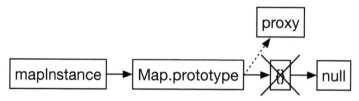

In the design we created in the previous section, the get() trap of our proxy had to do some extra work: taking care of both existing and nonexisting members. In the new design, the proxy does not have to worry about existing members—the original object, as the *receiver* of calls, will take care of that. The proxy, now serving as the state-appointed prototype, will be called on only for nonexistent members.

There is one other significant difference between the design of proxies in the previous section and here. In the previous one, the receiver was the proxy since the key was called on the proxy. Here, the receiver is the instance of Map. With those thoughts in mind, let's implement our new design.

metaprogramming/map-synthesis.js
```
const proxy = new Proxy(Map.prototype, {
  get: function(target, propertyName, receiver) {
    return receiver.get(propertyName);
  }
});

Reflect.setPrototypeOf(Map.prototype, proxy);
```

We created a new Proxy for Map.prototype—which houses all the instance methods for Map—instead of creating a proxy on one specific instance of Map. In the handler we trap get() and assume the given property represents a key. The trap method is much simpler than the one we created in the previous section. Then, we set the newly created proxy as the prototype of the Map's prototype.

Let's now see this proxy in action on an instance of Map, for example, langsAnd-Authors:

metaprogramming/map-synthesis.js
```
const langsAndAuthors = new Map([
  ['JavaScript', 'Eich'], ['Java', 'Gosling']]);

console.log(langsAndAuthors.get('JavaScript'));
console.log(langsAndAuthors.JavaScript);
```

We created an instance of Map and directly called the dynamic property on it after making the traditional built-in call with get. The instance happily responds to both the calls:

```
Eich
Eich
```

Let's verify that this solution works on a different instance of Map as well.

```
metaprogramming/map-synthesis.js
const capitals = new Map([
  ['USA', 'Washington. D.C.'],
  ['UK', 'London'],
  ['Trinidad & Tobago', 'Port of Spain']]);

console.log(capitals.UK);
console.log(capitals['Trinidad & Tobago']);
```

This example uses countries and capitals instead of languages and authors, with one twist; there's a country name with & in the middle. The proxy we created can handle that with no worries—remember to use [] to access the property with & since it does not conform to JavaScript property names syntax.

```
London
Port of Spain
```

Now we can declare our solution a great success.

Using Decorators

The Proxy class you saw so far in this chapter is very useful to synthesize or cook up your own dynamic methods and properties into existing classes. However, sometimes you want to bring a recipe of methods that someone else has created into your own classes and functions. In other words, you want to alter your classes or functions with metadata that, for example, a library or framework expects to find. This is where decorators come in.

JavaScript decorators serve a similar purpose as annotations in Java and attributes in C#—they offer a way to extend the capabilities of the subject that they decorate or annotate.

Let's take a quick look at an example function declaration from *Async and Await*, on page 183.

```
const callCompute = async function(number) {
```

To convey that a function may be making asynchronous calls, JavaScript offers the keyword async to decorate the code. Nice decoration, but it came as a keyword in the language. We, as users of the language, can't add keywords or change the semantics at the compiler/interpreter level. That's where decorators come to the rescue.

JavaScript offers decorators as a way for us to inject user-defined behaviors into classes and functions. Decorators are used in JavaScript libraries and frameworks, like React and Angular, for example. Decorators may appear on a class, method, function, and so forth.

Decorators in JavaScript are new and evolving as a standard. Node.js does not support decorators yet. Programmers using libraries and frameworks that use modern JavaScript features often rely on transpilers, like Babel, to convert code they write to equivalent old-style JavaScript. That's what we'll do here, except we'll convert decorators into old-style method calls to simulate the behavior of decorators. For this purpose we'll use the transform-decorators-legacy Babel plugin.

Let's explore the benefits of decorators with a few examples and, along the way, learn how to implement the code behind decorators as well.

Simulating an Angular Component

In Angular a component is a class that stands between the view or template that is displayed in the browser and the service that talks to the back-end server. Programmers who use Angular often write many components. A component needs to provide a few details. For example, a selector that refers to the name of an element in an HTML file will be replaced by the contents of a template. Also, a templateUrl will provide the name and location of the template. Rather than expecting these to be fields or properties on the component class, Angular expects to see them as part of a @Component decorator on the component. Looking at the @Component decorator of Angular is a great way to learn about decorators, so we will explore that first.

If we write an Angular component, we'll have to bring in dependencies to the Angular library. Although that's not too hard, that step is rather redundant from the point of view of learning about decorators. So, instead we'll simulate an Angular component.

Here's an example of a class that looks like an Angular component; it specifies the name of a DOM element to manipulate, using selector, and the name of the template file to use for that purpose, with the templateUrl property.

decorators/src/sample.component.mjs
```
import { Component } from './component';

@Component({
  selector: 'contents',
  templateUrl: './sample.component.html'
})
export class SampleComponent {}
```

If this were truly an Angular component, then the first line with import would be referring to '@angular/core' instead of './component'. Furthermore, the file would have the extension .js or .ts instead of .mjs. But the rest of the code looks pretty identical to what a programmer would write when creating an Angular component.

Angular uses @Component to decorate classes and stores the details provided with the decorator as *metadata* for the class. If you wonder how Angular does it, the rest of this example will answer that.

Angular stores the properties like selector into an annotations metadata key. For this, it uses a library called reflect-metadata that provides functions to store and retrieve metadata.

A decorator is simply an intercepting function that is executed at runtime. When JavaScript sees a decorator, it places a call to a function with the name of that decorator—for example, a function named Component() when it encounters the decorator @Component. That function will then be executed for its effects during runtime.

Angular internally already has the @Component decorator defined as a function within the framework. Since we're simulating a component without actually depending on Angular, we don't have access to that decorator. But we can easily write our own version that's very similar to Angular's @Component decorator. Again, the implementation of a decorator is simply an interceptor function that in turn returns a function to manipulate the target of decoration. That sounds a bit complicated, but an example will help you to see how it all works.

decorators/src/component.mjs
```
import 'reflect-metadata';

export const Component = function(properties) {
  return function(target) {
    Reflect.defineMetadata('annotations', properties, target);
    return target;
  };
}
```

The Component() function receives properties as its parameter but immediately returns yet another function—the decorator function. That function, in turn, takes a target—that is, the class being decorated—as its parameter. Within that decorator function, we define metadata named annotations for the target class and assign the received properties to it. Finally we return the decorated class from the function. A class decorator always returns the class.

Introspecting the Decorated Class

Once a class is decorated with Angular decorators like @Component, @Pipe, @Directive, and so on, Angular can read the metadata to figure out what to do with them. In our example where we simulated the Angular @Component decorator, we stored the properties given to the decorator into the metadata. Let's verify that the decoration actually worked.

decorators/src/inspect-component.mjs

```
import { SampleComponent } from './sample.component';

const metadataKeys = Reflect.getMetadataKeys(SampleComponent);
console.log(`MetadataKeys: ${metadataKeys}`);

const annotations = Reflect.getMetadata('annotations', SampleComponent);
console.log('Annotations:');
console.log(`selector: ${annotations.selector}`);
console.log(`templateUrl: ${annotations.templateUrl}`);
```

We import SampleComponent and query for its metadata keys by calling Reflect.getMetadataKeys()—this method is added to the Reflect class by the reflect-metadata library that we imported earlier. Then we obtain the metadata for the property annotations using the Reflect.getMetadata() method.

Let's summarize the effect of all the decorator-related example code before we try to run it. The component.mjs file defines the functions that will be executed for the @Component decorator. The sample.component.mjs file contains a class named SampleComponent that's decorated with the @Component decorator. The net effect of this is that the properties provided with the decorator—selector and templateUrl—will be injected into the class SampleComponent's metadata when the decorator is processed by JavaScript. The code in inspect-component.mjs simply verifies that the decorator added the metadata to the SampleComponent class.

Using Babel to Transpile

Since decorators are not currently supported natively by Node.js, before we can run the code we have to transpile it. The easiest way to do so is to configure Babel to transpile the code with decorators into functions that can run on Node.js. Babel is available as an npm package. We can install it using the command npm install, but we have to install a few related plugins as well. Instead of manually running commands to install each one of them, we can configure a package.json file to easily install Babel and the related plugins we need. For your convenience, the book's website has a preconfigured package.json file.

Download the following file from the book's website:

```
decorators/package.json
{
  "name": "decorators",
  "version": "1.0.0",
  "description": "",
  "main": "index.js",
  "scripts": {
    "build": "babel src -d lib --keep-file-extension"
  },
  "author": "",
  "license": "ISC",
  "devDependencies": {
    "babel-cli": "^7.0.0-beta.3",
    "babel-plugin-transform-decorators-legacy": "^1.3.4",
    "babel-preset-es2016": "^6.24.1"
  },
  "dependencies": {
    "reflect-metadata": "^0.1.12"
  }
}
```

The package.json file mentions the necessary dependencies—the Babel command-line (CLI) tool, the Babel package for supporting modern JavaScript, and the plugin for transforming decorators into legacy functions. The build script specifies the commands to run Babel, to transpile code in the src directory and place the generated code into the destination lib directory.

To install the Babel-related tools, from within the decorators directory where the package.json file is located, issue the following command:

```
npm install
```

Once the install completes, run the following command to transpile the files src/component.mjs, src/sample.component.mjs, and src/inspect-component.mjs into files with the same name and extensions into the lib destination directory.

```
npm run build
```

This command runs the Babel transpiler, using the build script in the package.json file. Take a peek at the lib directory for the generated files.

Now, let's run the transpiled code to see the decoration in action. Enter the following command at the command prompt from within the decorators directory:

```
node --experimental-modules ./lib/inspect-component.mjs
```

The @Component decorator that we created, which mimics the decorator of Angular with the same name, added the metadata to the class, as we see from the output:

```
(node:2561) ExperimentalWarning: The ESM module loader is experimental.
MetadataKeys: annotations
Annotations:
selector: contents
templateUrl: ./sample.component.html
```

This example showed us two things: how decorators inject behavior to extend the subjects they decorate and how frameworks like Angular make use of decorators. While Angular knows what to do with these metadata, our example merely showed the act of injecting metadata into a class.

"We need some action," you demand. I'll oblige—let's bring some behavior in using decorators next.

Creating a Custom Decorator

Suppose we have a Person class that has a few fields. Let's create an instance, peter, of the class and invoke the toString() method on it, like so:

```
console.log(peter.toString());
```

The output of this call will be

```
[object Object]
```

That's disappointing if we were hoping to get a glimpse of the fields and their values. If we printed the instance without .toString(), then we would have seen all the fields, but maybe that's too much. It would be great to dictate what toString() should return, but without having to write it for each class we create. What if we could decorate classes with a ToString() decorator? Seems like a nice idea.

The ToString() decorator we will design and implement here will take an array of fields/properties to exclude. In the decorator function, we will inject a toString() method into the prototype of the class. This toString() method will iterate over all the keys of the object and create a string representation, while excluding any field/property that's in the exclude array.

Since decorators are really functions, we should start by writing a ToString() decorator factory, as we did for the @Component decorator.

decorators/src/decorators.mjs
```
export const ToString = function(properties) {
  const exclude = (properties && properties.exclude) || [];
```

```
    return function(target) {
      target.prototype.toString = function() {
        return Object.keys(this)
          .filter(key => !exclude.includes(key))
          .map(key => `${key}: ${this[key]}`)
          .join(', ');
      };

      return target;
    }
  }
```

In the ToString() decorator factory, we save the exclude property passed through the properties. If none was present, we store an empty exclude array. Then in the decorator function we use that array to ignore some properties and join the name-value pair of the other keys together.

Now that we've defined the @ToString decorator, we can use it to dynamically add members to just about any class. Let's use this decorator in a Person class.

decorators/src/person.mjs
```
import { ToString } from './decorators.mjs';

@ToString({exclude: ['age']})
export default class Person {
  constructor(firstName, lastName, age) {
    this.firstName = firstName;
    this.lastName = lastName;
    this.age = age;
  }
}
```

Our Person class has three fields: firstName, lastName, and age. It is rather rude to ask someone's age, so we exclude that field from the toString() method that will be created. We achieve this by passing the age field name as an element in the array for the exclude property.

Let's create an instance of the Person class, which we decorated with ToString(), by providing all three necessary fields. Then we'll invoke the toString() method on the instance and print the result.

decorators/src/view-person.mjs
```
import Person from './person';

const peter = new Person('Peter', 'Parker', 23);

console.log(peter.toString());
```

To compile and run this file, we'll use the same package.json file we used earlier. Execute the following commands at the command prompt to run the code:

```
npm install
npm run build
node --experimental-modules ./lib/view-person.mjs
```

The output from this code shows the power of using the decorator to extend the class.

```
(node:2585) ExperimentalWarning: The ESM module loader is experimental.
firstName: Peter, lastName: Parker
```

The @ToString decorator injected the toString() instance method into the Person class and can do so on any class it decorates. That's yet another very powerful way to perform method injection.

Loving what this language can do compared to only a few years ago. Way to go, JavaScript.

Wrapping Up

Method synthesis is a way to add members to objects, at runtime, based on context and the current state of the object. Using this capability, you can enhance and alter the API and the behavior of objects, at runtime, far beyond the facilities offered by the author of a class. This powerful metaprogramming feature is now possible in JavaScript due to the addition of two classes: Reflect and Proxy. The Reflect class provides convenience methods to query for different metadata of a class. The Proxy class is an interceptor that can wrap around objects and manipulate interactions with the object. Decorators offer another way to do metaprogramming—when placed on a target, they are executed by the runtime to add predefined metadata and members to their target.

Exercises

Use these exercises to deepen your understanding of proxy and method synthesis. You can find answers to these exercises on page 250.

Exercise 1

Complete the following code to get the desired result.

```
'use strict';

class Counter {
  constructor() {
    this.count = 0;
  }

  incrementBy(value) { this.count += value; return this.count; }
  decrementBy(value) { this.count -= value; return this.count; }
}
```

```
//Implement the call method here

const counter = new Counter();

console.log(call(counter, 'incrementBy', 10)); //10
console.log(call(counter, 'decrementBy', 7)); //3
console.log(counter.count); //3
```

Exercise 2

Given the handler

```
const handler = {
  get: function(target, propertyName, receiver) {}
};
```

and the following code to use a proxy:

```
const sample = {};
const proxy = new Proxy(sample, handler);
const value = proxy.foo;
```

what do the three parameters—target, propertyName, and receiver—in the get trap refer to during the execution of the last line of this code?

Exercise 3

Implement the createRevocableProxy() method in the following code to create a proxy that may be used for up to 3 seconds. During that time, any method calls on the proxy should be directed to the target instance.

```
'use strict';

const createRevocableProxy = function(instance) {
        //Your code goes here
};

const proxy = createRevocableProxy(new Date());

const callGetYear = function() {
  try {
    console.log(1900 + proxy.getYear());
  } catch(ex) {
    console.log(ex.message);
  }
};

callGetYear(); //current year like 2018

setTimeout(callGetYear, 1000); //current year like 2018

setTimeout(callGetYear, 5000);
//Cannot perform 'get' on a proxy that has been revoked
```

Exercise 4

Create a proxy that will receive a method that starts with play and return a string "I love to play ..." message if the part after play is contained in an activities array field. For example, when playTennis() is called, the returned message will be "I love to play Tennis". If the activity is not contained in the array, then the "I don't play ..." message is returned. For any call that does not start with play, an exception should be thrown.

```
'use strict';

const createPlayMethodProxy = function(instance) {
  //Your code goes here
};

const proxy = createPlayMethodProxy({ activities: ['Football', 'Tennis'] });

console.log(proxy.playTennis());    //I love to play Tennis
console.log(proxy.playFootball()); //I love to play Football
console.log(proxy.playPolitics()); //I don't play Politics

try {
  console.log(proxy.dance());
} catch(ex) {
  console.log(ex.message); //dance is not a function
}
```

Exercise 5

Complete the following code to synthesize dynamic properties on Set to return true if the property exists as an element and false otherwise. If the property invoked is a predefined property on Set, then use that.

```
'use strict';

//Your code goes here

const fruits = new Set(['Apple', 'Banana', 'Orange', 'Jack Fruit']);

console.log(fruits.size);              //4
console.log(fruits.Apple);             //true
console.log(fruits.Banana);            //true
console.log(fruits.Orange);            //true
console.log(fruits['Jack Fruit']);     //true
console.log(fruits.Tomato);            //false
```

Answers to Exercises

Chapter 1

Here are the solutions to the *Exercises*, on page 13, for the *JavaScript Gotchas* chapter.

Exercise 1

```
return           //undefined
  2 * 3;

return 2         //6
  * 3;

return 2 * 3     //6
  ;
```

Exercise 2

```
//That's one strange comparison, but given the choices, choose ===
"2.0" / 2 * "2.0" === 2 / 2 * 2;
```

Exercise 3

```
'use strict';

const canVote = function(age) {
  if(age === 18) {
    return 'yay, start voting';
  }

  if(age > 17) {
    return "please vote";
  }

  return "no, can't vote";
};
```

```
console.log(canVote(12));      //no, can't vote
console.log(canVote("12"));    //no, can't vote
console.log(canVote(17));      //no, can't vote
console.log(canVote('@18'));   //no, can't vote
console.log(canVote(18));      //yay, start voting
console.log(canVote(28));      //please vote
```

Exercise 4

```
//The code as given in the exercise will not terminate.

//Here's the fix: use option strict and declare i before use in the two loops
'use strict';

const isPrime = function(n) {
  for(let i = 2; i <= Math.sqrt(n); i++) {//or < n instead of <= Math.sqrt(n)
    if(n % i === 0) return false;
  }

  return n > 1;
};

const sumOfPrimes = function(n) {
  let sum = 0;
  for(let i = 1; i <= n; i++) {
    if(isPrime(i)) sum += i;
  }

  return sum;
};

console.log(sumOfPrimes(10));
```

Exercise 5

ESLint reported the following errors for the given code:

```
   1:1   error  Use the global form of 'use strict'       strict
   1:1   error  Unexpected var, use let or const instead  no-var
   2:3   error  Unexpected var, use let or const instead  no-var
   4:7   error  'index' is not defined                    no-undef
   4:18  error  'index' is not defined                    no-undef
   4:35  error  'index' is not defined                    no-undef
   5:17  error  'index' is not defined                    no-undef
   5:23  error  Expected '===' and instead saw '=='       eqeqeq
   6:23  error  'index' is not defined                    no-undef
  11:5   error  Expected '===' and instead saw '=='       eqeqeq
  14:5   error  'i' is not defined                        no-undef
  14:12  error  'i' is not defined                        no-undef
  14:21  error  'i' is not defined                        no-undef
  15:23  error  'i' is not defined                        no-undef
  15:53  error  'i' is not defined                        no-undef

✖ 15 problems (15 errors, 0 warnings)
  2 errors, 0 warnings potentially fixable with the `--fix` option.
```

Here's the code after removing the errors—using const where possible and let instead of var:

```
'use strict';

const isPerfect = function(number) {
  let sumOfFactors = 0;

  for(let index = 1; index <= number; index++) {
    if(number % index === 0) {
      sumOfFactors += index;
    }
  }

  return sumOfFactors === number * 2;
};
for(let i = 1; i <= 10; i++) {
  console.log('is ' + i + ' perfect?: ' + isPerfect(i));
}
```

Chapter 2

Here are the solutions to the *Exercises*, on page 24, for the *Variables and Constants* chapter.

Exercise 1

The program will not terminate. It will output 0, 1, 2, 0, 1, 2,... forever until you terminate the program out of boredom.

Exercise 2

```
'use strict';

function first() {
  for(let i = 0; i < 5; i++) {
    second();
  }
}
function second() {
  for(let i = 0; i < 3; i++) {
    console.log(i);
  }
}
first();
```

Exercise 3

Runs the code in struct mode. Detects undeclared variables, errors due to setting read-only properties, and the use of any reserved keywords.

Exercise 4

Yes. The const field cannot be changed.

Exercise 5

No. Freeze is not deep. Only the top-level object is read-only. The program changes an object at a lower level.

Chapter 3

Here are the solutions to the *Exercises*, on page 43, for the *Working with Function Arguments* chapter.

Exercise 1

```
'use strict';

const amountAfterTaxes = function(amount, ...taxes) {
  const computeTaxForAmount = function(tax) {
    return amount * tax / 100.0;
  };

  const totalValues = function(total, value) {
    return total + value;
  };

  return taxes.map(computeTaxForAmount)
    .reduce(totalValues, amount).toFixed(2);

  //or, using arrow functions:
  //return taxes.map(tax => amount * tax / 100.0)
  //   .reduce((total, value) => total + value, amount)
  //   .toFixed(2);
};

const amount = 25.12;
const fedTax = 10;
const stateTax = 2;
const localTax = 0.5;

console.log(amountAfterTaxes(amount)); //25.12
console.log(amountAfterTaxes(amount, fedTax)); //27.63
console.log(amountAfterTaxes(amount, fedTax, stateTax)); //28.13
console.log(
  amountAfterTaxes(amount, fedTax, stateTax, localTax)); //28.26
```

Exercise 2

```
'use strict';

const purchaseItems = function(essential1, essential2, ...optionals) {
  console.log(essential1 + ', ' + essential2 + ', ' + optionals.join(', '));
};
```

```
purchaseItems('bread', 'milk');
purchaseItems('bread', 'milk', 'jelly');

const mustHaves = ['bread', 'milk'];
const andAlso = ['eggs', 'donuts', 'tea'];

//call purchaseItems so it prints bread, milk, eggs, donuts, tea
purchaseItems(...mustHaves, ...andAlso);
```

Exercise 3

```
'use strict';

const purchaseItems = function(essential1 = 'milk',
  essential2 = 'bread', ...optionals) {
  console.log(essential1 + ', ' + essential2 + ', ' + optionals.join(', '));
};

const items = ['cheese', 'milk'];
purchaseItems('cheese'); //cheese, bread,
purchaseItems(...items); //cheese, milk,
purchaseItems(); //milk, bread,
```

Exercise 4

```
'use strict';

const placeOrder = function(
  id, amount,
  shipping = (amount < 20 ? 5 : 10),
  date = new Date()) {
  console.log(' shipping charge for id: ' +
    id + ' is $' + shipping + ' Date:' + date.getDate());
};

//shipping, if not given, is $5 if amount less than 20 else $10
//date is today's date unless given
placeOrder(1, 12.10, 3, new Date('05/15/2018'));
placeOrder(1, 25.20, 10);
placeOrder(1, 12.05);
placeOrder(1, 25.30);
placeOrder(1, 25.20);
```

Exercise 5

```
'use strict';

const placeOrder = function(
  id, amount,
  shipping = (amount < 20 ? 5 : 10),
  date = new Date()) {
  console.log(' shipping charge:$' + shipping + ' Date:' + date.getDate());
};

placeOrder(1, 12.10, undefined, new Date('05/15/2018'));
```

Chapter 4

Here are the solutions to the *Exercises*, on page 66, for the *Iterators and Symbols* chapter.

Exercise 1

```
const letters = ['a', 'b', 'c', 'd', 'e', 'f', 'g', 'h'];

for(const [i, letter] of letters.entries()) {
  if(i % 3 === 0)
    console.log(letter);
}
```

Exercise 2

```
const numbers = [1, 2, 3];

console.log("The Symbol properties in arrays are:");

console.log(
  Object.getOwnPropertySymbols(Object.getPrototypeOf(numbers)));
```

Exercise 3

```
class Message {
  constructor(text) { this.text = text; }

  [Symbol.replace](word, substitute) {
    return this.text.replace(word, substitute);
  }
}

const message = new Message('There are no stupid questions.');

console.log('stupid'.replace(message, 's*****'));
//There are no s***** questions.

console.log(''.replace(message, 'Yes, '));
//Yes, There are no stupid questions.
```

Exercise 4

```
const fibonocciSeries = function*() {
  let current = 1;
  let next = 1;

  yield* [current, next];

  while(true) {
    const temp = current;
    current = next;
    next = next + temp;
```

```
    yield next;
  }
}

for(const value of fibonocciSeries()) {
  if(value > 25) break;
  process.stdout.write(value + ", ");
}
```

Exercise 5

```
const fibonocciSeries = function*() {
  let current = 1;
  let next = 1;

  let index = 0;

  yield *[[index++, current], [index++, next]];

  while(true) {
    const temp = current;
    current = next;
    next = next + temp;

    yield [index++, next];
  }
}

for(const [index, value] of fibonocciSeries()) {
  if(index > 8) break;
  process.stdout.write(value + ", ");
}
```

Chapter 5

Here are the solutions to the *Exercises*, on page 87, for the *Arrow Functions and Functional Style* chapter.

Exercise 1

For anonymous functions, this and arguments are dynamically scoped and other non-local, non-parameter variables are lexically scoped.

For arrow functions, all non-local, non-parameter variables are lexically scoped.

Exercise 2

Here's a solution to make the code concise and to use arrow functions:

```
'use strict';

const success = value => ({ value: value });
```

```
const blowup = value => { throw new Error('blowing up with value ' + value); };

const process = function(successFn, errorFn) {
  const value = Math.round(Math.random() * 100, 2);

  return value > 50 ? successFn(value) : errorFn(value);
};

try {
  console.log(process(success, blowup));
} catch(ex) {
  console.log(ex.message);
}
```

Keep process() as a regular function instead of a multiline arrow function, which does not offer much benefit.

Exercise 3

The given function, greet(), relies on this, which makes it harder to convert to arrow functions. We can rework the function as follows:

```
'use strict';

const greet = (message, ...names) =>
  console.log(message + ' ' + names.join(', '));

const helloJackJill = greet.bind(null, 'hello', 'Jack', 'Jill');

helloJackJill(); //hello Jack, Jill
```

Exercise 4

The output for the given code is

```
I am undefined, age undefined with ball
```

The function play() needs this in dynamic scope, the object on which it is called. Don't use an arrow function as an instance method. Here's the fix:

```
'use strict';

const sam = {
  name: 'Sam',
  age: 2,
  play: function(toy) {
    return 'I am ' + this.name + ', age ' + this.age + ' with ' + toy;
  }
};

console.log(sam.play('ball'));
```

The output of this modified code is

```
I am Sam, age 2 with ball
```

Exercise 5

From imperative to functional, using the higher-order functions in an array:

```
'use strict';

const numbers = [1, 5, 2, 6, 8, 3, 4, 9, 7, 6];

console.log(
  numbers.filter(e => e % 2 === 0)
    .map(e => e * 2)
    .reduce((total, e) => total + e));
```

Chapter 6

Here are the solutions to the *Exercises*, on page 110, for the *Literals and Destructuring* chapter.

Exercise 1

```
'use strict';

const greet = function(name, gender) {
  return `Hello, ${gender === Symbol.for('female') ? 'Ms.' : 'Mr.'} ${name}`;
};

console.log(greet('Sara', Symbol.for('female'))); //Hello, Ms. Sara
console.log(greet('Tom', Symbol.for('male'))); //Hello, Mr. Tom
```

Exercise 2

```
'use strict';

const stripMargin = function(texts, ...expressions) {
  const exceptLast = expressions.map(function(expression, index) {
    return `${texts[index]}${expression.toString().toUpperCase()}`;
  }).join('');

  const result = `${exceptLast}${texts[texts.length - 1]}`;

  return result.replace(/[\n][\t\s]+(\w)/g, ' $1').trim();
};

const name = 'Jane';

const processed = stripMargin` This is for
  ${name} and it needs to be
      delivered by December 24th.`;

console.log(processed);
//This is for JANE and it needs to be delivered by December 24th.
```

Exercise 3

```
'use strict';

const beforeAndAfter = function(number) {
  if(number < 0) return [];
  if(number === 0) return [1];

  return [number - 1, number + 1];
};

let before = 0;
let after = 0;

//Your code goes before =
[before, after] = beforeAndAfter(7);
console.log(`${before} and ${after}`); //6 and 8

[before, after] = beforeAndAfter(9);
console.log(`${before} and ${after}`); //8 and 10

[before, after = 0] = beforeAndAfter(0);
console.log(`${before} and ${after}`); //0 and 1

[before = 0, after = 0] = beforeAndAfter(-1);
console.log(`${before} and ${after}`); //0 and 0
```

Exercise 4

```
'use strict';

const purchaseItems = function(essential1, essential2, ...optionals) {
  console.log(`${essential1}, ${essential2}, ${optionals.join(', ')}`);
};

const mustHaves = ['bread', 'milk'];
const also = ['eggs', 'donuts'];
const andAlso = ['juice', 'tea'];

//call purchaseItems so it prints
//bread, milk, eggs, donuts, coffee, juice, tea
purchaseItems(...mustHaves, ...[...also, 'coffee', ...andAlso]);
```

Exercise 5

```
'use strict';

const getDetails = function(
  {name, born: { year: birthYear }, graduated: {year}}) {
  return `${name} born in the year ${birthYear}, graduated in ${year}.`;
};

const details =
  getDetails({name: 'Sara',
    born: { month: 1, day: 1, year: 2000 },
    graduated: { month: 5, day: 31, year: 2018 }});
```

```
console.log(details);
//Sara born in the year 2000, graduated in 2018.
```

Chapter 7

Here are the solutions to the *Exercises*, on page 133, for the *Working with Classes* chapter.

Exercise 1

```
'use strict';

class Book {
  constructor(title, author, pages) {
    this.title = title;
    this.author = author;
    this.numberOfPages = pages;
    this.sales = 0;
  }

  get pages() { return this.numberOfPages; }

  get copiesSold() { return this.sales; }
  set copiesSold(value) {
    if(value < 0) throw new Error(`Value can't be negative`);

    this.sales = value;
  }
}
const book = new Book('Who Moved My Cheese?', 'Spencer Johnson', 96);
console.log(book.title); //Who Moved My Cheese
console.log(book.pages); //96

try {
  book.pages = 96;
} catch(ex) {
  console.log(ex.message);
  //Cannot set property pages of #<Book> which has only a getter
}
console.log(book.copiesSold); //0
book.copiesSold = 1;
console.log(book.copiesSold); //1

try {
  book.copiesSold = -2;
} catch(ex) {
  console.log(ex.message);//Value can't be negative
}
console.log(book.copiesSold); //1
```

Exercise 2

```javascript
'use strict';

class Tax {
  static forAmount(amount) {
    return amount * Tax.stateRate;
  }
}

Tax.stateRate = '.08';

console.log(Tax.stateRate); //0.08
console.log(Tax.forAmount(100)); // 8

const forAmount = Tax.forAmount;
this.stateRate = 0.01;
console.log(forAmount.call(this, 100)); //8
```

Exercise 3

```javascript
'use strict';

class Todo {
  constructor() {
    this['learn JavaScript'] = 'done';
    this['write elegant code'] = 'work-in-progress';
    this['automate tests'] = 'work-in-progress';
  }

  get completedCount() {
    return Object.keys(this)
      .filter(key => this[key] === 'done')
      .length;
  }
}

const todo = new Todo();
console.log(todo['learn JavaScript']); //'done'
console.log(todo['write elegant code']);//'work-in-progress'
console.log(todo['automate tests']);//'work-in-progress'
console.log(todo.completedCount); //1
```

Exercise 4

```javascript
'use strict';

const createTodo = function() {
  const todo = new Map();
  todo.set('learn JavaScript', 'done');
  todo.set('write elegant code', 'work-in-progress');
  todo.set('automate tests', 'work-in-progress');

  return todo;
};
```

```
const completedCount = function(map) {
  return [...map.values()]
    .filter(value => value === 'done')
    .length;
};
const todo = createTodo(); //Returns a Map
console.log(todo.get('learn JavaScript')); //'done'
console.log(todo.get('write elegant code'));//'work-in-progress'
console.log(todo.get('automate tests'));//'work-in-progress'
console.log(completedCount(todo)); //1
```

Exercise 5

```
'use strict';

const create = function(sports) {
  return new Set(sports.map(sport => sport.toUpperCase()));
};

const toLowerCase = function(sports) {
  return new Set([...sports].map(sport => sport.toLowerCase()));
};

const sports = create(['Soccer', 'Football', 'Cricket', 'Tennis', 'soccer']);

console.log(sports.has('FOOTBALL')); //true
console.log(sports.has('Football')); //false
console.log(sports.size); //4

const inLowerCase = toLowerCase(sports);
console.log(inLowerCase.has('football'));
console.log(inLowerCase.size); //4
```

Chapter 8

Here are the solutions to the *Exercises*, on page 151, for the *Using Inheritance* chapter.

Exercise 1

```
'use strict';

class FunctionalSet extends Set {
  filter(predicate) {
    return new FunctionalSet([...this].filter(predicate));
  }

  map(mapper) {
    return new FunctionalSet([...this].map(mapper));
  }
```

```
    reduce(accumulator, identity) {
      return [...this].reduce(accumulator, identity);
    }
}

const set = new FunctionalSet(['Jack', 'Jill', 'Tom', 'Jerry']);

const jSet = set.filter(name => name.startsWith('J'));
const allCaps = set.map(name => name.toUpperCase());

const totalLengthOfJWords =
  set.filter(name => name.startsWith('J'))
    .reduce((total, word) => total + word.length, 0);

console.log(jSet); //FunctionalSet { 'Jack', 'Jill', 'Jerry' }
console.log(allCaps); //FunctionalSet { 'JACK', 'JILL', 'TOM', 'JERRY' }
console.log(totalLengthOfJWords); //13
```

Exercise 2

No code change is necessary. The add() method of Set returns an instance based on the runtime type. When add() is called on an instance of FunctionalSet, the returned instance is of the same derived type.

Exercise 3

```
'use strict';

class BoundedSet extends Set {
  constructor(capacity, initialValues) {
    super();
    this.capacity = capacity;

    if(initialValues.length <= capacity) {
      initialValues.forEach(value => this.add(value));
    }
  }

  add(value) {
    if(this.has(value)) return;

    if(this.size < this.capacity) {
      super.add(value);
    } else {
      throw new Error(`exceeded capacity of ${this.capacity} elements`);
    }
  }
}

const set = new BoundedSet(5, ['Apple', 'Banana', 'Grape', 'Mangoe']);

set.add('Orange');
set.add('Apple');
```

```
try {
  set.add('Tangerine');
} catch(ex) {
  console.log(ex.message); //exceeded capacity of 5 elements
}

set.delete('Grape');
set.add('Peach');
console.log(set.size); //5

const set2 = new BoundedSet(2, ['Apple', 'Banana', 'Grape']);
console.log(set2.size); //0
console.log(set2); //BoundedSet { capacity: 2 }
```

Exercise 4

```
'use strict';

class Base {
  copy() {
    const constructor =
      Reflect.getPrototypeOf(this).constructor[Symbol.species] ||
        Reflect.getPrototypeOf(this).constructor;

    return new constructor();
  }
}

class Derived1 extends Base {
  static get [Symbol.species]() {
    return Base;
  }
}

class Derived2 extends Base {
  static get [Symbol.species]() {
    return Derived2;
  }
}

const derived1 = new Derived1();
const derived2 = new Derived2();

console.log(derived1.copy()); //Base {}
console.log(derived2.copy()); //Derived2 {}
```

Exercise 5

```
'use strict';

class SpecialWordChecker {
  isSpecial(word) { return word !== word; }
}
```

```
class PalindromeChecker extends SpecialWordChecker {
  isSpecial(word) {
    return [...word].reverse().join('') === word || super.isSpecial(word);
  }
}

class AlphabeticalChecker extends SpecialWordChecker {
  isSpecial(word) {
    return [...word].sort().join('') === word || super.isSpecial(word);
  }
}

const checkIfSpecial = function(specialWordChecker, word) {
  const result = specialWordChecker.isSpecial(word) ? 'is' : 'is not';
  console.log(`${word} ${result} special`);
};

const palindromeChecker = new PalindromeChecker();
checkIfSpecial(palindromeChecker, 'mom'); //mom is special
checkIfSpecial(palindromeChecker, 'abe'); //abe is not special

const alphabeticalChecker = new AlphabeticalChecker();
checkIfSpecial(alphabeticalChecker, 'mom'); //mom is not special
checkIfSpecial(alphabeticalChecker, 'abe'); //abe is special

//Combine PalindromeChecker and AlphabeticalChecker here
const alphabeticalAndPalindromeChecker =
  Object.setPrototypeOf(
    Object.getPrototypeOf(new AlphabeticalChecker()),
    new PalindromeChecker());

checkIfSpecial(alphabeticalAndPalindromeChecker, 'mom'); //mom is special
checkIfSpecial(alphabeticalAndPalindromeChecker, 'abe'); //abe is special
```

Chapter 9

Here are the solutions to the *Exercises*, on page 166 for the *Using Modules* chapter.

Exercise 1

1. false. Each module is loaded at most once in the execution flow.

2. false. No; to export as default, we need to place the keyword default. Inlined export creates a named export.

3. false. The importing module provides names for the defaults, so there are no conflicts.

4. true. Inline exports are less verbose than explicit exports.

5. false. A module may have at most one default export, but it may have any number of nondefault exports.

Exercise 2

Use explicit import when you want to export

1. only select variables from multiple declarations

2. a variable with a different name than its declared name

Exercise 3

The importing module sees the name of the default exported item as default, but the importing module may assign whatever name it likes for that item.

Exercise 4

The module that has the code

```
export * from 'some-module';
```

will reexport all exports, except the default export, from the module named some-module. The module that imports the exporting module will be able to see all the exported items (except default) from some-module without a direct import to some-module.

Exercise 5

Let's pick a name, deliver, for the default item exported by fasttrack and give a namespace fasttrack for housing the items exported by the module fasttrack. Here's the code to import that module:

```
import deliver, * as fasttrack from 'fasttrack';
```

Chapter 10

Here are the solutions to the *Exercises*, on page 185, for the *Keeping Your Promises* chapter.

Exercise 1

No. Promise.race() will complete with the state of the first promise to complete. If the first resolves, then race() will resolve. If the first rejects, so will race().

Exercise 2

No. If any of the candidate promise rejects, then all() will reject. However, if no candidate promise has rejected, then all() will resolve when all candidate promises resolve.

Exercise 3

```
/*
npm install fs-extra
*/

'use strict';

const fs = require('fs-extra');

fs.readFile(__filename)
  .then(contents => console.log(contents.toString()))
  .catch(err => console.log(err.message));
```

Exercise 4

```
'use strict';

const fs = require('fs-extra');
const request = require('request-promise');

const countPrimes = function(number) {
  if(isNaN(number)) {
    return Promise.reject(`'${number}' is not a number`);
  }

  return request(`http://localhost:8084?number=${number}`)
    .then(count => `Number of primes from 1 to ${number} is ${count}`);
};

const createTimeout = function(timeInMillis) {
  return new Promise(function(resolve, reject) {
    setTimeout(() => reject(`timeout ${timeInMillis} MS`), timeInMillis);
  });
};

const logAndTerminate = function(err) {
  console.log(err);
  process.exit(1);
};

const countPrimesForEachLine = function(pathToFile) {
  fs.readFile(pathToFile)
    .then(content => content.toString())
    .then(content =>content.split('\n'))
    .then(lines => Promise.race(
        [Promise.all(lines.map(countPrimes)), createTimeout(1000)]))
    .then(counts => console.log(counts))
    .catch(logAndTerminate);
};

countPrimesForEachLine('numbers.txt');
```

Exercise 5

```javascript
'use strict';

const fs = require('fs-extra');
const request = require('request-promise');

const countPrimes = function(number) {
  if(isNaN(number)) {
    return Promise.reject(`'${number}' is not a number`);
  }

  return request(`http://localhost:8084?number=${number}`)
    .then(count => `Number of primes from 1 to ${number} is ${count}`);
};

const createTimeout = function(timeInMillis) {
  return new Promise(function(resolve, reject) {
    setTimeout(() => reject(`timeout ${timeInMillis} MS`), timeInMillis);
  });
};

const logAndTerminate = function(err) {
  console.log(err);
  process.exit(1);
};

const readFileContents = function(pathToFile) {
  return fs.readFile(pathToFile)
    .then(content => content.toString())
    .then(content =>content.split('\n'));
}

const countPrimesForEachLine = async function(pathToFile) {
  try {
    const lines = await readFileContents(pathToFile);

    const counts = await Promise.race(
      [Promise.all(lines.map(countPrimes)), createTimeout(1000)]);

    console.log(counts);
  } catch(err) {
    logAndTerminate(err);
  }
};

countPrimesForEachLine('numbers.txt');
```

Chapter 11

Here are the solutions to the *Exercises*, on page 199, for the *Exploring Metaprogramming* chapter.

Exercise 1

```
'use strict';

const printProperties = function(obj) {
  for(const property of Object.getOwnPropertyNames(obj)) {
    console.log(`${property} is ${obj[property]}`);
  }
};

printProperties({language: 'JavaScript', typing: 'dynamic'});
printProperties(
  {tool: 'Redux', language: 'JavaScript', purpose: 'transpiler', });
```

Exercise 2

```
'use strict';

Number.prototype.percent = function() {
  if(this >= 1) {
    throw new Error('value should be less than 1');
  }

  return `${this * 100}%`;
};

const value1 = 0.35;
const value2 = 0.91;

console.log(value1.percent()); //35%
console.log(value2.percent()); //91%

try {
  const value3 = 44;
  console.log(value3.percent());
} catch(ex) {
  console.log(ex.message); // value should be less than 1
}
```

Exercise 3

```
'use strict';

Object.defineProperties(Number.prototype, {
  integerPart: {
    get: function() {
      return this.toString().split('.')[0];
    }
  },
```

```
    fractionalPart: {
      get: function() { return this.toString().split('.')[1] || 0; }
    }
});

const printParts = function(number) {
  console.log(
    `whole: ${number.integerPart} decimal: ${number.fractionalPart}`);
};

printParts(22.12);     //whole: 22 decimal: 12
printParts(.14);       //whole: 0 decimal: 14
printParts(-23.19);    //whole: -23 decimal: 19
printParts(42);        //whole: 42 decimal: 0
```

Exercise 4

```
'use strict';

Set.prototype.combine = function(otherSet) {
  const copyOfSet = new Set(this);

  for(const element of otherSet) {
    copyOfSet.add(element);
  }

  return copyOfSet;
};

const names1 = new Set(['Tom', 'Sara', 'Brad', 'Kim']);
const names2 = new Set(['Mike', 'Kate']);

const combinedNames = names1.combine(names2);

console.log(names1.size);
console.log(names2.size);
console.log(combinedNames.size);
console.log(combinedNames);
```

Exercise 5

instance.methodName = function... instead of ClassName.prototype.methodName = function....

Adding a method to an instance instead of to the class's prototype has a few benefits:

- It's less intrusive and less risky.
- You can limit the scope of your change.
- You avoid the risk of replacing an existing method.
- It's useful to create a test double when doing automated testing—replace the method with a stub or a mock to facilitate ease of testing a function that depends on the function that was replaced.

Chapter 12

Here are the solutions to the *Exercises*, on page 226, for the *Deep Dive into Metaprogramming* chapter.

Exercise 1

```
'use strict';

class Counter {
  constructor() {
    this.count = 0;
  }

  incrementBy(value) { this.count += value; return this.count; }
  decrementBy(value) { this.count -= value; return this.count; }
}

const call = function(counter, method, ...data) {
  const methodToCall = Reflect.get(counter, method);
  return Reflect.apply(methodToCall, counter, data);
};

const counter = new Counter();

console.log(call(counter, 'incrementBy', 10)); //10
console.log(call(counter, 'decrementBy', 7)); //3
console.log(counter.count); //3
```

Exercise 2

- target refers to sample
- propertyName refers to "foo"
- receiver refers to proxy

Exercise 3

There's a small twist in this exercise. At first thought, merely Proxy.revocable(instance, {}); appears to be sufficient. However, that approach will result in an incompatible type error when proxy.getYear() is called. The type of the proxy is not the same as the type of Date. To fix this we have to use the bind() method, like so:

```
'use strict';

const createRevocableProxy = function(instance) {
  const handler = {
    get: function(target, propertyName /*, unusedReceiver */) {
      return Reflect.get(target, propertyName).bind(target);
    }
  };

  const { proxy, revoke } = Proxy.revocable(instance, handler);
```

```
    setTimeout(revoke, 3000);

  return proxy;
};

const proxy = createRevocableProxy(new Date());

const callGetYear = function() {
  try {
    console.log(1900 + proxy.getYear());
  } catch(ex) {
    console.log(ex.message);
  }
};

callGetYear(); //current year like 2018

setTimeout(callGetYear, 1000); //current year like 2018

setTimeout(callGetYear, 5000);
//Cannot perform 'get' on a proxy that has been revoked
```

Exercise 4

```
'use strict';

const createPlayMethodProxy = function(instance) {
  const handler = {
    get: function(target, propertyName) {
      if(propertyName.startsWith('play')) {
        const activity = propertyName.substring(4);

        if(target.activities.includes(activity)) {
          return () => `I love to play ${activity}`;
        } else {
          return () => `I don't play ${activity}`;
        }
      } else {
        throw new Error(`${propertyName} is not a function`);
      }
    }
  };

  return new Proxy(instance, handler);
};

const proxy = createPlayMethodProxy({ activities: ['Football', 'Tennis'] });

console.log(proxy.playTennis());   //I love to play Tennis
console.log(proxy.playFootball()); //I love to play Football
console.log(proxy.playPolitics()); //I don't play Politics

try {
  console.log(proxy.dance());
} catch(ex) {
  console.log(ex.message); //dance is not a function
}
```

Exercise 5

```
'use strict';

const proxy = new Proxy(Set.prototype, {
  get: function(target, propertyName, receiver) {
    return receiver.has(propertyName);
  }
});

Reflect.setPrototypeOf(Set.prototype, proxy);

const fruits = new Set(['Apple', 'Banana', 'Orange', 'Jack Fruit']);

console.log(fruits.size);          //4
console.log(fruits.Apple);         //true
console.log(fruits.Banana);        //true
console.log(fruits.Orange);        //true
console.log(fruits['Jack Fruit']); //true
console.log(fruits.Tomato);        //false
```

Web Resources

Babel ———————————————————————— https://babeljs.io
The website for Babel, the popular JavaScript transpiler.

Can I Use? ———————————————————— https://caniuse.com
A site that compares browsers and helps to find if a browser supports a particular feature.

ECMAScript 2015/ES6 Specification —— https://www.ecma-international.org/ecma-262/6.0
The specification document for the ES6 version.

ESLint ———————————————————————— https://eslint.org
Website for the ESLint tool.

ESLint Configuring Guide ——————— https://eslint.org/docs/user-guide/configuring
Webpage with details on configuring ESLint.

JSHint ———————————————————————— https://jshint.com
Website for the JSHint tool.

JSLint ———————————————————————— https://www.jslint.com
Website for the JSLint tool.

Kangax Compatibility Table ——————— https://kangax.github.io/compat-table/es6/
A site that provides details about feature compatibility for different browsers.

MDN web docs ———————————————————— https://developer.mozilla.org
A good source of documentation for various JavaScript features supported by different browsers.

Node.js _____ https://nodejs.org
The website for Node.js, the server-side JavaScript engine.

NFJS _____ https://www.nofluffjuststuff.com
A popular traveling conference in North America.

NVM _____ https://github.com/creationix/nvm
The Node Version Manager, which lets you manage multiple versions of node
on your system.

Pragmatic Bookshelf Resources for this book ___ https://www.pragprog.com/titles/ves6
The website for this book with link to source code download.

Redux _____ https://redux.js.org/
Popular JavaScript state container library that elegantly uses some of the
modern JavaScript features.

Bibliography

[Cro08]   Douglas Crockford. *JavaScript: The Good Parts*. O'Reilly & Associates, Inc.,
           Sebastopol, CA, 2008.

[GHJV95] Erich Gamma, Richard Helm, Ralph Johnson, and John Vlissides. *Design
          Patterns: Elements of Reusable Object-Oriented Software*. Addison-Wesley,
          Boston, MA, 1995.

[Sub16]   Venkat Subramaniam. *Test-Driving JavaScript Applications*. The Pragmatic
           Bookshelf, Raleigh, NC, 2016.

Index

Thank you!

How did you enjoy this book? Please let us know. Take a moment and email us at support@pragprog.com with your feedback. Tell us your story and you could win free ebooks. Please use the subject line "Book Feedback."

Ready for your next great Pragmatic Bookshelf book? Come on over to https://pragprog.com and use the coupon code BUYANOTHER2018 to save 30% on your next ebook.

Void where prohibited, restricted, or otherwise unwelcome. Do not use ebooks near water. If rash persists, see a doctor. Doesn't apply to *The Pragmatic Programmer* ebook because it's older than the Pragmatic Bookshelf itself. Side effects may include increased knowledge and skill, increased marketability, and deep satisfaction. Increase dosage regularly.

And thank you for your continued support,

Andy Hunt, Publisher

More on Java

Get up to date on the latest Java 8 features, and take an in-depth look at concurrency options.

Functional Programming in Java

Get ready to program in a whole new way. *Functional Programming in Java* will help you quickly get on top of the new, essential Java 8 language features and the functional style that will change and improve your code. This short, targeted book will help you make the paradigm shift from the old imperative way to a less error-prone, more elegant, and concise coding style that's also a breeze to parallelize. You'll explore the syntax and semantics of lambda expressions, method and constructor references, and functional interfaces. You'll design and write applications better using the new standards in Java 8 and the JDK.

Venkat Subramaniam
(196 pages) ISBN: 9781937785468. $33
https://pragprog.com/book/vsjava8

Programming Concurrency on the JVM

Stop dreading concurrency hassles and start reaping the pure power of modern multicore hardware. Learn how to avoid shared mutable state and how to write safe, elegant, explicit synchronization-free programs in Java or other JVM languages including Clojure, JRuby, Groovy, or Scala.

Venkat Subramaniam
(280 pages) ISBN: 9781934356760. $35
https://pragprog.com/book/vspcon

Better by Design

From architecture and design to deployment in the harsh realities of the real world, make your software better by design.

Design It!

Don't engineer by coincidence—design it like you mean it! Grounded by fundamentals and filled with practical design methods, this is the perfect introduction to software architecture for programmers who are ready to grow their design skills. Ask the right stakeholders the right questions, explore design options, share your design decisions, and facilitate collaborative workshops that are fast, effective, and fun. Become a better programmer, leader, and designer. Use your new skills to lead your team in implementing software with the right capabilities—and develop awesome software!

Michael Keeling
(358 pages) ISBN: 9781680502091. $41.95
https://pragprog.com/book/mkdsa

Release It! Second Edition

A single dramatic software failure can cost a company millions of dollars—but can be avoided with simple changes to design and architecture. This new edition of the best-selling industry standard shows you how to create systems that run longer, with fewer failures, and recover better when bad things happen. New coverage includes DevOps, microservices, and cloud-native architecture. Stability antipatterns have grown to include systemic problems in large-scale systems. This is a must-have pragmatic guide to engineering for production systems.

Michael Nygard
(376 pages) ISBN: 9781680502398. $47.95
https://pragprog.com/book/mnee2

Secure JavaScript and Web Testing

Secure your Node applications and see how to really test on the web.

Secure Your Node.js Web Application

Cyber-criminals have your web applications in their crosshairs. They search for and exploit common security mistakes in your web application to steal user data. Learn how you can secure your Node.js applications, database and web server to avoid these security holes. Discover the primary attack vectors against web applications, and implement security best practices and effective countermeasures. Coding securely will make you a stronger web developer and analyst, and you'll protect your users.

Karl Düüna
(230 pages) ISBN: 9781680500851. $36
https://pragprog.com/book/kdnodesec

The Way of the Web Tester

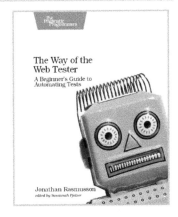

This book is for everyone who needs to test the web. As a tester, you'll automate your tests. As a developer, you'll build more robust solutions. And as a team, you'll gain a vocabulary and a means to coordinate how to write and organize automated tests for the web. Follow the testing pyramid and level up your skills in user interface testing, integration testing, and unit testing. Your new skills will free you up to do other, more important things while letting the computer do the one thing it's really good at: quickly running thousands of repetitive tasks.

Jonathan Rasmusson
(256 pages) ISBN: 9781680501834. $29
https://pragprog.com/book/jrtest

Learn Why, Then Learn How

Get started on your Elixir journey today.

Adopting Elixir

Adoption is more than programming. Elixir is an exciting new language, but to successfully get your application from start to finish, you're going to need to know more than just the language. You need the case studies and strategies in this book. Learn the best practices for the whole life of your application, from design and team-building, to managing stakeholders, to deployment and monitoring. Go beyond the syntax and the tools to learn the techniques you need to develop your Elixir application from concept to production.

Ben Marx, José Valim, Bruce Tate
(242 pages) ISBN: 9781680502527. $42.95
https://pragprog.com/book/tvmelixir

Programming Elixir 1.6

This book is *the* introduction to Elixir for experienced programmers, completely updated for Elixir 1.6 and beyond. Explore functional programming without the academic overtones (tell me about monads just one more time). Create concurrent applications, but get them right without all the locking and consistency headaches. Meet Elixir, a modern, functional, concurrent language built on the rock-solid Erlang VM. Elixir's pragmatic syntax and built-in support for metaprogramming will make you productive and keep you interested for the long haul. Maybe the time is right for the Next Big Thing. Maybe it's Elixir.

Dave Thomas
(410 pages) ISBN: 9781680502992. $47.95
https://pragprog.com/book/elixir16

Pragmatic Programming

We'll show you how to be more pragmatic and effective, for new code and old.

Your Code as a Crime Scene

Jack the Ripper and legacy codebases have more in common than you'd think. Inspired by forensic psychology methods, this book teaches you strategies to predict the future of your codebase, assess refactoring direction, and understand how your team influences the design. With its unique blend of forensic psychology and code analysis, this book arms you with the strategies you need, no matter what programming language you use.

Adam Tornhill
(218 pages) ISBN: 9781680500387. $36
https://pragprog.com/book/atcrime

The Nature of Software Development

You need to get value from your software project. You need it "free, now, and perfect." We can't get you there, but we can help you get to "cheaper, sooner, and better." This book leads you from the desire for value down to the specific activities that help good Agile projects deliver better software sooner, and at a lower cost. Using simple sketches and a few words, the author invites you to follow his path of learning and understanding from a half century of software development and from his engagement with Agile methods from their very beginning.

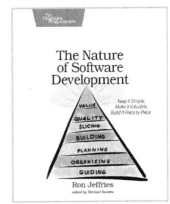

Ron Jeffries
(176 pages) ISBN: 9781941222379. $24
https://pragprog.com/book/rjnsd

The Pragmatic Bookshelf

The Pragmatic Bookshelf features books written by developers for developers. The titles continue the well-known Pragmatic Programmer style and continue to garner awards and rave reviews. As development gets more and more difficult, the Pragmatic Programmers will be there with more titles and products to help you stay on top of your game.

Visit Us Online

This Book's Home Page
https://pragprog.com/book/ves6
Source code from this book, errata, and other resources. Come give us feedback, too!

Keep Up to Date
https://pragprog.com
Join our announcement mailing list (low volume) or follow us on twitter @pragprog for new titles, sales, coupons, hot tips, and more.

New and Noteworthy
https://pragprog.com/news
Check out the latest pragmatic developments, new titles and other offerings.

Save on the eBook

Save on the eBook versions of this title. Owning the paper version of this book entitles you to purchase the electronic versions at a terrific discount.

PDFs are great for carrying around on your laptop—they are hyperlinked, have color, and are fully searchable. Most titles are also available for the iPhone and iPod touch, Amazon Kindle, and other popular e-book readers.

Buy now at *https://pragprog.com/coupon*

Contact Us

Online Orders:	*https://pragprog.com/catalog*
Customer Service:	*support@pragprog.com*
International Rights:	*translations@pragprog.com*
Academic Use:	*academic@pragprog.com*
Write for Us:	*http://write-for-us.pragprog.com*
Or Call:	+1 800-699-7764

Milton Keynes UK
Ingram Content Group UK Ltd.
UKHW050751210524
442990UK00007B/96

9 781680 505467